# Latin American Detectives against Power

# Latin American Detectives against Power

## Individualism, the State, and Failure in Crime Fiction

Fabricio Tocco

LEXINGTON BOOKS
*Lanham • Boulder • New York • London*

Published by Lexington Books
An imprint of The Rowman & Littlefield Publishing Group, Inc.
4501 Forbes Boulevard, Suite 200, Lanham, Maryland 20706
www.rowman.com

86-90 Paul Street, London EC2A 4NE

Copyright © 2022 by The Rowman & Littlefield Publishing Group, Inc.

*All rights reserved.* No part of this book may be reproduced in any form or by any electronic or mechanical means, including information storage and retrieval systems, without written permission from the publisher, except by a reviewer who may quote passages in a review.

British Library Cataloguing in Publication Information Available

**Library of Congress Cataloging-in-Publication Data**

Names: Tocco, Fabricio, 1985- author.
Title: Latin American detectives against power : individualism, the state, and failure in crime fiction / Fabricio Tocco.
Description: Lanham : Lexington Books, [2022] | Includes bibliographical references and index. | Summary: "This book examines Latin American detective fiction and how the genre produces a socio-political critique of individualism and the state"-- Provided by publisher.
Identifiers: LCCN 2021062033 (print) | LCCN 2021062034 (ebook) | ISBN 9781793651648 (cloth) | ISBN 9781793651662 (paperback) | ISBN 9781793651655 (ebook)
Subjects: LCSH: Detective and mystery stories, Latin American--Political aspects. | Detective and mystery stories, Latin American--Social aspects. | Latin American fiction--20th century--History and criticism. | Individualism in literature. | State, The, in literature. | Piglia, Ricardo--Criticism and interpretation. | Bolaño, Roberto, 1953-2003--Criticism and interpretation. | Fonseca, Rubem--Criticism and interpretation. | LCGFT: Literary criticism.
Classification: LCC PQ7082.D48 T63 2022  (print) | LCC PQ7082.D48  (ebook) | DDC 863/.08720906--dc23/eng/20220215
LC record available at https://lccn.loc.gov/2021062033
LC ebook record available at https://lccn.loc.gov/2021062034

*À memória de João Carlos Chiodini, ao seu sorriso, e à sua malandragem*

*Para Rita de Grandis, por haber hecho posible
palabras sabiendo que nunca podría leerlas*

# Contents

| | |
|---|---|
| Acknowledgments | ix |
| Introduction | 1 |
| Chapter 1: The Anglo-American Detective: Individualism against the State | 11 |
| Chapter 2: Argentina: The State against Individualism | 47 |
| Chapter 3: Chile: Individualism within the State | 91 |
| Chapter 4: Brazil: The State against the State | 123 |
| Chapter 5: Coda: The Mexican-American Border Seen from Chilean Eyes | 157 |
| Chapter 6: Final Thoughts: From Failure to Community | 195 |
| Notes | 203 |
| Bibliography | 207 |
| Index | 217 |
| About the Author | 235 |

# Acknowledgments

There is a community behind this book on detective fiction. Some of their members contributed so much that they should be considered (if not co-authors), at the very least, accomplices. *Latin American Detectives against Power* originated as a doctoral dissertation so, first and foremost, I would like to thank my supervisor Jon Beasley-Murray, whose support, instruction, wisdom, guidance, and friendship have been unique and fruitful during the past years. Jon has a rare ability to see through and beyond the texture of books. Only time will tell if he bequeathed me some of this ability; I would be satisfied with a very small portion. Along with Jon, I had the privilege of enjoying other wonderful readers, such as Alessandra Santos, Adam Frank, and Rosa Sarabia. They all made careful and acute readings of my manuscript, enriching it in substantial ways.

I am indebted to the Faculty of Graduate and Postdoctoral Studies and to the department of French, Hispanic, and Italian studies at the University of British Columbia, for funding the writing of this book in different ways: the Four-Year Doctoral Fellowship, the International Partial Tuition Scholarship, the Graduate Research Grant, the Travel Funds, Teaching Assistantships, and Sessional Lectureships without which my work would not have been possible. Their generous support allowed me to do research and share parts of my work in progress in Mexico City, Puebla, Rio de Janeiro, São Paulo, Buenos Aires, Montevideo, Barcelona, Victoria, Toronto, and Eugene. As important as the financial support were the professors who were close to me at different stages of the program: Joël Castonguay-Bélanger, Kim Beauchesne, Brianne-Orr Álvarez, Stephanie Spacciante, Ralph Sarkonak, Enrique Manchón, André Lamontagne, Anna Casas Aguilar, Raúl Álvarez-Moreno, Nancy Frelick, Iris Escuer, Andrea Roca, Pedro Dos Santos, Carlo Testa, María Adelaida Escobar Trujillo, Carolina Navarrete, Gabriel Saldías Rosel, all helped me to move forward. The same goes for the administrative office and their endless patience: Carole Schoenfeld, Michael Ferrazzi, Marjo Scheffer, and Emanuela Guerra and the helpful librarians of the Walter C.

Koerner's, the Irving K. Libraries, and the Mariano Moreno National Library of the Argentine Republic, in Buenos Aires. But perhaps my deepest gratitude is for someone who no longer works in the department, someone who believed in my potential when I was about to give up my career in academia and changed my life in ways only few people have: Rita De Grandis.

Many other friends are in the community of accomplices behind this book: Pablo Zölldan and Cristina Figueredo, who infused me with their passion for literature and without whom I could have never been able to write a whole book, let alone in English. Iván Cherjovsky, Jonathan Di Renzo, Mercedes Paz, José Barletta, Fernando Gómez Carchak, Tzeitel Puig Andreu, Gisela Eichbaum, Santiago Kalinowski, Matías Fernández, Catalina Rossini, Fernando Veríssimo, Giselle Aronson, Miguel Julià, Javier Moreno, Beñat Sarasola, Pere Turu, Constanza Flores, Mikel Aboitiz, Giselle Pablovsky, Javier Pereyra, Laeticia Rovecchio, Alejandro Pérez, Àlex Gonzàlez Aznar, Sara Ferrer, Guido and Sebastián Napolitano, Sebastián Maques, Mariano Nicotera, Diego Páez, Daniel Molinari, Julián Battista, Juan Aguilera, Aleix Castellví, Paula Álvarez and Judit Algueró, they all maintained a permanent presence despite the enormous time zone differences.

I can call Vancouver home, where I wrote most of this book, thanks to Nandy Fajardo, Erfan Rezaie, Patricio Robles, Gustavo Halaburda, Ross Swanson, Alan Marx, Olga Albarrán Caselles, Matt Schmidt, Valeria Narváez, Melisa Múñoz, Marcos Moscoso, Anabella Forte, Doris Egúsquiza, Magali Blanc, Karen O'Regan, Luca Oluic, Upasana Thakkar, Camilo Castillo, Ricardo García, Han Fei, Verónica Dahl, Edmundo González, Will Burke, Frank and Wendy Palumbo, Faustino Fredes, Nikki Faint, Eric Jarvis, Rick García, María Carbonetti, Henri Giovanetti, Brayan Seixas, Eduardo Lucástegui, Nairy Arellano, Ana Vivaldi, and Rafael Wainer.

Several peers and professors' insight on Latin American literature, political and literary theory, anthropology, philosophy, psychoanalysis, poetry, history, and detective fiction, have provided me with a stimulating intellectual exchange which was indeed productive for this book: Nora Catelli, Elsa Drucaroff, Alejandro Soifer, Jorge Carrión, Iván Cherjovsky (again!), Susana Vallejo, David Viñas Piquer, Carolina Baffi, Maurizio Esposito, Max Hidalgo, Thomas Waldemer, Julio Premat, Vivian Mills, María Rosa Lojo, Miguel Vitagliano, Isis Sadek, David William Foster, Agustín Cosovschi, Erica Beckman, Tamara Mitchell, Robert Caner, Ezequiel Meler, Diego Trelles-Paz, Isabel Quintana, Alejo Steimberg, Cristina Fangmann, Sebastián Lalaurette, Federico Reggiani, Valeria Wagner, Adriana López-Labourdette, Natalí Incaminato, Rayén Nazareno, Daniela Ruiz, Alan Astropolsky, Diego Alonso, Teresa Ochavas, Àlex Matas, Bernat Padró, Antoni Martí, Paula Luciani, Cristian Piazza, Inés Ordiz, Luis Miguel Hermoza, Josias

Padilha, Roger Seró, Scott Anderson, Julio Hardisson, Victoria Baratta, and Júlia Gonzàlez.

I would like to thank the School of Literature, Language, and Linguistics at the Australian National University, for their support during the final stages, as well as my students, from Canada to Australia. I also thank Nicolette Amstutz, who became interested in bringing this project to Lexington Books and who was involved in the early stages of its publication and Alexandra Rallo, for her hard work as the final editor.

A special thanks goes to Sergi Viciana and Miguel Ángel Guerra for reading patiently and wisely the first chapters.

A heartfelt thanks to my mother Isamara Chiodini, my father José Alberto Tocco, my sisters Mirela Tocco and Romina Aira, and my extended family, whose love, sent from four different countries (all located thousands of kilometers away from Vancouver), kept me on track the whole time.

And last, but surely not least, thanks to Stacey Stevens, my most important reader.

# Introduction

In 1888, Friedrich Engels wrote a letter to British author Margaret Harkness, in which he claims to have learned more about French history from Balzac, than from all historians who studied the period combined. One century later, several Latin American writers have echoed Engel's quip. From the Mexican Paco Taibo II to the Argentine Mempo Giardinelli, including the Chilean Ramón Díaz Eterovic, there is a consensus in the Latin American critic that reading detective fiction is essential to understand the region in the present (Valle 100, Giardinelli 15, Díaz Eterovic 35). With these maxims as its starting point, the following book engages with texts that are part of a boom of detective fiction published recently in Latin America.

Originally a nineteenth-century genre conceived for the masses in the English-speaking world, detective fiction circulated in the region from an early stage, especially since the 1890s Spanish translations of the Sherlock Holmes series (Yates 1956, 229). However, the genre experienced a peak in local production only recently, during the past few decades. As Díaz Eterovic notes, detective fiction became in many Latin American countries "one of the most efficient literary forms to address the existing ties between power, criminality, truth and justice" (36). The landscape is certainly different from the 1950s, when the American scholar Donald A. Yates claimed that only around a 5 percent of detective stories were originally published in Spanish (1956, 228).

Whereas in the United States, classic hard-boiled fiction became popular during the 1920s–1940s; it is in the 1990s, (Valle 100, Stavans 11), when this boom takes place in Latin America, with the proliferation of many authors who engage with what the critics have called *neopolicial* or *nueva novela negra*, that is, the new hard-boiled fiction. Major publishing houses have promoted the works of the Peruvian Mario Vargas Llosa, the Mexican Paco Taibo II, the Cuban Leonardo Padura, the Colombian Santiago Gamboa, the Brazilian Luis Alfredo García-Roza, the Chilean Ramón Díaz Eterovic, and the Argentine Claudia Piñeiro, to name a few.

Since its foundations, there has been many prejudices surrounding the literary quality of detective fiction. Perhaps one of the most famous belongs to German playwright Bertolt Brecht, who regarded the genre as nothing but aesthetic escapism, a dose of exciting adventure against the prosaisms of modern daily life (343). As Giardinelli notes, Arthur Conan Doyle himself disavowed the genre he practiced so extensively (24). Far from such prejudices, that Argentine literary critic Beatriz Sarlo terms "hierarchical superstitions" (41), this book follows the Borgesian tradition that ever since the 1930s takes detective fiction seriously. After all, "the critical disdain against the genre has not thwarted its universal prevalence," as Giardinelli puts it (15). Even though Giardinelli acknowledges that "commercial success does not necessarily amount to literary quality," the prominence of detective fiction does make literary quality possible, much like what happens in other genres that became popular over the course of history (16).

These are the narratives I analyze below: they are part of this genre boom, but they also go beyond it, providing a literary quality that problematizes genre formulas. They are, in this sense, "anti-Brechtian detective stories," borrowing Rodríguez Pérsico's term (121): even though some of them became bestsellers, like Roberto Bolaño's *2666*, they are best described as complex texts that surpass the formulaic conventions of the genre, to comment on the political and the historical in a more problematic way. In Argentine writer Ricardo Piglia's terms, the detective is not merely reduced to solving the mysteries of a crime, it also reveals the structures of society and power, in ways that other genres cannot (2002, 9). Seeking what Engels found in Balzac, this book focuses on the Argentine Ricardo Piglia, the Chilean Roberto Bolaño and the Brazilian Rubem Fonseca, and the ways in which they build on and break with their precursors in the detective story tradition, from Edgar Allan Poe to Jorge Luis Borges.

This book, then, covers a wide historical period, across many countries, trying to fill the "understudied ties" that Giardinelli sees "between North and Latin American detective fiction traditions" (215). It begins in the 1830s with the American Poe's Dupin (set in Paris) and it ends in the 2000s with the Chilean Bolaño's *2666* (set on the American/Mexican border). Throughout, however, it focuses on a very particular aspect of the genre: the historical and aesthetic tensions between individualism and the state. In the following chapters, I examine two main problems: on the one hand, I study how Piglia, Bolaño, and Fonseca reproduce and re-imagine these traditional tensions. On the other, I delve into how their stories help us understand differently the portrayal of the state and individualism in classic English and North American detective fiction.

Despite its historical range, this book puts a special stress on novels and short stories produced and published in the 1990s, that is, at the end of and immediately after the Cold War 1970s–1980s dictatorships that ravaged a specific part of the region, namely, the Southern Cone countries: Argentina,

Brazil, and Chile. The "Latin American detective fiction," referred to in this book's title, excludes parts of the region where the genre was prominent, such as Mexico or Cuba. On the one hand, this exclusion responds to the fact that Mexican and American scholars, such as Ilan Stavans and Persephone Braham, to name a few, studied the genre (and its relationship with failure and the state) in Mexican and Cuban national literatures, in their wonderful books *Antihéroes* and *Crimes against the State, Crimes against Persons*, respectively.

On the other hand, the book focuses on Southern Cone national literatures because the region shares a common a past, marked by the transnational Operation Condor, which helped to implement neoliberal economic policies through these 1970s–1980s dictatorships. By the time that Piglia, Bolaño, and Fonseca have written most of these detective stories, Argentina, Brazil, and Chile had abandoned the military rule. By contrasting these post-dictatorial stories with their models, this book aims to give an account of what Latin American authors can tell us about detective fiction written in the world's oldest modern democracies: drawing on the historical distinction that neither the United States nor the United Kingdom have experienced military interruptions of their democratic rule or dictatorial re-shaping of their political institutions (unlike Argentina, Brazil, and Chile), I hope to show how Southern Cone detective stories offer a radically different critique of the state, that sheds a new light to their models.

For Giardinelli, these models should be found mainly in the literature of the United States (218). This is not to say that European counterparts have not left their trace, too. Manuel Vázquez Montalbán's detective novels have especially shaped the works of Taibo, Padura and Díaz Eterovic. In fact, the Spanish author writes from a post-dictatorial context, too, i.e.,: during the 1970s and 1980s, the years of the Spanish transition to democracy. However, his influence is less present in Piglia, Bolaño, and Fonseca. Hopefully this book will help start a comparative conversation about the detective genre in Spanish and Latin American post-dictatorial literatures.

This book has five chapters, each of which deals with detective fiction written in the context of different national literatures. The first chapter, "The Anglo-American Detective: Individualism against the State" traces the inception and consolidation of the tension between individualism and the state and the way it developed in the English and North American literary traditions as a stable rivalry. I explore the historical causes of these tensions, connecting them with their representations in the founding authors of the genre—Edgar Allan Poe, Arthur Conan Doyle, Agatha Christie, Dashiell Hammett, and Raymond Chandler—from the 1840s to the 1930s.

I include these specific canonical expressions of the genre due to a problem of literary reception: apart from Agatha Christie, all these writers were white and male. During the late nineteenth century and the early twentieth century, these pre-requisites were essential to ensure the circulation of their work through literary translations, and their eventual influence in the public discussion of foreign literary fields. By the time that the Latin American authors examined in this book were producing their own work, these canonical Anglo-American authors were established as "safe" models to look to. Their detective fictions were translated into Spanish and Portuguese multiple times, read, imitated, and frequently criticized.

Of course, reducing Anglo-American detective fiction to these five canonical authors entails excluding other important works, such as those partaking in the African American tradition. Authors such as Chester Himes (in the 1950s and 1960s) and more recently Walter Mosley or Hugh Holton Jr. (1990s and the beginning of the twenty-first century), engaged with detective fiction, sometimes in substantially different ways, compared to their white counterparts, namely, to denounce the unwritten politics of race that are fundamental to understand the American state.

Although an interesting comparative study could arise from their points of contact with Latin American authors, the work of Himes, Mosley, and Holton Jr. did not constitute a central part of the genre's reception in the Southern Cone. While their influence is strong in the work of the Cuban Leonardo Padura or the Mexican Paco Taibo II (Taibo 38); it is less so in Piglia, Bolaño, or Fonseca. In *Escritores norteamericanos*, for instance, Piglia values the quality of Himes's writing, but he considers his contribution to the genre to be a repetition or exasperation of the formulas established by the classics of the genre, especially Chandler (2013, 148). In turn, Bolaño explicitly comments in *Entre paréntesis* how Mosley's detective-like individualistic hero, Easy, always ends up succeeding, like Himes's and Chandler's, not seeing a noticeable difference between them (2004b, 144).

The first chapter, then, focuses on these canonical authors, fleshing out a close reading of their work through the prism of the tensions of individualism and the state, and it establishes a constellation of concepts that will reappear throughout the book. To begin with, this chapter owes a great deal to the British scholar Ian Watt's *Myths of Modern Individualism*. But whereas Watt focused on earlier mythical figures of European literature (Faust, Don Quixote, Don Juan, and Robinson Crusoe), I adopt his opposition of the individualistic hero against the world, an *ego contra mundum*, for an analysis of the literary, historic, and political tactics of classic detective fiction. Equally, Watt's individualistic myths informs my reading of Latin American detectives in that they share a common trans-Atlantic heritage: Don Quixote's individualism against the world, which features explicitly in Fonseca's final scene in *Agosto*, and more subtly in Piglia and Bolaño.

I am particularly interested in the work of personification in detective stories, i.e.,: the embodiment of political abstractions (individualism, the state) in specific literary characters (the private eye, the policeman). I examine these metonymical embodiments as problematic narrative strategies, in which the classic Anglo-American detective is imagined as a mind without a body, and the state, as a body without a mind. Poe's Dupin or Conan Doyle's Holmes are intellects divested of a corporeal frame (we barely hear about their physical appearance), but they are still able to give a concrete body form to the mythical attributes of individualism.

I explore this intellect without a body in terms of Italian philosopher Roberto Esposito's concept of *immunitas*, i.e., as a privilege of being exonerated of one's debts towards society. I argue that the classic private eye endorses individualism through this exoneration. By contrast, I examine how Anglo-American detective stories portray the modern state in terms not of positive attributes but of negative lacks, that I call "symbolic disabilities," i.e., corporeal mutilations or incapacities that impede or diminish a body's agency at a metaphorical level. Classic detective fiction's main critique of the state is rooted in this figuration of a maimed body, located in disfigured characters, mainly policemen, who cannot speak, see, read, listen, act, or think, and who, as a result, are always perceived to be inferior to an always successful and undivided self-incarnated in the detective.

The second chapter, "Argentina. The State against Individualism," explores the transformation of this classic tension, highlighting an inversion of subject and object, which is not a whimsical play on words. Instead, it aims to capture the way in which Argentine detective fiction emphasizes the all-pervasive agency of a criminal state against an impotent failing self. Like the first chapter, Chapter 2 engages with canonical authors of the genre, through the prism of this rivalry. Equally, it spans a long period of time, from the 1940s to the 1990s, trying to establish the genealogy that Ricardo Piglia chooses to inherit (Jorge Luis Borges and Rodolfo Walsh), to later offer a close reading of two of his detective stories in which dictatorial state and failing individualism are put center stage: "La loca y el relato del crimen" and *Plata quemada*.

I hope to show how Piglia exhibits a productive rewriting of *ego contra mundum*: his texts show an *ego* that has lost the immunity it once had in the classical detective story. Private eyes, here, fail at the hands of the state because they paradoxically rely on the same aspect that makes the Anglo-American detectives succeed: knowledge and literacy, the ability to read signifiers, and make sense of them to solve a case. Instead, Argentine detectives inherit the symbolic disabilities that in Anglo-American stories were a monopoly of the state. In Borges, Walsh and Piglia, it is the private eyes who cannot read, speak or see, and their symbolic illiteracy, muteness and blindness, are what cause them to fail against the state. Knowledge, once useful, is now irrelevant or itself a cause of failure. I link the rewriting of the rivalry between *ego* and *mundus* to the dictatorial experiences that crowded the country's twentieth century and the way they re-shaped the understanding of what individuals can do and what a modern state is or can be. Through the lens of Argentine detective fiction, I offer a re-reading of the Anglo-American tradition and the way it imagined the state in contractualist terms.

These first and the second chapters explore the tensions between individualism and the state through a panoramic survey of texts and periods. The third, the fourth and the fifth chapters, by contrast, each offer a close reading of one text. The third chapter, "Chile. Individualism within the State," addresses the invasion of destabilizing individualistic forces inside the state. The boundaries between individualism and the state that once were solid in Anglo-American detective stories, and even in Argentina (where despite the subversion, the rivalry prevailed), start to crumble in Chile. This chapter focuses on Roberto Bolaño's *Estrella distante*, examining the way the author reproduces the tensions between a criminal mastermind (who works for the dictatorial state) and the private detectives who chase him.

Once more, the notion of symbolic disabilities helps us to read this tension: Bolaño imagines a state whose criminal members endure the symbolic muteness required by the censorious rule of Augusto Pinochet's dictatorial regime. At first, the novel seems to meet the conventions of the detective story and its horizon of expectations in Latin America. But I show how *Estrella distante* breaks with tradition by displaying a selective state muteness. These variations of the symbolic disabilities of the state are but symptoms of a literary and a political device that no longer works: personification. The malfunction takes place on both levels of representation: aesthetic and political. Characters who are supposed to embody the state disobey their mandate, relinquishing that pact of absolute silence.

Challenging genres that go beyond detective fiction, such as the dictator novel, I show how Bolaño puts at center stage a state (whose crimes against humanity remain beyond comprehension) that paradoxically cannot be represented. Similarly, private investigators fail to incarnate the heroic individualism they are expected to, becoming instead reluctant detectives, still affected by paralysis and illiteracy, like their Argentine counterparts. The crumbling of the boundaries that once separated individualism and the state is expressed in terms of the opposite of personification: fragmentation and a tendency towards depersonalization. In the third chapter, the concept of the multitude, a depersonalized agent, features for the first time. The *ego* of the criminal mastermind and the private eyes blend into one, diluted into the amorphous multitude of the Chilean diaspora in Europe as well as of the *desaparecidos*, the missing victims of the crimes against humanity.

The fourth chapter, "Brazil. *The State against the State*," reads another instance in which this rivalry crumbles, in Rubem Fonseca's *Agosto* (1990), where the boundaries between individualism and state are again challenged (as in Bolaño) from within the agents of the state. But whereas in *Estrella distante* the state's contours are defined by one individual actor, in *Agosto* this defiance is multitudinous. The tensions between two philosophical concepts, the multitude and the people, are at stake here: once individualism starts melting into the thin air of the acephalous multitude, the crumbling state desperately tries to recapture individuals, enclosing them under the Hobbesian category of "the people." Here, again, the trope of personification is prominent as it is intertwined with its political dimension: personalism.

After all, the cult of personality is rooted in the figure of the individualistic leader that the state and the people presuppose. This paradox is one of the issues that this chapter addresses in the figure of a detective (who works not privately but within the state) and his double: one of the most important personalist politicians of Latin American history, Getúlio Vargas. Fonseca's text shares with the other Latin American narratives that both individualistic heroes and state officers experience symbolic disabilities, such as muteness, blindness, illiteracy, and paralysis. In this chapter, I also examine the blurred boundaries between national mythology and historiography as well as the mythification of personalist leaders through the narration of the past. I study the novel as a device that exposes the literary dimension of historiographic accounts narratives, which ultimately resorts to personification to the same extent as detective stories.

The fifth chapter, "Coda. The Mexican-American Border seen from Chilean Eyes," analyzes Roberto Bolaño's *2666*, specifically "The Part about the Crimes." The chapter concludes that Bolaño presents the final collapse of the *ego contra mundum* opposition. In *Estrella distante* and *Agosto* this rivalry crumbled but ultimately it remained in force. By contrast, Bolaño's narrative strategy in his posthumous novel is to dissolve both private detectives and public policemen, rendering this traditional tension obsolete. Even though he still reproduces the traditional symbolic disabilities, (amongst which the most important is unintelligibility), there is in this novel a shift in the author's literary project, which now differs radically from his previous detective stories: there is no room left for any remaining vestiges of individualism and personification, not even in fragments, as there was in *Estrella distante*.

By contrast, the main novelty of "The Part about the Crimes" can be attributed to the consolidation of depersonalization as a force that affects all agents involved in crime equally: criminals, bystanders, police officers, but also the victims, all lose their personhood. Yet although this all-pervasive depersonalization affects all these figures, it does so with opposing results, always at the service of constituted power. Finally, I meditate on a more emancipatory outcome of this depersonalized world, by reading the body of the victims as a multitude, as a driving force of constituent power. The conclusion that follows, "*From Failure to Community,*" explores what is left after the poetics of failure: neither individualism nor the state, but a multitudinous community.

The predominance of male authors in this corpus can be explained following the double axes previously mentioned: aesthetics and politics. In terms of the former, as the Finnish critic Jopi Nyman claims, Hammett and Chandler's detectives partake in "the chain of fictions of American masculinity," which, similarly to "its precedents such as the Western," aims "to provide the male character with social dominance" (35). A similar phenomenon takes place in terms of the political. Argentine Feminist anthropologist Rita Segato, in her recent essay *La guerra contra las mujeres* (2016), claims that "the history of men, the historical process of masculinity, constitutes the DNA of the state and its masculine genealogy reveals itself daily" (94). As Nyman notes, detective fiction displays, too, a masculine DNA, since it "aims at a reaffirmation of a disrupted masculine social order" and it does so through "the privileging of a masculine language to a vision of social order based on a masculine authority" (3). Nyman links these traces "the masculine fantasy of all-knowing omnipotence" as "a dream that comes through in hard-boiled narratives" (4). In other words, he understands masculinity, in detective stories, as a delusion of sovereignty.

There are, of course, many female authors who engage with the genre in Latin America. Especially in Argentina and Uruguay, novelists such as Luisa Valenzuela, Claudia Piñeiro, Myriam Laurini, Mercedes Rosende, to name a few, have enjoyed a positive critical and commercial reception. I chose not to include them in this book because the problem of individualism and the state, understood as a conflict (and a fantasy) of masculine sovereignty, is not particularly explored in their novels. My male corpus is relevant to my research questions on the one hand because, as Segato claims, state sovereignty has traditionally been thought and embodied by men and men only. On the other hand, the fantasies and anxieties of masculinity are incarnated in the figure of the private detective and the policemen, while women (especially in hard-boiled fiction) are often relegated to the trite and misogynist figure of the *femme fatale*.

The theoretical framework behind this book is eclectic and, like its corpus, wide-ranging. Nonetheless, there is an underlying logic that follows a consistent path. My analyses draw on and aim to contribute to recent debates on political and literary theory, concerning the people and the multitude, the community and the state of exception, personhood, and depersonalization. This is why my framework relies on two distinct branches of Continental Philosophy: French Post-Structuralism and Italian Post-Marxism. The names of Michel Foucault, Jacques Lacan, Jacques Derrida, Pierre Bourdieu, Tzvetan Todorov, and Roland Barthes will often appear next to those of Roberto Esposito, Giorgio Agamben, Paolo Virno, and Antonio Negri. Beyond this, the work of a previous generation of thinkers was also useful to shed light on the detective stories examined here: above all, essayists who belong to the Marxist and the Structuralist tradition, such as György Lukács, Theodor W. Adorno, Walter Benjamin, Ernst Mandel, Émile Benveniste, Claude Lévi-Strauss, and Louis Althusser, not to mention the founding fathers of these traditions, Marx and Saussure themselves. I read their work, nonetheless, through the lens of Post-Structuralism and Post-Marxism. Perhaps, the author with whom this book resonates the most is Roberto Esposito: a whole arc could be drawn following his books, from *Immunitas* (2002) to *Communitas* (1998), via *The Origins of the Political* (1996) and *The Third Person* (2012), all of which are key to read the literary projects of Piglia, Bolaño, and Fonseca.

In the end, I argue that post-dictatorial Southern Cone detective fiction offer a transnational "poetics of failure." But how can "failure" be the material for a poetics? A close reading of their works shows the extent to which these authors put failure at center stage: all these Latin American detectives fail to solve their cases, in one way or another, at the hands of the state. Yet their portrayal of failure must not be understood in a neo-Romantic way. These authors do not celebrate failure, but nor do they condemn it. Instead, they take it as a common problem that is, once more, twofold: aesthetic and political. Failure, after all, is an intellectual anxiety that goes beyond literature, reaching political historiography, too. Tulio Halperín Donghi understands Argentine historical revisionism as a "decadentist matrix," a recurring sense of national failure that is constantly haunting the national way of perceiving and retelling history.

These stories partake in what late Argentine critic Horacio González best described as "a shift in critical writing, which now deals almost exclusively with the failures of the law" (499). The poetics of failure is a re-elaboration of detective fiction. It is a poetics because it is also a theorization of failure, and its narrative impacts in the literary and the political. It is a poetics that resonates with a common political counter-discourse that crosses the Triple Frontier, the Andes, the Río de la Plata, even the Río Bravo. A poetics that reformulates an obsolete literary convention, because it understands it as a conservative endorsement of individualism and a veiled apology for the oppressive mechanisms of the state. Paraphrasing Walter Benjamin, the poetics of failure responds to this convention by dismantling its narratives: it unmasks the fictional silhouette of the state while simultaneously underlining the structuring structures that coerce individuals. By re-appropriating an Anglo-American genre, it makes it plausible in Latin America, where the modern liberal state cannot possibly be understood through the lens of those who once created it.

*Chapter 1*

# The Anglo-American Detective
## *Individualism against the State*

### A LITERARY ANTAGONISM

**A Stable Rivalry**

"The facility with which I shall arrive, or have arrived, at the solution of this mystery, is in the direct ratio of its apparent insolubility in the eyes of the police" (Poe 1980a, 120), announces proudly Chevalier August Dupin. Here, the first detective in literary history is not solely claiming to have solved a crime. Edgar Allan Poe's hero is also inaugurating a rivalry that will be reproduced by many of his successors in different geographical settings and historical situations, from the mid-nineteenth century onwards. For although detective stories have often been read as a modern translation of an old literary opposition (the conflict between good and evil, the cop chasing the thief), there is in fact a second underlying battle at stake: a rivalry between a sleuth who confronts not only the criminal but also the police.

Since Poe, detective stories exhibit a tension between an individualistic hero and the state, embodied respectively in a private detective and an officer of the law. Although for Argentine detective fiction writer Mempo Giardinelli, individualistic heroism is one of the elements that would feature mainly in twentieth-century hard-boiled fiction (25) as a by-product of the Great Depression (19), this metonymic treatment of individualism in the figure of the detective already appears much earlier with Poe. The first manifestations of such a rivalry can be seen at the dénouement of "The Murders in the Rue Morgue," Poe's first detective story, published in 1841. When Dupin solves this locked-room mystery case, he shows a sense of achievement not only because he has solved the puzzle, but more importantly because he draws satisfaction from having defeated G—, the Prefect of the Parisian Police. In other words, he has successfully beaten the state. As the Argentine essayist Josefina Ludmer claims in her essay on detective fiction, *El cuerpo del delito* (1999), what defines "the constellation of crime, in literary speech," is precisely "the tense and contradictory correlation between subjects [. . .] and the state" (15). Dupin attributes his victory to a series of deficiencies in his opponent. Unlike himself, G—is "too cunning to be profound," his wisdom shows no "*stamen*" and he has a "reputation for ingenuity" (1980a, 139; Poe's italics). At the close of this story, the narrator, Dupin's anonymous sidekick, describes G—, "the functionary," as a failed officer who "could not altogether conceal his chagrin at the turn which affairs had taken" (138–139). This emphasizes the importance of a hierarchy, setting the foundations for the genre, in which solving a crime is a twofold task: what is important is not merely restoring social order but doing so in the face of the state.

Arthur Conan Doyle's *A Study in Scarlet*, the first novel featuring Sherlock Holmes, reproduces the rivalry created by Poe, almost half a century later, in 1887. Holmes admits to his famous companion Dr. Watson his reluctance to join the Scotland Yard officers, Tobias Gregson and Inspector G. Lestrade (whose middle name, "G.," evokes Poe's Parisian police prefect), when they beg for his help. The hesitation fades when he accepts the case in the hope that he will "have a laugh at them, if I have nothing else" (1993, 25). In the same way that Dupin seems more concerned about outwitting G—, Holmes, beyond his duty of investigating a crime, is also defined by his superiority over his state counterpart.

This rivalry reappears in an inverse way in another of Doyle's stories, one of the rare times in which Holmes almost fails to solve a case: "The Adventure of the Norwood Builder" (1903). The original element of this story is that the suspected murderer is Holmes's own client, McFarlane, who goes to the private eye asking for help to prove his innocence by investigating the crime at the same time as the police do. In that McFarlane is the main heir of the murdered man, the Scotland Yard goes for the obvious and assumes he is guilty. When every hint seems to point to this conclusion, Holmes tells Watson, with a "haggard and anxious face" (2014, 309), feeling "pale and harassed" (309): "It's all going wrong. I kept a bold face before Lestrade, but

[. . .] I believe that for once the fellow is on the right track and we are on the wrong [. . .]. I fear

[. . .] our case will end ingloriously by Lestrade hanging our client, which will certainly be a triumph for Scotland Yard" (312). What anguishes Holmes here is striking. It is almost irrelevant whether the suspect is guilty or innocent. What matters for Holmes is that he should be the one deciding that, not Lestrade. The eventual punishment of an innocent man, or a guilty one for that matter, should be funneled through him and him only. Of course, Holmes eventually reveals that McFarlane is innocent, but his initial bemoaning shows that he cares not so much about justice itself as about being the one responsible for making that justice.

Conan Doyle continued to write Sherlock Holmes stories almost until his death, in 1930, nearly a century after Edgar Allan Poe imagined the first private eye. It was then that the successors of Dupin and Holmes multiplied profusely, especially in the United Kingdom, where the genre burgeoned during the so-called "Golden Age of Detective Fiction," sometimes also described as the classic era of Murder Mystery narratives. Agatha Christie, G. K. Chesterton, Dorothy L. Sayers, to name a few, created private detectives who replicated this tension between individualism and the state, now in the British countryside.

In the United States, on the other hand, the impact of the Great Depression produced a variation of the genre that has been much more influential during the rest of the twentieth century well beyond the Anglo-American literary field: hard-boiled fiction. Aside from the formal differences between British and American authors, in Dashiell Hammett's foundational novel of hard-boiled fiction, *Red Harvest* (1929), the traces of the opposition between the individualistic hero against the state officers are still there. For instance, the Continental Op, the novel's private eye, blackmails a murderer into a confession: "If you won't talk, I will, to Noonan. If you'll come through to me, I'll do what I can for you" (113). Noonan is Hammett's version of G—or Lestrade: an incompetent Chief of Police. All these examples show the extent to which proving the police wrong is a fundamental goal for the classic detective in Anglo-American stories, a motivation that often exceeds the mere resolution of the puzzle or the identification of a guilty suspect.

From the 1840s to the 1930s, both the United States and the United Kingdom went through substantial historical transition and international conflict, from crucial warfare to the reconfiguration of their territories (civil war, annexation of neighboring regions, loss of colonies, etc.). Faced with a state whose contours and political nature were constantly being altered, these authors set the foundations of a literary rivalry that remained stable. All seem to agree that what was at stake was who opened the way for justice, not justice itself.

Regardless of the specific realizations of the American or the British state that Poe, Doyle or Hammett were writing about, they all give a similar importance to confronting state officers in their fictional worlds through a male protagonist that they imagine as a solid individualistic hero, "a complete man and a common man and yet an unusual man" (2014, 41), as Chandler defined him in his essay *The Simple Art of Murder* (1950). For Giardinelli, the hard-boiled detective is rather a response to individualism. According to him, the Continental Op or Marlowe are best described as antiheroes, that reproduce the North American literary tradition of the classic heroic man who is always young and successful (223). However, neither Hammett nor Chandler completely disengage from that individualistic tradition, as their sleuths may well be "common" but are still "unusual."

It is true that there were also women detectives: the historical Pinkerton National Detective Agency, (the largest private law enforcement organization at the beginning of the twentieth century), located in Chicago, hired women as early as 1856. In literature, female detectives feature as early as 1841, when British novelist Catherine Crowe published an anonymous series of stories featuring a female private eye, which quickly became a best-selling book, *The Adventures of Susan Hopley*. Yet Crowe's initiative had few heirs, to the point that even famous women authors writing in the twentieth century, such as Agatha Christie, Dorothy Sayers, Margery Allingham or Ngaio Marsh, the four "Queens of Crime," would imagine their sleuths under the precepts of masculinity, as strong men—apart from Christie's Miss Marple.

In Anglo-American detective stories, women were usually portrayed not in the active function of the private eye but that of the passive role either of the *femme fatale* (especially in hard-boiled fiction) or the victim of a murder. In Poe's "The Murders in the Rue Morgue" and "The Mystery of Marie Rogêt," for instance, the murdered characters are women. In his essay "The Philosophy of Composition," Poe himself reflects on his own poem "The Raven" concluding that "the death [. . .] of a beautiful woman is, unquestionably, the most poetical topic in the world—and equally is it beyond doubt that the lips best suited for such topic are those of a bereaved lover" (2017, 25). Obviously, this has nothing to do with what for us today would constitute a feminicide (Poe talks about a dead, not necessarily a murdered, woman) that I will study in Chapter 5 in terms of gender violence and the state. But it is still an aesthetic fetishization of dead women, rooted in the Romantic ideas of the sublime, that is central to the genre. In any case, it is masculinity, associated with power, knowledge and force, that dominated the constitution of the private eye as an individualistic myth, the only one capable of truly challenging the state.

## FROM HISTORY TO LITERATURE: INDIVIDUALISM AGAINST THE STATE

The rivalry between individualism and the state has historical roots that go beyond literary production. In fact, it would be unfair to say that the tensions between the individual and the state neither belong to nor start with detective stories. For the German historian Jacob Burkhardt, both individualism and state are concepts that arose together as an opposition in Renaissance Italy, the former being a reaction, a product, of the latter. Particularly in Florence, where "the despotic states [. . .] created a personal desire for eminence [. . .] and also fostered a new emphasis on the values of private life" (qtd. in Watt 121). The origins of individualism are closely related to an emerging social class, the European bourgeoisie, and the ways in which it constructed itself against the state.

In the 1940s, the Italian philosopher Antonio Gramsci observes in his analysis of Poe's detective stories a disdain "towards the judicial apparatus, which is always discredited and thus paves its way with the private detective or amateur" ("Sul romanzo poliziesco"; my translation).[1]

In the same decade, Jorge Luis Borges and French author Roger Caillois had a heated debate in the Argentine literary magazine *Sur*, about whether the origins of detective fiction should be traced within or outside of the literary field (Capdevila 65–78). Whereas Borges circumscribes the origins of detective fiction to literary tradition (isolating it strictly to Dupin's stories); Caillois understands the emergence of the genre within the broader perspective of the sociology of literature. Caillois sees the apparition of the French secret police (a by-product of the French Revolution that eventually spread to other parts of Europe and North America), as a "condition of possibility for the dissemination and success of the detective story ever since the second half of the nineteenth century" (Capdevila 66–67).

Following in Gramsci and Caillois's footsteps, German philosopher Ernest Mandel opens his *Social History of the Crime Story* (1986) by linking this discredit to more specific socioeconomic causes. He dates this hostility towards the police to the first half of the nineteenth century, precisely the period in which Poe founds the genre. According to Mandel, "the great majority of the middle classes and the intelligentsia" (12) feds this contempt against the state. Both for Gramsci and Mande, the origins of this tension can be found in an element that appears already in Poe and Conan Doyle: class. "In most Western countries," says Mandel, "the state apparatus was still anachronistically, semi-feudal, an institution against which the bourgeois class had to fight [. . .] to consolidate its economic and social power" (12).

In this light, Dupin's arrogance towards the Parisian Prefect of Police or Holmes's sense of competition with Scotland Yard can be seen as a literary translation of a historical struggle to consolidate a emerging class in front of a still decaying social order. Mandel goes on to claim that "where the state was already bourgeois (Britain, France, Belgium, Holland and the infant United States) the liberal bourgeoisie preferred it to remain weak, confident that the laws of the market would suffice to perpetuate its rule" (12). Not coincidentally, it was in the national literatures of those countries that detective fiction rose as a popular literary genre almost two hundred years ago. This chapter deals especially with Anglo-American detective stories, but even some of their heroes are from Francophone Europe, such as Christie's Hércules Poirot, a retired Belgian policeman who moves to London.

In the mid-nineteenth century, Mandel argues, the vestiges of the feudal order are mirrored in the way the emerging European and North American bourgeoisie regarded the bureaucratic modern state, whose "spending was considered [. . .] an unproductive deduction from surplus value that would do no more than reduce the amount of capital that could be accumulated" (12) and whose "police was considered a necessary evil, intent on encroaching upon individual rights and freedoms [. . .] The motto of the bourgeoisie was that the weaker the state was, the better" (12). Nonetheless, there is a remarkable historical transformation while Poe creates Dupin and G—. It is then, according to Mandel, when "all that began to change between 1830 and 1848 [. . .]. The violence and sweep of [. . .] rebellions struck fear into the bourgeoisie for the first time" (12). In other words, the social reputation and the political value of the police change as a result of uprisings led by an agent that was traditionally seen as diametrically opposed to the individual: the multitude.

For this reason, the bourgeoisie realized that "perhaps their power would not reproduce itself eternally through the operation of market laws alone [and] a stronger state and a correspondingly more powerful police force were needed to keep a watchful eye on the lower orders, on the classes that were ever restive, periodically rebellious, and therefore criminal in bourgeois eyes" (Mandel 12). Once the bourgeoisie managed to snatch the modern state from its aristocratic remains and took full control of its resources, it mimicked the robust size of the apparatus that they inherited. Thus, they would preserve their power in the face of a new class they themselves produced: the proletariat, especially, when it gathered to demonstrate in the increasingly crowded cities. In short, the European bourgeoisie would strengthen a social order that relied heavily on impersonal bodies (the law and its enforcement agencies, the parliament and the police) to contain and subjugate undesired agents that were equally impersonal, such as the multitude.

Drawing from Burkhardt, Gramsci, and Mandel, the conflict underlying the rivalry between individualism and the state should not be read merely as textual antagonism but also as the literary representation of an unresolved socio-historical conflict. For it is precisely during the mid-nineteenth century that the consolidation of the modern state takes place as well as the emergence of detective stories as a literary genre. Both phenomena are inextricably linked at their very core. As the Welsh literary historian Ian Watt notes in his essay on *Myths of Modern Individualism* (1996), the word "individualism" happens to appear in the English language during the same time that Poe writes the first detective stories. Watt notes that the French diplomat Alexis de Tocqueville's *On Democracy in America* (a book first published in

French in 1835) features in its English translation of 1840 a footnote apologizing for the literal adoption of *individualisme*, because the translator is unaware of any equivalent in English (Henry Reeve, qtd. in Watt 240). It is no coincidence that it is also in the 1840s that the word "individualism" first appears in English dictionaries (Watt 283), to almost simultaneously appear embodied in Poe's Dupin. Significantly, according to Watt, not only the word individualism but also the appearance of the word "myth" can be dated to the same decade (228).

The two poles of the opposition I address in this book, then, are strongly intertwined. Early detective stories deploy individualism in direct relationship with a hostility towards the state without which it would have no *raison d'être*. One piece of the story cannot be conceived or justified without the other. In "The Purloined Letter," Dupin introduces G—as a "contemptible" man even though he "had not seen him for several years" (Poe 1980c, 200), while Watson says about Lestrade that his "insolence was maddening" (Conan Doyle 2014, 314). Both G—and Lestrade are not really individuals but mere representatives of the state, while the detectives are the true individuals that stand for individualism itself due to their idiosyncratic and peculiar personalities. Dupin and G—feature in the three detective stories written by Poe during the 1840s, which will become the foundational tales of the detective genre: "The Murders in the Rue Morgue" (1841), "The Mystery of Marie Rogêt" (1842), and "The Purloined Letter" (1844). In each case, they incarnate a rivalry that will later be embodied by sundry private detectives and policemen from late-nineteenth to early-twentieth-century Anglo-American detective stories. In this chapter, I will focus on a series of examples in which this rivalry is prominent: Poe's Dupin against G—; Doyle's Sherlock Holmes against Inspector Lestrade; Christie's Hércules Poirot against Inspector Japp (also an officer of Scotland Yard); Hammett's Continental Op against Personville's crooked Chief of Police Noonan; and Chandler's Philip Marlowe against LAPD Lieutenant Nulty.

The monotonous attributes of these state men without qualities are often announced in their names. Poe names G—following the early nineteenth-century Romantic trend of redacting names to make them look vaguer. The Parisian Prefect of Police does not even have a full name, only an initial and a dash. Unlike his counterpart the Chevalier Dupin, who holds a nobility title, G—does not have a lineage. He is almost anonymous. He is a non-entity, a nothing, which is recaptured a century later by Raymond Chandler when he names his LAPD Lieutenant "Nulty," evoking the word "null." Similarly, "Lestrade," which in Italian (*le strade*) points to the streets, is the man who only possess a mundane knowledge. Lestrade and his colleague Gregson (again, a simple son of a Greg, an ordinary person) are in clear opposition with Sherlock, who in turn carries in his name the mark of the Old English "scir," i.e.,: "bright" (*Online Etymology Dictionary*): the private eye defines them as "the pick of a bad lot" (Conan Doyle 1993, 24), the most you could expect from what he considers to be a mediocre institution such as Scotland Yard. Lestrade is "quick and energetic, but conventional" (24), that is, he has a prosaic personality incapable of even a minimum degree of imagination.

For all the nuances that can be found in each author's work, there is in each of them a common construction of the police as an entity that, although necessary, represents an instance of inferiority in contrast to the singularity of their private sleuths. "I've always had a secret hankering to be a detective" confesses Poirot's sidekick, Captain Hastings, at the beginning of Christie's first novel *The Mysterious Affair at Styles* (1916). "Scotland Yard? Or Sherlock Holmes?" he is asked, to which he answers: "Holmes by all means" (12). This trend for private eyes, and their proliferation as the individualistic heroes of early detective fiction, echoes the historical conflicts of the period examined by Mandel: the characters that incarnate the state police force are a necessary foil to the private eye. They are textual functions: none of them are interesting as characters in their own right, but for what they stand for. They all embody a doctrine, following a specific narrative strategy that is fundamental to understand detective fiction in Anglo-American literatures and beyond: personification. Like policemen, detectives, too, give a corporeal identity to immaterial abstractions: respectively, individualism and the modern state. Yet they do so in different ways, following opposing modes of personification: whereas the detective personifies individualism by being singular and remarkable, the policemen personify the state by being nothing, emptied nobodies. Hence the success of Dupin, a character filled with mythical attributes, who is "in the direct ratio" (Poe 1980a, 120) of the failure of the police, an institution defined by lack.

One of the main ideas that features in the *Theory of the Novel* (1920), by the Hungarian philosopher György Lukács, resides in a distinction between the types of hero appearing in the epic and in that genre's main successor: the modern novel. Lukács claims that "the epic hero is, strictly speaking, never an individual" (66) but a collective figure whose essential characteristic "is the fact that its theme is not a personal destiny but the destiny of a community" (66). By contrast, it is only the novel that depicts individuals as such. The world of the epic is "a homogeneous world" (32) in which there is no room for individual characters to emerge because "even the separation between man and world, between 'I' and 'you,' cannot disturb its homogeneity" (32). According to Lukács, the novelistic hero brings a distinct novelty: he is detached from his community. For Lukács, as French sociologist Lucien Goldmann says, "if there is to be a novel there must be a radical opposition between man and the world, between the individual and society" (171). The detective story's rivalry between individualism and the state could be understood as an exacerbation of Lukács's prerequisite: the genre poses an even more explicit opposition between a specific kind of individual and a precise form of organized society. The rivalry goes a step further: Dupin and his heirs are not solely individuals; they are individualism itself incarnated. G—and his successors are not individuals at all; instead, they evoke a depersonalized entity, the modern state.

The exacerbation of Lukács's opposition could also be read as a rewriting of a Renaissance trope, in Ian Watt's terms: the "posture of ego contra mundum" (122). Watt examines how Faust, Don Quixote, Don Juan, and Robinson Crusoe constitute the four myths that epitomize and endorse modern individualism. Since Watt focuses on classical literature examples, he does not include the different incarnations of the detective, which, I believe, reproduce this very same logic of a self against the world, only to a more specific purpose: to criticize the hindrances of the modern state. Like these myths, the classic detective operates "without any regard whatsoever to race, people, party, family or corporation," adopting "the posture of *ego contra mundum* [. . .] unaffected by, and hardly even noticing, the normative intermediaries between [itself] and the existential social and intellectual realities around" (122). Regardless of its incarnations (Dupin, Holmes, Nulty), it is the archetypical figure of the private eye as such that shares several of these features. Equally, Watt says his four myths "are not completely real, historical persons; yet their audience yields to them a kind of genuine existence" (233). The same applies, for instance, to Sherlock Holmes, whose "house" opened in 1990 at the fictional detective's address on Baker Street, London. Ever since, hundreds of thousands of tourists visit it from all over the world.

In his Seminar on 'The Purloined Letter,' French psychoanalyst Jacques Lacan already identifies these mythical dimensions when he defines G—as "a hapless prefect of police who plays the role, classic in this kind of mythology, of someone who has to find what is being sought after, but who cannot but end up losing the thread" and Dupin as "the character, more mythical still, who understands everything" (194). The mythical dimension of these founding characters holds for their heirs. Holmes, for example, even considers himself superior to his model: "No doubt you think that you are complimenting me in comparing me to Dupin [. . .]. Now, in my opinion, Dupin was a very inferior fellow" (Conan Doyle 1993, 21). This intertextual gesture reinforces the individualistic dimension of the private eye as a myth, unable to share with its forerunner a sort of symbolic title, only available to a sole heir: that of the wittiest detective.

Borrowing Watt's terms, the tradition inaugurated by Poe rewrites the *ego* through the figure of the private detective as an embodiment of individualism, *contra mundum*, against a world, now rewritten under the form of a modern state that coerces him. Watt identifies *mundus* with a specific period in European history: The Counter-Reformation. The mechanisms that coerce Watt's myths, essentially, are religious constraints. In turn, the counter-mechanisms that make them modern is the way in which they exert their agency. Watt cites French sociologist Émile Durkheim, who claims that ancestral myths unite societies. Their primary goal is to function as agglutinating agents "to maintain and strengthen social solidarity" (qtd. in Watt 230).

These individualistic myths, instead, do not unite societies but go against them. The paradigmatic example, perhaps, is Don Quixote's tilting at windmills or, even more clearly, his unilateral release of galley slaves that were imprisoned by the rule of the Spanish King. It matters little if the state is an absolute monarchy as in Cervantes or an emerging liberal republic as in Poe, the myths of modern individualism follow their own rule above the law. Beyond the different historical periods and geographical settings, what is at stake in Watt's *ego contra mundum*, is an issue that resides at the core of the political: the problem of sovereignty. Who is in charge? Who wields power? Don Quixote or the Spanish Monarch? Dupin or G—? Holmes or Scotland Yard? Alternatively, what is also at stake is the literary portrayal of this political conflict: how to represent representation? Early Anglo-American detective fiction problematizes this by personifying the impersonal institutions of the state in a body signifying nothing, opposing it to an individual that signifies, perhaps, much more than humans can, thus, producing an asymmetric rivalry.

## AN ASYMMETRIC RIVALRY

Literary rivalries are indeed problematic: the line that separates the individualistic hero and the state is frequently crossed in the classic detective story. The rivalry between *ego* and *mundus* is configured under the assumption that the boundary between individual and state is stable. Yet the permeability of this boundary appears when G—hires Dupin to solve the murders of the Rue Morgue and his success is such that he is called upon once more by the Parisian Police to solve "The Mystery of Marie Rogêt" (1842). As his sidekick says, Dupin "found himself the cynosure of the policial [sic] eyes; and the cases were not few in which attempt was made to engage his services at the Prefecture" (Poe 1980b, 144). In Anglo-American detective stories, the *ego* is not only constrained but it is also coveted by *mundus*. Lestrade says of Holmes that he has been "of use to the force once or twice in the past, and we owe you a good turn at Scotland Yard" (Conan Doyle 2014, 303). The state officers do not only contend against their individualistic competitor; they are also fascinated by him: Hammett's Continental Op is hired as an associate member of the Continental Detective Agency's San Francisco office to solve the murder of newspaper publisher Donald Wilson. In the fictional town of Personville (ironically renamed by the narrator as Poisonville, a city filled with vice), he works closely with the city police, under the supervision of Chief Noonan.

According to Argentine novelist and critic Ricardo Piglia, "since Dupin, the detective is

[. . .] the police's trustworthy man" (1986, 69). Nonetheless, even when the police rely on the private detective to collaborate with them, this power relationship is more of an asymmetrical competition than an amiable collaboration. The private eye may be a confidant of the state police, but this does not mean that he is on their side. The private detective is on his own side and his side only. If he works with the police, it is to take advantage of them and outwit them as much as he can. Dupin, for instance, operates as a privileged individual who "shall have no difficulty in obtaining the necessary permission" from the Prefect of Police to see "the premises with our own eyes" (1980a, 118). Similarly, when he visits the crime scene with Dupin, his sidekick mentions: "We came again to the front of the dwelling, rang, and having shown our credentials, were admitted by the agents in charge" (1980a, 119). But what are these so-called "credentials"? Because these first detective stories do not conform with the conventions of literary realism, the sidekick does not say, as the narrator takes for granted that his characters are somehow entitled to them.

The classic private detective does not need an explanation to justify this quasi-supernatural privilege: neither Dupin nor the narrator work for any private or public institution that can attest for their legitimacy to investigate crime. Yet they manage to be admitted by the authorities to go everywhere they please. This privilege shows the extent to which Dupin is not just another citizen, but someone who holds power enough to surmount the hindrances usually applied by the state to its citizens. His individual wit is so strong, it surmounts the chain of command that a whole institution has for itself: it is difficult to imagine a junior officer, for instance, repeating the words of the private detective—not to mention, the tone of his voice. It is in the sleuth's voice that the asymmetry of this rivalry is put centre stage: its amplification, its incidence, its confidence, are in clear contrast with the silence of the state officers.

This asymmetry looks even sharper in the hostility and fascination that shape the relationship between sleuths and policemen. Especially in the fact that these hostility and fascination are usually unidirectional. Sleuths often use the thin line that separates them from state officers as a strategy to obtain information that might help them solve their case and take personal credit. The permeability of this boundary reappears in Hammett's *Red Harvest*: When he is interrogating a witness, the Continental Op says: "'I want five minutes' talk with you. I've got nothing to do with Noonan except to queer his racket. I'm alone'" (52). Even if he is ultimately working for the city police, he manipulates the witness by underlining his autonomy from the state.

Conversely, police officers do not display the same grudge towards the individualistic hero that he holds for them. By contrast, they admire private investigators: G—, Lestrade, and Japp are fascinated by Dupin, Holmes, and Poirot. By contrast, Holmes only esteems a challenging opponent, such as the criminal mastermind, Professor James Moriarty. When Holmes finally solves "The Adventure of the Norwood Builder," Lestrade utters his astonishment: "This is the brightest thing that you have done yet, though it is a mystery to me how you did it" (2014, 318). Instead of regretting his defeat, he is relieved that Holmes has proven him wrong: "You have saved an innocent man's life, and you have prevented a very grave scandal, which would have ruined my reputation in the force" (318). Similarly, Scotland Yard inspector Jimmy Japp acknowledges "there's no man's judgement I'd sooner take than" Poirot's (Christie 115). Both parties are aware of their rivalry; but neither the hostility nor the fascination are reciprocal.

Yet this asymmetry evolves as the genre does. In hard-boiled fiction, the unrequited fascination vanishes. In *Red Harvest*, Chief Noonan convinces the Continental Op to get involved in a shooting only to try and get him killed because the Police Prefect anticipates his antagonist is "going to make a nuisance" of himself (53). From Hammett onwards, police officers are not as enthralled by private detectives. All the idealization of the private eye's unmatchable wit begins to slowly fade away, clearing the way for a more realistic representation of the agents involved with crime investigation. Regardless of the degree of idealization of the classic detective, in Hammett and Chandler, the state still needs the individualistic hero; who in turn does not truly need the state. In other words, the state is symbolically dominated, in Bourdieu's terms, by the private individual. It is not without reason that G—or Lestrade must go to Dupin's or Holmes's offices to get their cases solved. The facility with which these rivals are so detached from each other resides on the one hand in a set of "symbolic disabilities" ascribed to the body of the state and on the other hand a supplementary series of mythical attributes assigned to the private detective, related in one way or another to individualism.

# THE ANGLO-AMERICAN PRIVATE DETECTIVE: A DISEMBODIED MIND

## Loneliness and Immunity: The Mythical Attributes of Individualism

Lukács (117), Goldmann (64), and Watt (238) all agree that individualism reaches its peak only when modernity is consolidated, during the nineteenth century, at the very same time that the first detective stories were shaping the classic model of the detective. According to Lukács it was then when "the inner importance of the individual has reached its historical apogee: the individual is no longer significant as the carrier of transcendent worlds [. . .] he now carries his value exclusively within himself" (117). No wonder, therefore, that it is then when the private detective emerges as a triumphant character. When Tocqueville travels through the United States, he distinguishes individualism (which he sees as an unprecedented historical phenomena) from selfishness, an "exaggerated love of self, which leads a man to connect everything with himself and to prefer himself to everything in the world" (qtd. in Watt 240). For Tocqueville, individualism "disposes each member of the community to sever himself from the mass of his fellows and to draw apart with his family and his friends" (qtd. in Watt 240). Whereas egoism is "a psychological term," individualism is "a social description" (235), the institutionalization of egoism.

Individualism is a by-product of a new social order, an unprecedented way of structuring societies that must be understood as a consequence of major historical events and processes, e.g.,: The Colonisation of the Americas, the selective industrialisation of European cities, the American Independence, the French Revolution, all of which reshaped the West during its gradual abandonment of feudal economy. "Individualism," obviously, is not the same as "individual." Whereas the latter is already present in Descartes' *cogito ergo sum*, which was established in the 1630s; the former is a programmatic idea that does not appear as such until after the Romantic movement, nor it can be understood without these historic events.

One of the main attributes of individualism that leads to the detective's success against the state is loneliness. Dupin's anonymous sidekick describes the prevailing atmosphere of the sleuth's house in these terms: "Our seclusion was perfect. We admitted no visitors. [. . .] We existed within ourselves alone" (Poe 1980a, 108). Equally, when Watson meets Holmes, he thinks "my companion was as friendless as a man as I was myself" (Conan Doyle 1993, 17). Hastings introduces himself and his master Poirot as individuals also lacking "near relations or friends" (Christie 5). In one scene in *Red Harvest*, the Chief of Poisonville Police Noonan offers the Continental Op a few policemen to help him: "Would you like me to leave a couple of the boys with you, just to see nothing else happens?" (Hammett 67). Yet the Continental Op refuses to work in a team, because he takes pride in his loneliness; he is, quintessentially, a lonesome male (Chandler 2014, 42).

Indeed, the ways Western societies have regarded individualism underwent many transformations from the 1840s till the 1930s. When Tocqueville writes about individualism in the United States, he is one of the few not to describe it in derogatory terms. But both from the left and the right, individualism originated as a negative concept, criticized by thinkers of a diverse spectrum, from counter-revolutionary authors such as the Scottish philosopher Edmund Burke and the French writer Xavier de Maître to one of the founders of utopian socialism, the Welsh philanthropist Robert Owen. Despite their political differences, they all used the noun "individualist" as an insult to describe their political opponents. As Watt reminds us, it is only after the 1830s that the idea of putting the individual at the center of the political evolved to a more positive light. From Tocqueville to the Manchester School, individualism changed the reception of Watt's four myths, whose individualistic drive was initially conceived and perceived as excesses, sins, or, more generally, as behavior that their readers were not supposed to mimic, but later shifted to a more desirable trait.

The first period of detective stories, specifically with Poe and Doyle, is a direct inheritor of this post-Romantic sensitivity. Watt claims that Romantics saw his myths in a favorable light, as "they presented individualism as the most desirable human quality" (172). Inaugurated by Poe, perhaps the most Romantic of American authors, it is no coincidence that the detective genre extols the uniqueness of this illustrious upper-class individual. Even if hard-boiled detectives are far from being Romantic characters in the same way as Poe's, their individualistic subjectivity still is an unquestionable given, an inheritance of Romanticism. Of course, after the Great Depression, the celebration of individualism in hard-boiled fiction is mitigated and reshaped in terms of survival within a hostile urban setting.

Like Watt's mythic figures, these detectives are generally "stripped of any family connection" (123): they "exist in a domestic vacuum [. . .] either they have no recorded parents, siblings, wives or children, or they are alienated from other family members," sharing the same "degree of isolation from the wider world around" (123). In a nutshell, they are a paradigmatic exacerbation of individualism, which is encapsulated in domestic isolation. But why is this endorsement of isolation so prominent in the configuration of the classic detective? Perhaps, the reasons can be found in that seclusion allows for one of the main driving forces of individualism: individual freedom. Thanks to his seclusion, the private detective is more effective than the teams led by the state police. Being stripped of society, detached from any family or community, allows him to get rid of the bureaucratic constraints that would hinder his efficiency. Beyond the differences that separate the distant periods (from the 1840s to the 1930s), private eyes work alone, after all, because it is more praiseworthy to solve a case by oneself than as part of a team.

It is true that their loneliness is never absolute. Like Watt's individualistic myths, while the private eye does not "have close and trusting relationships with like-minded men or women," he "form[s] [his] only close tie with a male servant" (123). Though detached from society due to his unmatchable wit, the detective seldom works fully alone: he tends to be accompanied by a sidekick, who is often the narrator of the stories that tell his tale. Nevertheless, they are two lonelinesses together, or as Watt describes Don Quixote and Sancho, they "form a duality of solitaries" (234). And despite their isolated position, there is still a hierarchy that establishes another asymmetrical relationship: unlike the one facing the detective against the state policeman, the detective and his sidekick should be understood not as a rivalry but as an uneven alliance.

The fascination the detective exerts on his subordinate is conspicuous and unidirectional. Holmes, for instance, describes himself as "a conjurer [who] gets no credit once he has explained his trick." He admits to Watson that "if I show you too much of my method of working, you will come to the conclusion that I am a very ordinary individual after all" (1993, 36), to which his companion replies: "I shall never do that [. . .] you have brought detection as near an exact science as it ever will be brought in this world" (36). The cynical tone of hard-boiled fiction transforms this uneven alliance: Hammett introduces the Continental Op's sidekick, Mickey Linehan, as someone who comes from the "Continental's San Francisco branch [because the private eye] had wired for help" (117). This may lead us to think that the Continental Op is not as self-sufficient as his predecessors, but his sidekick again functions mainly as an inferior counterpart, described in ways that are not that different from a state antagonist. Linehan was "a big slob with sagging shoulders and a shapeless body that seemed to be coming apart at all its joints. His ears stood out like red wings, and his round red face usually wore the meaningless smirk of a half-wit. He looked like a comedian and was" (116).

As I explore below, there are significant similarities between the ways in which the narrator depicts the private's eye sidekick and state officers: through lacks and distortions, a "shapeless body," disproportionately big ears, etc. All these physical features highlight the detective's superiority. After all, the sidekick never influences his master's elucidations. When the time comes to solve crimes, all the credit goes solely to the private detective who, impervious to the constrictions of society (be it the policemen's or his sidekick's), turns into an immune superhero.

The second attribute of individualism that defines the private eye is immunity. In "Typologie du Roman policier," a structuralist analysis of detective stories, Tzvetan Todorov discusses "the detective's immunity" to death (1971, 44). According to Todorov, "we cannot imagine Hercule Poirot [. . .] threatened by some danger, attacked, wounded, even killed" (44). Holmes is "temporarily killed" in "The Adventure of the Final Problem" (1893) only to return in The Hound of the *Baskervilles* (1901) because Conan Doyle needed the money only his most famous invention could bring in. This imperviousness to threats and vulnerability transcends early detective stories, and it remains a convention that continues in hard-boiled fiction. This is why the Continental Op boasts that he has "framed millions, and nothing happened to me" (132).

Piglia, in turn, establishes a different type of immunity, this time, against corruption: "In Chandler, everything is corrupted except for Marlowe, an honest professional who does his job well and does not get contaminated; he actually seems an urban expression of the cowboy" (1986, 70). Chandler himself puts it in this way: the detective is "a man [. . .] who is [. . .] neither tarnished nor afraid" (2014, 41). This is true for Chandler's detective as well as for his forerunner: Hammett's The Continental Op, who is impervious to Noonan's corruption. In brief, the immortality and the honesty of the private eye add another layer that configures him not only as another modern myth of individualism, but also as a forerunner of twentieth-century superheroes, which is why Lacan defines Dupin as a "prototype of a latter-day swashbuckler, as yet safe from the insipidity of our contemporary superman" ("Seminar on 'The Purloined Letter'"). While Watt's myths of modern individualism all die, and their death is a punishment (except for Crusoe) because of the abuse of their individualistic drive, classic detectives endure and even if they get involved with questionable means, it is for the sake of honest ends that distinguish them from criminals.

The Italian philosopher Roberto Esposito revises in his work the concept of "immunity" by returning to its original Latin meanings. He argues that immunity should be understood as a "protective response in the face of a risk" that he labels "contagion," i.e.,: "the rupture of a previous equilibrium and the consequent need for its reconstitution" (2011, 2). He goes beyond the medical and political sense of immunity and contagion, merging them in a biopolitical meaning: "Latin dictionaries tell us that the noun *Immunitas* [. . .] is a negative or privative term whose meaning derives from what it negates or lacks, namely, the *munus*. [. . .] (a task, obligation)." Someone who is immune is "exonerated, exempted [. . .] from the *pensum* of paying tributes or performing services for others [. . .] Those who are immune owe nothing to anyone" (5). What is the private eye exempted from paying? To begin with, he does not seem to be obligated to obey the same rules that apply for the rest of society, as seen, for instance, when Dupin gets by without credentials to visit the crime scene of "The Purloined Letter." The *munus* negated by the private eye is related to the duties imposed by the modern state to its citizens. Following Esposito's reading of immunity as a privileged and unilateral autonomy towards the community, it could be argued that the classic private detective displays a fourfold immunity: not solely to death and corruption as Todorov and Piglia argue, but also to the state and to failure. None of these four elements affect the classic detective. This proto-superhero's immunity turns him into an exception: he is entirely lonely and immune when restoring social order, i.e.,: when he gathers in the fruits of his labour.

## LABOUR AND MONEY

Following Max Weber, Watt sees modern individualism as a "force which Protestantism had done much to bring to birth" (40). It is no coincidence that Crusoe, Watt's last myth of modern individualism (the only one detached as a secular myth), shares the fact of being conceived in Protestant societies with Dupin, Holmes, Poirot, The Continental Op, or Marlowe. By the nineteenth century, religious morals have been out of the scope for such a long time that the threat to individualism no longer comes from religious *doxa* but from political *habitus*, linked not to the church but to the modern bureaucratic state.[2]

Unlike Faust, Don Quixote, or Don Juan, none of the early private detectives struggle against their sinful deeds (such as their pride, for instance). In this sense, they share with Watt's myths their *arete* but are exempt from their *hubris*. In other words, private detectives share the individualistic excellence of Counter-Reformation heroes without inheriting their arrogance. In consequence, they are closer to the also unpunished Crusoe, conceived in the early eighteenth century, "in the context of developing individualism" (Watt xv). Because of the private eye's immunity to death, the punitive element (closely linked to death or hell) is no longer at stake in early detective stories. If there is punishment, it is circumscribed to the criminal. What is at stake is the relation that private detectives establish with a *habitus* that, as Weber shows in *The Protestant Ethic and the Spirit of Capitalism* (1905), is closely linked to religion: labour.

Richard Henry Tawney, in *Religion and the Rise of Capitalism* (1926), states that "the distinctive note of Puritan teaching was [. . .] individual responsibility [whose] qualities arm the spiritual athlete for his solitary contest with a hostile world" (qtd. in Watt 163). This teaching informs the early private detective's Calvinist sense of self-importance and strenuous commitment to the lonely task of detection. As I explore in Chapter 4, subsequent detective stories exacerbate both this loneliness and this commitment to labour in the shape of neoliberal workaholism, by depicting individuals who are deeply (and solely) engaged with their jobs, disregarding their families when and if they have them, ratifying Lukács's motto that "to be a man in the new world is to be solitary" (36), and prolonging the domestic vacuum that Watt ascribes to his myths.

From the first scene of *A Study in Scarlet*, Holmes's singularity resides in a paradox involving his commitment to perform labour in a successful fashion: he appears to have no clear profession but at the same time he shows an obsessive devotion to his cases. When Watson first encounters him, he is "absorbed in his work" (1993, 9), spending his days at the medical laboratory "from morning till night" (8). Similarly, when the Continental Op is invited by a female character to "go down to Salt Lake" he refuses: "Somebody's got to stay here to count the dead" (Hammett 158). A strict work ethic permeates both. The very professions of detectives, far from being arbitrary, are part of the endorsement of individualism against the bureaucratic corporatism of the state. While Dupin, Holmes, and Poirot work for themselves as amateur freelance investigators (never fully joining any team or working as employees), the Continental Op and Marlowe are professional independent agents hired by corporations. Beyond these variations a common factor remains: they all work for the private sector. By contrast, G—, Lestrade, Japp, Nulty, and Noonan are public policemen. They all work for the metropolitan police of their cities: the Parisian Prefecture, London's Scotland Yard, Los Angeles or the fictional Poisonville's Police Department. In short, while detectives are immersed in the market, policemen are constricted by the state.

Christie's initial description of Poirot, in *The Mysterious Affair at Styles* (1920), mentions that he "had been in his time one of the most celebrated members of the Belgian police" (19). The fact that he is no longer an officer of the state but a retired policeman, based in London to run a private detective agency, is no coincidence. It reproduces the literary boundaries between individual and state that are at the core of the asymmetric rivalry between them. Similarly, if the Continental Op does not work strictly for himself but for a private agency, that does not diminish his sense of individualism: "It's right enough for the Agency to have rules and regulations, but when you're out on a job you've got to do it the best way you can" (Hammett 117), he says, contrasting his individual effectiveness to the structures of the Continental Operation Agency, a fictional corporation, inspired by the historical Pinkerton National Detective Agency. The same can be said about Philip Marlowe, whose cases start only once he becomes a private sleuth after being dismissed, for insubordination, from the District Attorney's office of Los Angeles County.

According to Mandel, private detectives and state policemen perform a labour that is linked to an underlying class distinction between them. G—or Lestrade were modeled on state policemen who "were not rich entrepreneurs or gentlefolk; [nor] members of the ruling class, but generally belonged to the lower middle class" (14–15). Instead, "the real hero of the criminal detective story [. . .] had to be not the plodding cop but a brilliant sleuth of upper-class origins. And that is what Dupin and Holmes [. . .] are" (14–15). As Poe's narrator becomes acquainted with Dupin, social class is precisely one of the first attributes he notices: "This young gentleman was of an excellent—indeed of an illustrious family" (1980a, 107). Inversely, Marlowe introduces Lieutenant Nulty with the comment that he "looked poor enough to be honest" (Chandler 1988, 212). The class abyss that separates them is visible from both sides.

The private eye's subjectivity should be understood as the product of a twofold cultural shift of attitudes towards individualism. Firstly, in its relationship with labour: "Whereas *Genesis* had presented labour as a curse for Adam and Eve's disobedience to God's command," says Watt, "the Protestant ethic taught that untiring stewardship of the gifts of God was a paramount and religious obligation" (122). This resignification of labour, from the Jewish to the Protestant worldview, is clearly present in Dupin or Holmes, especially, the sense of work as duty to oneself. This brings to the second aspect of this twofold cultural shift: namely, the one that individualism establishes with loneliness. Watt notes that Ancient Jewish and Greek culture regarded "leaving home a punishment," and to be banished from society, "a personal catastrophe" (112). He traces back to Aristotle's *Politics* the idea that self-sufficient humans, who were not fit to live gregariously, were considered "either a beast or a god" (112). After Romanticism, working by oneself is no longer a negative attribute. While for Lukács, the modern novel's "loneliness [. . .] is the torment of a creature condemned to solitude and devoured by a longing for community" (38), the private eye's loneliness enhances his commitment to his labour and the merit of his detecting skills, because he solves most of his cases alone, often barely needing to move from his desk.

Even in hard-boiled fiction, when the detective leaves his office and goes to the mean streets his loneliness remains unaltered. Daniel Defoe, in a chapter of his *Robinson Crusoe* (1719) entitled "Of Solitude," argues that seclusion is not only to be relished but also experienced in contact with others: "I enjoy much more solitude in the middle of the greatest collection of mankind in the world, I mean, at London [. . .] than ever I could say that I enjoy'd in eight and twenty years confinement to a desolate island" (qtd. in Watt 150). Loneliness and labour are thus inseparable from their necessary contrast: the people and its formal representation in the modern state. This helps to explain why the classic detective performs his solitary work in Europe's most populous cities, London and Paris, the only ones whose population surpassed a million inhabitants from the 1850s till the 1870s (Chandler and Fox 303–342).

The relationship between this lonely individual and society cannot but be tense, due to the role and the ever-shifting contours of both market and state.

Holmes describes himself as "an unofficial personage" (1993, 25), highlighting the parastatal nature of his job. Hesitating to take on the case of *A Study in Scarlet*, he portrays his task almost as if it was a clandestine one performed in the shadows: "Supposing I unravel the whole matter, you may be sure that Gregson, Lestrade, and Co. will pocket all the credit [. . .]. He knows I am his superior and acknowledges it to me; but he would cut his tongue out before he would own it to any third person" (25). Public recognition becomes vain for Holmes. After all, what is its value when compared with his own private delusion of greatness? Despite being this "unofficial personage," he acts as if he were a supervisor of the Scotland Yard officers. For instance, when Lestrade and Gregson remove the corpse of a victim, they only do so once Holmes authorizes them. The following dialogue illustrates the asymmetry that involves both parties and cast doubts on the "unofficial" nature of Holmes's position:

"Have you made any inquiries as to this man Stangerson?"

"I did at once, sir," said Gregson. "I have had advertisements sent to [. . .] newspapers"

"Have you sent to Cleveland?"

"We telegraphed this morning."

"How did you word your inquiries?"

"We simply detailed the circumstances." (30)

Rather than simply taking advice from an external consultant, Lestrade and Gregson seem to be reporting to their boss. Likewise, the Continental Op treats his sidekick as his subordinate: "I don't want you birds to send any writing back to San Francisco without letting me see it first" (Hammett 118). The power structure is clear: the classic Anglo-American detective commands crime investigation with an entitlement of authority that seems naturally obtained. Dupin, Holmes, the Continental Op, they are all egos who order the world, in the twofold meaning of the verb: they put in and give orders.

Before his failure to locate the purloined letter, G——confesses that he is driven to succeed because "the reward is enormous" (Poe 1980c, 203). In early pre-hardboiled detective stories, money might motivate crime, but rarely its investigation. Even if G——offers this generous reward admitting he is "perfectly willing to take advice and to pay [. . .] fifty thousand francs to anyone who would aid me in the matter" (207) and Dupin replies "fill me up a check for the amount mentioned. When you have signed it, I will hand you the letter" (207), payment is not the *sine qua non* that it is in Hammett or Chandler. Dupin welcomes the money as a reward, as a financial recognition of his unmatched knowledge, not because he needs it for his survival. As French philosopher Jacques Derrida reminds us, Dupin holds "a remnant of his paternal inheritance, apparently surrendered without calculation to the debtor who knows how, by calculating ('rigorous economy'), to draw from it a *rente*, an income, the surplus-value of a capital that works alone" (1975, 105). So Dupin does not really need income.

Instead, hard-boiled detectives, because they are depicted in terms of a more realistic aesthetics, must engage with more prosaic financial concerns. As Piglia argues, Hammett and Chandler display "a narrative mode [. . .] that is linked to a materialistic [. . .] sense of reality" (1986, 69). According to Piglia, Marlowe or the Continental Op are professionals, "someone who does a job and receives a salary whereas in Poe or Holmes the detective is often an amateur who 'selflessly' volunteers to decipher an enigma" (69). Although, it should be nuanced that the hard-boiled private detective does not, strictly speaking, earn a salary but an occasional remuneration for his services: he is not a working-class wage earner; he is an upper-class freelancer, which puts him in a superior dimension in front of the state officers. Holmes sees himself as above bureaucratic and material hindrances, thus aiming to be regarded beyond social material recognition, not even claiming credit once he has solved "The Adventure of the Norwood Builder." When Lestrade asks him: "And you don't want your name to appear?" he replies: "Not at all. The work is its own reward. Perhaps I shall get the credit also at some distant day, when I permit my zealous historian to lay out his foolscap once more—eh, Watson?" (2014, 319). Of course, the irony of the scene is that this "distant day" is re-signified and actualised with every reading of the story. Holmes is satisfied with what he regards as a much more valuable reward than mundane compensations: literary glory, a key component to make him another myth of modern individualism.

The absence or presence of money entail the twofold nature of the classic detective. With hard-boiled fiction, money becomes dominant in the configuration of the investigation and the condition that allows the resolution of crimes. Poirot emerges as an eccentric character when Hastings first describes him as "a great dandy" (Christie, 12). Dupin and Holmes could also be seen as dandies: precisely because of their lack of need for money. As Piglia mentions, in "early detective stories [. . .] material relationships appear sublimated: crimes are 'free' precisely because the gratuitousness of the motive strengthens the enigma" (1986, 70).

This sublimation could also be understood beyond money, in terms of gender: as queer studies scholar Elisa Glick defines, the dandy is "at the center of debates about the history of the homosexual in the West" (129). In other words, the dandy, "the premier model of modern gay subjectivity" (129), is in the antipodes of the state, whose DNA not only is masculine but is also perceived as straight, even though that is not always necessarily the case. As Rita Segato claims, to define the masculine sovereign in terms of "'heterosexuality' is not accurate, because, strictly speaking, we know little about his sexuality" (2016, 94). I will go back to the problem of the classic detective's queerness opposed to the state's perceived heteronormativity in Chapter 2.

That Holmes does not need financial compensation directly relates to the fact that despite his commitment to perform labour successfully, he is still an idle aristocrat who can afford to be "the most incurable lazy devil that ever stood in shoe leather" (Conan Doyle 1993, 25). Holmes is not a medical doctor or student, but an amateur whose profession is not that different from his other addictions linked more to dandy leisure: cocaine, chess, or the violin. Like Dupin, he might receive money for his work, but he values more the immaterial recognition of having bested the state.

By contrast, the Continental Op and Philip Marlowe could not conceive of working without financial compensation. When Hammett's detective discusses the case with his client, even if working alone is still an imperative, isolation is not enough: "You really want the town cleaned up? [. . .] I'd have to have a free hand [. . .] run the job as I pleased. And [. . .] a ten-thousand-dollar retainer [. . .]. If you want the job done, you'll plank down enough money" (42–44). The Continental Op is no longer an amateur sleuth working for pure intellectual pleasure. Unlike his predecessors, he is a professional hired to solve a case in exchange for money. While the presence of money will lead not only to professionalization but also to corruption, its absence paves the way for an obsessive passion for knowledge.

## FROM KNOWLEDGE TO SUCCESS

In *The Figure of the Detective* (2013), Charles Brownson defines the classic private eye as someone who "embodies the context of rationality as a spokesman for the power of thought and intelligibility of the universe, which is possible a more important function than solving the crime" (14). The private eye's individual uniqueness is linked to this "passion for definite and exact knowledge" (Conan Doyle 1993, 8), a feature that conversely ends up isolating him: "No man lives or has ever lived who has brought the same amount of study and of natural talent to the detection of crime which I have done" (22). Even if Holmes may regard the results of this uniqueness as negative because sometimes "there is no crime to detect, or, at most, some bungling villainy with a motive so transparent that even a Scotland Yard official can see through it" (22), his complaints are superficial. They introduce a case to be solved, a case that interrupts an absence of challenges, thus highlighting the privileged zenith in which he is in thanks to his knowledge.

The private eye's is the voice of truth because it is the voice of positivist science: the laws of physics, biology and forensics, are embedded in his speech, which dissects the arguments of his opponents, proving them wrong and illogical. While according to Australian anthropologist Michael Taussig, it is the state that is supposed to be the Hegelian "embodiment of Reason" (115), in these early detective stories the opposite is true: it is not the state that embodies reason but its antagonist, this intellectual, mythical superhero who stands for individualism.

This is the case since the first detective story: before getting into the intricacies of the plot of "The Murders in the Rue Morgue," the narrator introduces Dupin's psychological traits, exclusively in a positive light. He goes on to underline his thought-reading process, which will lay the foundations for the detective as an intellectual myth: "At such times I could not help remarking and admiring [. . .] a peculiar analytic ability in Dupin" (Poe 1980a, 109), he asserts, favouring the reader's identification with his puzzlement and fascination towards the private eye. When he first meets Dupin, he remarks: "I was astonished, too, at the vast extent of his reading; and, above all, I felt my soul enkindled within me by the wild fervour, and the vivid freshness of his imagination" (105). The Anglo-American private detective's virtues are first and foremost cerebral. While he gives corporeal entity to individualism, at the same time he is but cerebral drive, pure wit and reason bereft of an actual body and emotions but filled with the by-products of knowledge: imagination, literacy, erudition, empathy, intelligibility, eloquence, powers of observation.

As for his eloquence, Derrida argues that Dupin "is the only one who 'speaks' in the story. His discourse dominates with loquacious, didactic braggadocio, truly magisterial, handing out directives, giving directions, righting wrongs, teaching everyone" (1975, 110). Lukács, at his turn, claims that "the language of the absolutely lonely man is [. . .] monological" (38). Once more, loneliness is depicted in a positive light: talking alone does not imply alienation but power. Knowledge, in Foucauldian terms, confers power on the private eye, because it bestows upon him a direct control of truth.

Holmes's knowledge is directly linked not only to his eloquence but mainly to his ability to read. Literacy is fundamental to understand the detective as another myth of modern individualism. In "The Adventure of the Red Circle" (1911), Scotland Yard's Gregson shares intelligence with a Mr. Leverton, an American officer of the Pinkerton Detective Agency. Despite the strength of this alliance, the Gregson expects that "as usual, [Holmes] knows a good deal that we don't" (1917, 8). Holmes, mysteriously, always knows.

Knowledge is by no means an innocent attribute. In "The Purloined Letter," knowledge takes a different shape: slyness. It is fair to say that Dupin frequently acts like a criminal to outwit his interlocutors, G—and D—, the state officer and the criminal mastermind. In order to identify the location of the purloined letter, he robs the robber. He becomes a rogue, mirroring the criminal. By the same token, in order to attract the potential criminal of *A Study in Scarlet,* Holmes uses Watson's name to post an ad because "if I use my own, some of these dunderheads [Scotland Yarders] would recognize it and want to meddle in the affair" (1993, 42). Dupin's and Holmes's slyness are at the service of a behaviour that may sometimes be considered outlawry but in the end shares the aim of contributing to solving the crime at all costs. This sly use of knowledge will only be exacerbated in the Continental Op and Marlowe, the urban rascals.

As Brownson claims, "the classic detective ultimately provides his rational explanation" (58), which is always the correct interpretation of the case, making him the one and only triumphant character. Knowledge, in all these forms, guarantees success to the individual who knows how to manage it. Hence Mandel's observation: "The detective story is the realm of happy ending. The criminal is always caught. Justice is always done. Crime never pays. Bourgeois legality, bourgeois values, bourgeois society, always triumph in the end. It is soothing, socially integrating literature, despite its concern with crime, violence and murder" (47). Similarly, several decades previously, Siegfried Kracauer, in his philosophical treatise *The Detective Novel* (1923), had claimed that "the end of the detective novel is the undisputed victory of reason" (73). In this rational knowledge lies the expectation that the classic detective will eventually reveal "who has done it." An expectation that is always met: in contrast with the failing state, Dupin solves each of the three cases in which he features. This same high rate of success can be seen in subsequent detectives: Holmes and Poirot, strictly speaking, fail only once and, even then, only partially.

The success of this myth of individualism is taken for granted as a normalized product of his disembodied flawless mind. And these expectations are often met thanks to a mastery of knowledge, which will eventually triumph, if only after confronting a series of obstacles. Argentine thinker Daniel Link describes this process in terms of supernatural powers of observation: "Poe's Dupin is the one that can see what no one else can. Other authors will camouflage this boastfulness portraying the detective as someone who, even if he does so belatedly, eventually sees what is evident. That is Marlowe's case [. . .] one of the reasons why

[. . .] he became famous: like the common man, [he] does not see things immediately. But in the end, he knows" (7). Thus, the genre's horizon of expectations define success and failure.

In Hammett's *Red Harvest*, the private eye must solve a murder but, more importantly, he is hired to clean up the fictional Poisonville, a task that he accomplishes, among other things, by getting people killed. "You know now that your son was killed by young Albury [. . .]. All's lovely and peaceful again" (64) says the Continental Op to his client to later insist "I'm not licked, old top. I've won. You came crying to me that some naught men had taken your little city away from you [. . .] Where are they now?" (202). In reading these final sentences of the book, it is hard not to concur with Kracauer and Mandel: social order is successfully restored thanks to the private detective who, immune to death, state interference and failure, imposes the rational mastery of his knowledge, making individualism succeed against a failing state.

## THE ANGLO-AMERICAN STATE: A DISMEMBERED BODY

### From Blindness to Illiteracy: The Symbolic Disabilities of the State

Whereas Anglo-American detectives embody individualism through a set of mythical attributes, policemen are characterized by symbolic deficiencies. Whereas attributes magnify the private eye's aura, lacks shrink the state's dimensions. Dupin displays an omnipresent and strong voice; G—, by contrast, is notable for his muteness. Holmes shows a high level of literacy that allows him to read situations faster and better; Lestrade, instead, is essentially unlettered. Whatever private sleuths have is conspicuous by its absence in state officers. This asymmetry offers a foil for the main character: policemen are eclipsed by the mythic attributes of the private eye, who shines all the more thanks to the mediocrity of his counterparts. It is because of these lacks that state officers are doomed to failure at the hand of the individualistic hero.

Private detectives, however, are not the only ones to define the different embodiments of the Anglo-American state. Beyond the mutually necessary relationship that both poles hold, officers can still be read as characters that follow a twofold pattern. A set of encompassing metonymies constitute them. To begin with, these metonymical officers (Lestrade, Gregson, etc.) cite the institution of the police in its entirety. In turn, the police personify the modern state. Like a Russian doll, they are a part for the whole, which at the same time is a part of an even greater whole. In short, these metonymies show a gradual personification of the state.

Western philosophical discourse, especially the contractualist tradition, rooted in European thinkers of the seventeenth and the eighteenth century, had equally imagined the modern state in corporeal terms. Anglo-American detective fiction shows a continuity in which this imagination persists. The title of British philosopher Thomas Hobbes's *Leviathan* (1651), the most important early modern treatise on sovereignty, is named after a mythic creature, a sea monster of Jewish tradition. A supernatural animal of huge proportions in Jewish scriptures, the Leviathan embodied the sovereign in European Contractualism insofar as the sovereign was humanized and, more specifically, masculinized, in the frontispiece of Hobbes's book. Designed by French artist Abraham Bosse, the image famously features a giant crowned body of a bearded male, composed of many other men.

These specific attributes, charged with masculinity in the same way as early detective stories, show the extent to which, sovereignty, as Segato often observes, has traditionally been a matter circumscribed to men (2016, 94). Similarly, a century after Hobbes, in his treatise on the *Social Contract* (1762), Swiss thinker Jean-Jacques Rousseau relies heavily in the medieval trope of the body politic, a rewriting of the equation of the King with the state, in which the human body acts as a metaphor for the republican sovereign. Yet both Hobbes and Rousseau imagine the state as amorphous, abstract, and depersonalized. As Samuel Mintz mentions, "Leviathan and Hobbes's sovereign are unities compacted out of separate individuals" (2), they are not individuals themselves. Early detective stories personify the mythic figure of the omnipotent state, who would no longer be shaped in the prestigious figure of the King but in mundane policemen. The very same recourse to personification that Poe and his heirs use to build private sleuths as embodiments of individualism is present in the construction of characters such as G—, Lestrade or the Inspector Japp. What distinguishes them is that while the private eye has a well-defined personality, the policemen's individuality is blended into the amorphous and depersonalized image that philosophers used to imagine the state.

The personification of the state in mutilated bodies shows the hollowness of the state. And it does so through a set of symbolic disabilities. As German philosopher Walter Benjamin argues, "a consideration of the police institution encounters nothing essential at all. Its power is formless, like its nowhere tangible, all-pervasive, ghostly presence in the life of civilized states" (1978, 287). This is the imagery that Anglo-American classic detective stories use to perform their critique of the state: the permanent dismembering of policemen's body as a symptom of the lacks that the modern state exhibits on a more general level. While Dupin, Holmes, or Poirot are pure wit, bereft of a corporeal entity, the state has a body marked by figurative mutilations.

Sometimes these symbolic disabilities are phrased as blindness, sometimes as deafness: Lacan describes the Parisian Police as the "glance that sees nothing" and, particularly, G—as "a deaf man" ("Seminar on 'The Purloined Letter'"). One of the most prominent symbolic disabilities is related to the inability to speak, i.e.,: symbolic muteness. Hence Dupin's characteristic mode is soliloquy; while the other characters are left silenced for most of the stories in which he features. After hearing Dupin's speculations on "The Murders of the Rue Morgue," his sidekick says: "I stared at the speaker in mute astonishment" (Poe 1980a, 120). A similar silent fascination characterizes G—, the Prefect of the Parisian Police. Their silence enhances Dupin's individual force to the detriment of the voice of the state, which remains speechless, and thus powerless, unable to utter narratives.

The body of the state also faces paralysis when Dupin claims that the apparently unsolvable murders of the Rue Morgue "have sufficed to paralyze the powers" (1980a, 120) of the police. Immaturity could be read as another symbolic disability such as when Dupin says of G— that "many a schoolboy is a better reasoner than he" (Poe 1980c, 208). Likewise, Watson compares Lestrade to "a child asking questions of its teacher" (Conan Doyle 2014, 320). The individualistic hero's seniority, which is more symbolic than literal as most characters are middle-aged men, assumes more knowledge on the side of the private eye. This asymmetry of knowledge evidences the hierarchy in which the private sleuth and the state officers are embedded.

Because of these symbolic disabilities, the body of the state also produces negatively charged affective encounters. "I found that [Holmes] had many acquaintances, and those in the most different classes of society. There was one little sallow, rat-faced, dark-eyed fellow, who was introduced to me as Mr. Lestrade" (1993, 17), says Watson of his first meeting with the Scotland Yard inspector. The Continental Op describes the looks of Poisonville police officers similarly: "The first policeman I saw needed a shave. The second had a couple of buttons off his shabby uniform. The third stood in the centre of the city's main intersection [. . .] with a cigar in one corner of his mouth" (Hammett 4). The negative affect of these encounters goes beyond the surface of the policemen's physicality. Policemen are not merely "a shabby, shifty-eyed crew" but one "without enthusiasm for the job ahead of them" (51). Their body, then, informs the apathy that will lead to their incompetence to solve crimes. The Continental Op introduces Noonan to the readers as "a fat man with twinkling greenish eyes" (22). The sleuth constantly reminds the reader of Noonan's weight, bestowing on him an unpleasant negative affect that follows in his wake.

All through these narratives, the reader is reminded of the physical characteristics displayed by the different incarnations of the dismembered state. As for the detectives' body, the reader knows that the Continental Op is a "fat, middle-aged, hard-boiled, pig-headed guy" (85). Equally, Poirot is famous for his moustache, but references to the detective's body are rare compared to the attention given on the one hand to his flawless mind and on the other hand to the policemen's symbolic disabilities. Similarly, Marlowe describes LAPD

Lieutenant Nulty's office as a "smelly little cubbyhole" (Chandler 228), its floor covered with "dirty brown linoleum" (212). He first introduces him as a "lean-jawed sourpuss with long yellow hands" (211).

The state officers' bodies and the spaces in which they move insist on these kinds of physiological anomalies, that often echo their negative psychological features. Both Lestrade and G—were based on the same historical state policeman: the first chief of French SÛreté Nationale, Eugène-François Vidocq, who published his memoirs in 1828, i.e.,: only a few years before the Dupin stories, as Giardinelli reminds us (20). Dupin first describes Vidocq by conceding that he is "a good guesser, and a persevering man" (Poe 1980a, 118). Nonetheless, because he lacks "educated thought, he erred continually by the very intensity of his investigations" (118). His constant ineffectiveness is rooted in his physicality, specifically in his symbolic blindness: "He impaired his vision by holding the object too close. He might see, perhaps, one or two points with unusual clearness, but in so doing he, necessarily, lost sight of the matter as a whole" (118). G—or Vidocq, unlike Dupin, do not have sufficient knowledge to see properly. Dupin can "see" in the sense of having the ability to observe beyond the surface. For this reason, more than a century later, Derrida will call Dupin "the purveyor of truth" (1975, 65). The historical and the literary policemen, by contrast, share a common deficiency linked to blindness: "impaired [. . .] vision," "lost sight."

The state's symbolic disabilities go beyond physical characteristics. The state policemen lack all the by-products of knowledge (imagination, literacy, erudition, empathy, intelligibility, eloquence, powers of observation) that are so iconic of the sleuth, almost as though these by-products were attached to his body. In fact, the most prominent disability of the policemen is not physical but intellectual and rooted in class: the inability to read. Symbolic illiteracy is grounded in the historical process that Mandel and Derrida underline when they describe the socio-economic differences separating the prototype of the private eye and the state officer. Vidocq is illiterate ("without educated thought") and it is this disability that prevents him from solving cases.

To put it differently, because the state cannot read in Anglo-American detective stories, it is not fit to maintain power, or more broadly, it cannot uphold sovereignty. The inability to interpret clues accurately is often reproduced in early depictions of policemen. G—, Lestrade, Gregson, Japp all share this structural illiteracy. Lacan claims that in G—"everything is arranged to induce in us a sense of his imbecility. Which is powerfully articulated by the fact that he and his confederates never conceive of anything beyond what an ordinary rogue might imagine" ("Seminar on 'The Purloined Letter'"). Lacan's description of the Parisian policeman also holds for his inheritors. In *A Study in Scarlet,* Holmes asks Gregson if he remembers a particular case, to which the officer of course replies negatively. "Read it up—you really should," responds Holmes (1993, 29). The private eye has often read everything there is to be read well before his adversaries. If literacy is a source of pride for him, there is something at stake in this advantage.

In "The Adventure of the Norwood Builder" (2014, 306), Lestrade is unable to read documents containing important clues, he seems to be incapable of inferring more inventive conclusions that could go beyond his first impression. Lestrade defines himself as "a practical man" (315): "When I have got my evidence I come to my conclusions," he acknowledges (314). He is depicted as someone who refuses to problematize reality. He does not subject himself to the complexities of the written word. Similarly, Nulty admits he "ain't quite bright" (Chandler 1988, 233). These are the non-attributes that define the classic policemen in Anglo-American detective stories: they are naive, overly literal, incapable of perusing reality as a text to grasp its connotations, unable to interpret creatively or think laterally as the individualistic hero does.

The police's illiteracy resides in that they are incapable of understanding a language in which the private detective is perfectly fluent. This becomes literal in *A Study in Scarlet*, when Holmes goes beyond the easiest explanation thanks to his linguistic knowledge, as he reveals that "Rache" is not an allusion to a "Rachel" (as Lestrade thinks) but the German word for "revenge" (1993, 34). In "The Adventure of the Red Circle," Holmes's knowledge of Italian enables him to solve the case. But what is at stake here are not merely specific skills such as being good at German or Italian. It is not a problem of tongues but of language, more broadly, an element that detective stories will reproduce well beyond the Anglo-American tradition. The fundamental reason why the police fail is strongly connected to this symbolic illiteracy: G—, Lestrade, and Japp are unable to read because they fail to interact with what Lacan calls the Symbolic Order, the realm of language. While symbols remain illegible for the police, "Dupin makes linguistic, mathematical, religious observations, he constantly speculates about the symbol" ("Seminar on 'The Purloined Letter'"). Language and force, the Symbolic and the Real, incarnated in the private eye and the state policemen respectively, are constantly opposed in detective fiction.

The Continental Op, for instance, is rebuked by his client in those terms: "You're a great talker [. . .] A two-fisted, you-be-damned man with your words. But have you got anything else? Have you got the guts to match your gall? Or is it just the language you've got?" (Hammett 42). Of course, this opposition should be nuanced, as The Continental Op displays more than the mastery of symbols. In fact, one of the main innovations that Hammett offers to distinguish his private sleuth from his forerunners is that he is a tough man on the mean streets. His toughness, more connected with force, seems to mark the difference between the "hard-boiled" detective and the "armchair investigator." But even so, The Continental Op's eloquence is in direct opposition to force, encapsulated in "the guts." From Poe to Hammett there is a transition in the figure of the detective, who is portrayed gradually more and more as an aggressive man, but his intellectual wit remains a common attribute. As Benjamin claims, "state power [. . .] has eyes only for effects" (1978, 292). Its blind body has been designed not to decode but to execute, to perform, even if it does so with another main component that structures the portrayal of the state in Anglo-American detective stories: ineptitude.

## FROM INCOMPETENCE TO CORRUPTION

In one of the very first scenes of *A Study in Scarlet*, Holmes mocks Scotland Yarders as follows: "'You are doing so well now that it would be a pity for anyone to interfere.' There was a world of sarcasm in his voice as he spoke" (1993, 33). His air of superiority is mainly rooted in his counterpart's incompetence. Similarly, Poirot complains about Japp, confessing that he is "disappointed" in him since "he has no method!" (Christie 131). Having no method entails lacking rationality, knowledge of how to structure the interpretation of a case. In Poe, Doyle, and Christie, the state's incompetence is rooted in this lack. Poe's Parisian police are always late to understand the crime scene, where everything has been solved by the private eye even before their arrival—a genre convention that will be reproduced during decades even until nowadays.

By contrast, hard-boiled detectives and policemen display something that is absent in their forerunners: a loss of innocence. They add a less naive layer to the state's maimed body: its evident ties with criminality. In *Red Harvest*, policemen are no longer incompetent agents, unable to solve crime; on the contrary, now they are crooked agents who help to cover up for criminals or they sometimes are even criminals themselves. Hammett's novel opens with this paradigmatic shift in the detective story tradition: The Continental Op, leafing through the newspapers, reads: "*The Herald* said the chief of police could best show his own lack of complicity by speedily catching and convicting the murderer of murderers" (Hammett 13). Here, the fact that the state police are unable to solve crime is no longer due to their illiteracy or their incompetence, but to their structural corruption that must be concealed for them to survive.

Piglia believes that in Hammett and Chandler, "crime [. . .] is always surrounded by money: murders, theft, scams, blackmailing, kidnapping, they are all grounded in economics" (1986, 69–70). And as Giardinelli observes, the appearance of money is inseparable from the rise of corruption (222). In hard-boiled stories, the state's inability to solve crime is no longer linked to bureaucratic ineptitude. What the dismembered body lacks is now no longer competence, but an ethical stance. Poisonville's police, for example, receive bribes from the criminals. By contrast, the Continental Op (a hero, like Piglia says, immune to corruption) does not accept even a bonus from his client because the private agency that hired him has "rules against taking bonuses or rewards" (Hammett 63). Corruption is thus circumscribed to and is a monopoly of the state.

The lack of participation of the private eye in these state affairs is what magnifies his figure still more, in contrast to the ordinary interests of his adversaries. Infected with corruption, the state's body ends up resorting to force so as to conceal its own criminal structure. In *Red Harvest*, "there's no use taking anybody into court, no matter what you've got on them. They own the courts, and, besides, the courts are too slow for us now" (Hammett 118). The state, in hard-boiled fiction, here embodied in Chief Noonan, exacerbates its criminal nature, when the policeman wants to saddle innocent bystanders with corrupt schemes.

"I flatter myself that I can distinguish at a glance the ash of any known brand, either of cigar or of tobacco. It is just in such details that the skilled detective differs from the Gregson and Lestrade type" (Conan Doyle 1993, 35), says Holmes. In other words, what distinguishes *ego* and *mundus* is that the private eye holds the knowledge to interact with language while the police only know (and it is trained to) interacting with what is not susceptible to symbolized through language, that is, force. Inversely, as Benjamin claims, "a sphere of human agreement that is nonviolent to the extent that it is wholly inaccessible to violence: the proper sphere of 'understanding' language" (1978, 289), to which the state officers are somehow unable to access. Whereas knowledge would bring success to the sleuth; force would doom the policemen to failure.

## FROM FORCE TO FAILURE

The state's symbolic disabilities and corrupt nature result in the recourse to force and its subsequent failure. The maimed state tries to compensate for its disabilities by displaying its right to sheer force. Watson defines the Scotland Yarders as "official detectives" who "may blunder in the matter of intelligence but never in that of courage" (Conan Doyle 1917, 10). When Holmes is momentarily paralyzed, unable to solve "The Adventure of the Norwood Builder," Lestrade threatens him by saying: "you may look for your tramp, and while you are finding him, we will hold on to our man" (2014, 306). Because Scotland Yard has the right to coerce, it seems that this temporarily inverts the asymmetric rivalry between the individual and the state. But ultimately, the monopoly of corruption and force is what makes them fail.

Anglo-American detective stories perceive the state's monopoly to apply force not as powerful but as a lack, not as an asset but as a flaw, not a mythical attribute but as another symbolic disability. Facing his frustration to locate "The Purloined Letter," G—only can seek refuge to the fact that he is in possession of a set of keys, "with which I can open any chamber or cabinet in Paris" (Poe 1980c, 203). However, state power becomes useless without the literacy of symbols: being able to open any door is not enough to solve cases. When G—shows up at Dupin's office to hire him for the case, his frustration becomes explicit: "He had been piqued by the failure of all his endeavours to ferret out the assassins" (1980b, 146) says the sidekick.

G—admits that they have even searched for the purloined letter with "a most powerful microscope" (1980c, 205) and have still failed to find it. Even when the police have the latest technology available, the individualistic hero's interaction with symbols beats the disabled state in the end. Dupin compares G—'s proceedings to "a sort of Procrustean bed" (1980c, 208), to illustrate his rigid methodology of looking for clues that lacks the right dosage of creativity. In the Greek myth, Procrustes would physically attack visitors to make them fit the size of his bed, and so he stands for a whimsical standard to which agreement is forced. G—holds "a certain set of highly ingenious resources [. . .] to which he forcibly adapts his designs. But he perpetually errs by being too deep or too shallow" (1980c, 208). Here, once more, force is inextricably linked to failure as its main cause.

In his Collège de France lectures about the state, Pierre Bourdieu rewrites Weber's canonical definition of the state as "the only human *Gemeinschaft* which lays claim to the monopoly on the legitimated use of physical force" (2005, 79). For the French sociologist, the state does not detain the use of force only. The state could also be described as the "monopoly of legitimate physical and [also] symbolic violence" (Bourdieu 2014, 4). In this sense, the rivalry encapsulated in the *ego contra mundum* consists in a competition in which an individualistic hero (focused on symbols) defeats a series of embodiments of the state (centred on physical force) by solving crime. The early detective aims to become an agent more powerful than the state. It aims to replace and occupy its task of imposing a narrative or an interpretation that could explain the causes of a given crime. In a nutshell, it aims to become the sovereign.

Except that this individualistic hero has a head-start on the competition due to his mythical relationship with symbols. Force, without knowledge, becomes sterile and leads invariably to failure as when Parisian policemen are unable to find the purloined letter. As Lacan notes, "every legitimate power always rests, as does any kind of power, on the symbol" ("Seminar"). Even though "the police, like all powers, also rest on the symbol [. . .] there's a small difference between police and power. Namely that the police have been persuaded that their efficacy rests on force" It is "thanks to [that], they are as powerless" ("Seminar"), because they cannot decode signifiers.

The private eye dwells in a different dimension, in which everything is legible, any element of reality can become a signifying text, a clue, a hint that would help him to solve crimes. This is the reason why detectives fail only exceptionally. At the beginning of "The Adventure of the Yellow Face," Watson excuses Holmes's failures: "In publishing these short sketches [. . .] it is only natural that I should dwell rather upon his successes than upon his failures" (Conan Doyle 2014, 1), he admits, only to clarify that "this not so much for the sake of his reputations [. . .] but because where he failed it happened too often that no one else succeeded, and that the tale was left forever without a conclusion. [. . .] It chanced that even when he erred, the truth was still discovered" (1). Even when Holmes, his failures are relative, exceptional and innocuous: unlike Lestrade's structural misreadings, Holmes's causes no collateral damage. No innocent man is imprisoned because his account of the puzzle does not match what really happened.

At the end of the case, he tells Watson: "If it should ever strike you that I am getting a little over-confident in my powers [. . .] kindly whisper 'Norbury' in my ear, and I shall be infinitely obliged to you" (2014, 9). Individual failure irrupts here in the classic detective only to humanize the private eye, to underline his limitations, aiming for a more realist tone that will become gradually prominent in subsequent detective stories, especially in hard-boiled fiction. As with any literary genre, the detective story must evolve to renew the reader's horizon of expectations. In Christie's The Murder of Roger *Ackroyd* (1926), Poirot does not discover that the narrator, Dr. Sheppart, is the murderer until it is too late. The killer commits suicide before he can be punished. Nevertheless, in the end he is still identified as the criminal and the promise of restoration at the hands of the individualistic hero remains intact: individualism, embodied by Poirot, eventually finds the truth. During these early stories, even if some hard-boiled authors occasionally introduce a degree of failure to provide their narratives with a more realist tone, unsolved cases are rare, individual failure is not dominant but peripheral, in Jakobson's terms (77–85), unlike the state's failure which is constant and unavoidable, even inherent to its structure.

## FINAL THOUGHTS: THE PERSISTENCE OF INDIVIDUALISM

Watt considers the exemplars of his modern myths of individualism to be holders of "an undefined kind of ideal, [who] do not succeed in reaching it. They are [. . .] rather emblematic failures. Moreover, they are either punished for their attempt to realize their aspirations" (234). The individualistic private eye, ever successful, presents a shift away from these myths. While still embodying individualism, they portray it in a more favourable light. By contrast, there is a displacement of failure to the Anglo-American state.

In the late-nineteenth century, individualism was still far from being understood as a doctrine prone to failure, but just a few decades later, literary approaches to individualism will differ considerably: for Goldmann, the First World War brings a philosophical crisis that challenges the very foundations of individualism, in that "whatever were the individual values on which one claimed to found human existence, they now appear insufficient and outdated" (166). As with any other intellectual trend, a historical and dynamic concept, individualism has undergone significant changes ever since.

The first traces of this historical transformation in detective fiction appears in Hammett's *Red Harvest* and Chandler's *Farewell, My Lovely*, in which the degree of individualism gradually moves away from their forerunners' blind endorsement of its boundless powers. Chandler's typically cynical rhetoric is translated in Marlowe not taking himself seriously, as when he overthinks his deductions and says to himself "shut up, dimwit" (1988, 251), an attitude that would be inconceivable for Holmes. Marlowe knows the constraints of his wit, for instance, when while listening to Lieutenant Nulty, he acknowledges: "I turned over a few witty sayings in my mind, but none of them seemed amusing" (269). Similarly, when negotiating the fee that he expects for the case, the Continental Op manages to convince his client to hire him, by stating that he would be able to do the job since "when I say *me*, I mean the Continental [Agency]" (Hammett 44). The Continental Op, in this sense, is less individualized than, say, Dupin. He still works alone, but when he needs to back up his image, his self is no longer enough, he needs to resort to a private corporation to endorse him.

Hammett's shift is consistent with Goldmann's ideas on the attenuation of individualism in the interwar period, with its "disappearance [. . .] on an economical level (a process that Marxists have observed as [. . .] the transition from classic to imperial capitalism) and the analogous transformation in the novel precisely marked by the disappearance of the individual character and the biographical account" (my translation).[3] Despite its attenuation, individualism remains triumphant in Anglo-American fiction. Chandler exalts

Marlowe's emblematic uniqueness when he says that there are "seventeen hundred and fifty cops" in Los Angeles and "they want [Marlowe] to do their leg work for them" (1988, 236). Ultimately, whereas the realist narratives mentioned by Goldmann dilute the individual character, detective stories preserve it.

This triumph of individualistic narratives in Anglo-American detective fiction is valid even today, almost two centuries after Poe. For instance, in recent mainstream TV crime shows, whether from the United States or the United Kingdom, such as *Twin Peaks* (1990–1991), *Sherlock* (2010–2017), *The Killing* (2011–2014), *True Detective* (2014–2019), *Broadchurch* (2013–2017) and *Mare of Easttown* (2021), to name a few, sleuth always end up solving the case, outwitting the state, even when they work within it. All these contemporary narratives, heavily influenced by the hard-boiled tradition, recapture the intrinsic corruption of the state in that murderers are often policemen themselves. But they still rely on the individualistic hero, who ultimately vanquishes the coercive state.

There are, of course, a few exceptions, in which detectives fail, the most emblematic of which is perhaps David Simon's *The Wire* (2002–2008), where Baltimore police officers may catch drug dealers here and then but fail to fight against structural racialized crime. More recently, *Unsolved. The Murders of Tupac and the Notorious B.I.G.* (2018), the storyline that explores the failed attempts by LAPD and the FBI to find a single culprit for the killing of the hip-hop legends after two decades of investigation. Of course, *Unsolved* partakes not so much in the detective story tradition but more in the non-fictional genre of true crime. But even then, individualism remains unquestioned, since failure to solve the case is explained in terms of structural issues that have more to do with race in American society than with the insufficiency of individualism.

In Latin America, individualism holds a more problematic status. This is especially true in the Southern Cone, where the Anglo-American detective story has been deeply influential. Alternatively, in mainstream Latin American detective fiction, like Cuban novelist Leonardo Padura's quartet of novels *Four Seasons in Havana*, both the successful detective and the conventional endorsement of individualism are very much preserved as in their North American models. "A man can't expect always to have it his own way" Lestrade warns Holmes (2014, 314). This is probably the biggest lesson that writers from Argentina, Brazil, and Chile have incorporated in their take on the genre, that goes beyond the demands of market-oriented fiction.

Specifically, during the past few decades, above all from the 1990s onwards, in the period of post-dictatorship, failure seems to permeate Southern Cone detective stories, constituting a transnational "poetics of failure." Failure no longer affects only the state officers' performance but also the private detectives. Of the different treatments of individualism in the modern novel, Watt sees Faust as a "symbolic figure upon whom were projected the fears of anarchic and individualistic tendencies of the Renaissance and the Reformation" (46). Watt goes on to say that Counter-Reformation tried to execrate individualistic figures such as Faust, but this "anathema [. . .] was itself to fail" (46), since individualism became gradually a mainstream way to understand, to imagine and to conceive not only the literary but also the political. Classic Anglo-American detective stories, inaugurated with Poe's announcement of Dupin's victory "in the eyes of the police" (1980a, 120), dwell in this historical period, where individualism was not execrated but celebrated, to the apparent detriment of the state.

As the following chapters will show, in Latin America, this anathematization of individualism reappears, divested of religious connotations, as part of a critique of the state, much more radical than the one we can see in Anglo-American detective stories. The following detective narratives subvert and surmount the latter, offering a stronger comment on the neoliberal state, understood as a complex by-product of post-dictatorship. Reading the variations of individualism and the state in the work of Argentine, Brazilian and Chilean authors enable a re-interpretation of Poe, Doyle, Christie, Hammett and Chandler and the ways they imagined the modern state.

*Chapter 2*

# Argentina

## The State against Individualism

*Hay que hacer la historia de las derrotas.*

Ricardo Piglia, *Respiración artificial* (1980)

### APPROPRIATING A FOREIGN GENRE THROUGH PARODY

Addressing a client, Don Isidro Parodi takes up "his favorite gripe: he railed on and on against the Italians, who had wormed their way into everything—not excluding the state penitentiary" (19). Argentine writers Jorge Luis Borges and Adolfo Bioy Casares's detective offers a series of parodic overtones. The most literal is echoed in his surname, but the strongest parody resides in that, much like the Italians he rails against, Parodi (himself an Argentine with Italian ancestry) is also imprisoned in jail. These two characteristics are parodic in themselves: especially during the first half of the twentieth century, Italians connoted uncultured immigration in the eyes of the Argentine *criollo* elite, to which Borges and Bioy certainly belonged to.

Their book *Seis problemas para Don Isidro Parodi* (1942) belongs to a series of 1930s and 1940s Borgesian texts, which, as Argentine critic David Viñas notes, feature "a peculiar reluctance towards everything that is associated with the 'new man,' [. . .] the immigrant, a violator of the traditional sacredness" (33). It is important to remember that by the 1940s, when they write these short stories, most of the Italian migrant's origins shifted from the wealthier North (that had given the country some of their founding fathers, from Manuel Belgrano and Juan José Castelli to Carlos Pellegrini), to the Mezzogiorno, Italy's poorest, Southern region—which brought to the country undesirable elements, such as anarchism, uneducated peasantry, and organized crime (García 4). The historical change of perception towards Italians allows Borges and Bioy to imagine a different type of detective. As Viñas notes, "the typical *gringo rioplatense* (newly arrived from Genoa or Eastern Europe's Galicia) leads to parody" (33).

A hairdresser who solves cases while serving time in jail for a crime he has not even committed, Parodi is diametrically opposed to his sophisticated Anglo-American models. To begin with, because the latter come from kindred origins that are significantly distant to Southern Italy: Dupin is from Paris; Holmes from London, British; and Poirot, from the Belgian Ardennes. Borges and Bioy belonged to an Argentine intellectual tradition (that can be traced to Sarmiento's *Facundo* [1843]), which often associated these Northern European cities and towns with upper-class refinement and, subsequently, a desirable migration to populate Argentine land. These opposing poles, between national and international lineage, Southern and Northern Europe, Anglo and Latin America, are nothing but some of the many layers of the civilization and barbarism dichotomy that is at the core of Argentine literature, from Sarmiento onwards, permeating even detective fiction.

The main aspect that Parodi's stories shares with its models is their playful relationship to knowledge and enigma, in which solving cases is imagined like winning a chess tournament. Nevertheless, because the reader cannot take Parodi as seriously, Borges and Bioy pave the way for a radical shift in the ways Latin American literatures imagine the private eye (and individualism), from the second half of twentieth century onwards: whereas Dupin or Holmes were upper-class dandies, Parodi is a newcomer, a vulgar character. Even when contrasted with rough hard-boiled detectives, Parodi, an ordinary barber, seems more mundane. As the Argentine critic Cristina Parodi describes him, "Don Isidro is an illiterate, simple, silent man who has a practical knowledge made of sensibility, incredulity and skepticism" (13). Yet it is these very prosaic features that Don Isidro's successors (in Argentina and beyond) reproduce.

Thinking about Parodi's stories and, more broadly, about Borges and his literary group, Donald A. Yates argues that the center of local production of Latin American detective fiction is Buenos Aires (1956, 228). However, there were other detectives in Argentine literature before Parodi. The earliest detective stories written in Spanish can be traced as early as the late nineteenth century in Buenos Aires (see Setton, Picabea, Mattalia), that is, soon after the emergence of their Anglo-American models and the translation of their work to Spanish. The Argentine literary historian Román Setton makes the case that Borges and Bioy imposed a critical narrative, through *Sur* (a 1930s–1990s literary magazine in which they were editors), putting themselves as the first authors of detective stories in Spanish. Setton also mentions how the later critic would reproduce this gesture in an acritical way (2012, 249). By contrast, building on Pedro Luis Barcia's 1980s studies, Setton locates the birth of Argentine detective fiction in the earlier Luis Vicente Varela's novels, written and published in Buenos Aires in the 1870s. It is not a coincidence that Varela writes under the pseudonym Raúl Waleis, an English-sounding anagram of his own Hispanic name, which could be read as another symptom of the civilization and barbarism dichotomy, mentioned above.[1] The critic (Setton, Mattalia, and J.J. Delaney) agrees in the prevalence of parody as one of the main elements that distinguishes this early production, for instance in Paul Groussac's "El candado de oro" (1884) and Eustaquio Pellicer's "El botón del calzoncillo" (1918).[2]

Yet beyond these early examples, it was only with Borges and Bioy that the genre attained its unparalleled canonical status and international visibility, making Argentine detective fiction circulate well beyond Argentine borders. Their *Seis problemas* reproduces this tradition of parody, as a means of sullying the private eye's aura, thus producing what theorists Itamar Even-Zohar and José Lambert define as an "imported genre," i.e.,: a literary form created in a foreign context, often seen as a dominant aesthetic field in a complex network of poly-systems. For Even-Zohar, the importation of cultural productions is mainly related to translation. Snatching a literary work from other literary fields often entails an acknowledgement that the exporting party of the transaction, in this case, the United States, the United Kingdom, and even France—as Setton notes in the influence of Gaboriau's novels (2012, 250). This party often holds a higher symbolic capital than the importing party. It shows an implicit reverence for the foreign literary system, an element that is often present in parody.

Literary translations, then, lead to the translated works being "detached from their home contexts" (Even-Zohar 18). But for Lambert, by contrast, importing a genre "exceeds mere translations" (250, my translation). Yet both critics agree that importing a literary work is a re-appropriation that transforms the alien setting in order to incorporate it to a national repertoire. Borges and Bioy Casares's series of 120 translations (published between 1945 and 1955, as Pablo Brescia reminds us, i.e.,: one book per month over a decade [268]) under the name of "The Seventh Circle" (evoking the circle that Dante allocated to criminals in his *Inferno*) can be read as way of literary importation, but even more so their own production, e.g., these six stories featuring Parodi.

But, perhaps, more than a legal importation, Borges and Bioy's operations could best be described as a *"contrabando,"* in Brescia's terms, as they "smuggled" detective novels, trespassing the Argentine Good Taste Customs of the time. As Brescia notes, Borges's aim was to "achieve the legitimation of detective fiction as a narrative strategy and to contextualize the reception of his own work in the 1940s and 1950s Argentine literary field" (266). In short, Borges is an authentic "proselytizer of detective fiction" (Brescia 267) and Don Isidro Parodi is his most explicit attempt to materialize this proselytism.

Whereas Holmes is an enthusiastic investigator, Don Isidro is a reluctant detective, another characteristic that will be subsequently reproduced in other parts of Latin America. As Cristina Parodi notes, Don Isidro "does not seem to enjoy his task of detection: he gets worn out by his clients" (14). Unlike Holmes, he "is not interested in fame" (14) or literary glory. Don Isidro, whose "wisdom does not come from a supernatural intelligence nor from an extraordinary knowledge" (13), lacks the mythical attributes that his Anglo-American forerunners had. In short, he is a hero despite himself, he does not want to embody the myth of modern individualism that the horizon of expectations mandates him to be.

Parody is inextricably linked to tribute. While, at first glance, ridicule gives the impression of disrespect, as Linda Hutcheon remarks, "parody [. . .] is a form of imitation [. . .] characterized by ironic inversion, not always at the expense of the parodied text" (6). Borges and Bioy were subject to an ambivalent influence: on the one hand, parody entails a great deal of fascination; but on the other, it implies an awareness of the implausibility of importing/smuggling a genre without strenuous appropriation. The mix of a playful tone and absurd situations mock and yet at the same time pay tribute to their foreign models. Their successors will reproduce this gesture in Argentine literature in subsequent decades, from the 1940s to the 1980s, under a series of dictatorships, although incorporating new parodied influences, mainly North American hard-boiled fiction. Here as elsewhere, parody functions as "a method of inscribing continuity while permitting critical distance, [. . .] as a conservative force in both retaining and mocking" its models, and as a "transformative power in creating new syntheses" (Hutcheon 20). As Cristina Parodi reminds us, Don Isidro, like Dupin, is also an "armchair detective," except that his "office" is a jail (14). Borges's inheritors will also draw heavily on this integration of criminality and the law, or rather the dissolution of their imagined boundaries.

One of these inheritors, Velmiro Ayala Gauna, a journalist from the rural Argentine province of Corrientes, created an inspector named Don Frutos Gómez a few years after Don Isidro Parodi's stories were published. The Slovenian philosopher Slavoj Zizek, writing about the more contemporary Swedish detective fiction writer Hanning Mankel's parallax position between Scandinavia and Africa, claims that: "The main effect of globalization on detective fiction is discernible in its dialectical counterpart: the powerful re-emergence of a specific *locale* as the story's setting—a particular provincial environment." Zizek notes that contemporary detective fiction places its stories anywhere: "in the Native American reservations in the US [. . .] in Venice and Florence, in Iceland" ("Mankell . . . "). He clarifies that "there is, of course, in the history of detective fiction, a long tradition of eccentric locales," and he cites Christie's *Death Comes at the End* (1944), set in Ancient Egypt. "However," he continues, "these settings clearly had the status of eccentric exceptions, [. . .] their appeal [. . .] relied on the distance towards the paradigmatic locations," such as London, Paris or New York City. Writing during the 1950s, several decades before the very idea of "globalization," and the distinction between "global" and "local," set in, Ayala Gauna engages with this "particular provincial environment" *avant la lettre*.

Displacing the figure of the detective to a countryside filled with *gauchos*, he portrays Don Frutos solving his cases in the (fictional) small town of Capibara Cué, somewhere near the Paraná River. Ayala Gauna's short stories pay attention to local details and folklore to a degree that would be inconceivable in either the urban Californian settings of Chandler and Hammett, or the sophisticated English countryside atmosphere devised by Christie, as the Argentine critic Jorge Lafforgue notes (149). And it is through parody that Ayala Gauna bridges this vast geo-cultural distance. Like Don Isidro, Don Frutos is an ordinary and parodical character, a man without qualities, who is more reminiscent of Anglo-American policemen than of mythical private eyes.

The short story "Don Frutos's Investigation" (1955) gives the reader a glimpse of this rural environment in which everything seems to be inverted when compared to the Anglo-American models: "With his noisy spurs, Don Frutos Gómez [. . .] entered his wrecked office

[. . .] and sat in an old straw chair [. . .] waiting for the *mate* that one of his lazy agents was preparing" (52). Following Zizek, this scene can be read merely as an "eccentric exception." But, unlike Christie, Ayala Gauna does not rely "on the distance towards the paradigmatic locations" in the same way that Christie writing about Egypt does. Ayala Gauna creates Don Frutos as a rural Argentine translation (in Lafforgue's words, "a nationalization" [151]) of Dupin. Far from exploiting exoticism to seduce urban readers, Don Frutos highlights an anti-heroic setting, evoking the amateur and precarious conditions in which individualism must be embodied in Latin America.

When one of Don Frutos's assistants asks him why he does not use fingerprinting, he responds: "What footprints, son? [. . .] We do not use them footprints here. We keep it simple" (55). Although fingerprinting had in fact come to Buenos Aires several decades earlier, introduced by the Croatian-born Argentine anthropologist and police official Juan Vucetich, such technological imports have yet to arrive in Capibara Cué, that I read here as a metonymy of rural Latin America. Through this gap, Ayala Gauna underlines the class abyss that separates his rural detective and the sophisticated myth of modern individualism created in the Anglo-American literary field. Parody, in Ayala Gauna, goes even further than in Borges and Bioy, since he ridicules not only the detective but also murderers: in "Don Frutos's Investigation," this turns out to be (like Parodi) an Italian immigrant. Don Frutos manages to solve the crime because the victim's injuries show the criminal's ignorance of local knife-work: "the injuries were small and here [. . .] a knife is a work instrument, we use it to butcher, to cut herbs [. . .]. As soon as I checked, I knew that the incision was made from top to bottom, and I said to myself: *Gringo*" (59).

This tension between foreign and local, between *gringos* and *criollos*, another rewriting of the civilization and barbarism dichotomy, constantly reappears in Argentine detective stories. Borges explores it in his essay "Our Poor Individualism" (1946) and concludes that the hero of classic Hollywood crime cinema, an honest journalist who is endorsed because he "seeks out the friendship of a criminal in order to hand him over to the police," is seen by the Argentine spectator as an "incomprehensible cad" (34). According to Borges, this is due to the consensus that in Argentina "the police is a *maffia*" and that "the Argentine, unlike the Americans of the North and almost all Europeans, does not identify with the State" (34). By contrast, Borges proposes Sergeant Cruz from *Martín Fierro* (1872) as the ultimate national hero, even though Cruz is a traitor who helps a deserter, an anti-hero who is worlds away from the flawless and immune Anglo-American detective, whose slyness instead is used for benevolent purposes to restore social order.

If, for Hutcheon, parody entails the creation of a "new synthesis," what synthesis does the Argentine parody of Anglo-American detective fiction create? The synthesis of Borges, Bioy, Ayala Gauna, and others, reimagines the tensions between individualism and the state, by subverting its traditional features: an Argentine synthesis that derides and at the same time perpetuates Poe's archetype, venerating him by creating a bridge with a foreign tradition. In turn, this bridge ensures the transnational continuity of the genre through its radical transformation. As I hope to show, on the one hand, the private eye, once a successful hero, eventually becomes a failing individual who has lost any mythical stature and immunity his Anglo-American literary precursors may once have had. On the other hand, the state is no longer portrayed as an entity that despite its incompetence or corruption is still willing to collaborate with the detective in solving crime; instead, the state, the main source of crime itself, is the main agent that causes the detective's systemic failure. This subversive synthesis is particularly prominent in Borges's reformulation of Poe, his short story "La muerte y la brújula" (1942), and later in Rodolfo Walsh's *Operación masacre* (1957), a book of non-fiction journalism that, despite its explicit intention to represent reality without the mechanisms of literary artefacts, echoes hard-boiled fiction.

## THE LOSS OF IMMUNITY

According to Persephone Braham, "innovation in the detective story has coincided with political upheaval from its beginnings" (68). Braham cites 1848's European revolutionary movements as a starting point for Poe's Dupin stories, and Argentina's neutrality in the Second World War for Borges and Bioy's *Don Isidro Parodi* (1942). In the same year, Borges publishes his "La muerte y la brújula," in *Sur*, the most canonical detective story of Latin American literature, according to Yates (1964, 134) and, along with "El jardín de los senderos que se bifurcan" (1941) and "Abenjacán el Bojarí, muerto en su laberinto" (1951), one of the few detective stories that Borges wrote strictly speaking (Brescia 267).

Perhaps a more relevant political trigger for genre innovation in the Argentine case is that the text appears towards the end of the so-called "Infamous Decade" (1930–1943), the period that began with the first dictatorial interruption of Argentina's constitutional order. Luz Rodríguez Carranza explores the connections between the *década infame* and Borges's *Historia universal de la infamia*, a book that was published in 1935—i.e.,: well before 1945, when Argentine journalist José Luis Torres nicknamed the period as an "infamous decade." In that book, Borges tests his narrative approach to crime stories, although without portraying detectives. Instead, he tells the story from the murderer's perspective, as in "El hombre de la esquina rosada." While writing about his infamous villains and heroes, Rodríguez Carranza observes, Borges held strong ties with the supporters of the ousted Hipólito Yrigoyen, a 1930 coup that inaugurates the *década infame*. Below, I will go back to how this political context (much more than the Second World War) informs "La muerte y la brújula," too.

Borges introduces his private eye in "La muerte y la brújula" with a concise antithesis, that fully engages with the problems of the individualistic hero's failure and success: "It is true that Erik Lönnrot did not succeed in preventing the last murder, but that he foresaw it is indisputable" (1962, 76). Borges depicts Lönnrot's attempt to solve a series of enigmatic murders that follow a cabalistic pattern in a fictional city that is unnamed but allegorical of Buenos Aires.

On a third of December, someone murders Marcelo Yarmolinsky, a Hasidic rabbi and a scholar. Lönnrot is in charge of solving his murder. On the rabbi's typewriter, there is a message. Its content is hermetic, echoing the Talmudic tradition of interpreting cryptic passages of the scriptures. It states: "The first letter of the name has been uttered" (Borges 1962, 76). Lönnrot's story is a story of failure caused by misreading. Initially, he believes the murder is related to the Tetragrammaton, YHVH, the four-letter name of God, that features in several books of the Torah. On the third of January and of February, a second and a third murder take place. In each case, a similar message is left stating that "the second" and "the third letter" have been uttered. Lönnrot, convinced of his reading, predicts that there will be a fourth murder on the third of March. The prediction is accurate, except that the fourth victim is himself. Lönnrot falls into the trap of the criminal mastermind he is chasing, Red Scharlach. Whereas it was Yarmolinsky who writes the first message, Scarlach is the author of the other ones, as part of a strategy to lead Lönnrot to his death.

Lönnrot's failure to solve his case is paradoxical: in fact, he *does* successfully reveal the murderer's identity and foresees the last crime of a series, but it is in doing so that he fails to prevent his own death and to stop the murderer from committing a crime. As Cristina Parodi puts it, Lönnrot "triumphs because he has failed" (9). We can discern here the emergence of a poetics of failure, as the private eye's success is what makes him fail.

A first reading may make us think that Lönnrot is diametrically opposed to Parodi, in that his Scandinavian-sounding surname evokes civilization. Besides, while Lönnrot is a bibliophile, Parodi is almost illiterate. However, both detectives are parodic in the sense that they pay tribute to their forerunners, while at the same time they mock their individualistic mythical attributes. Borges defines Lönnrot as Dupin's heterodox heir: "Lönnrot thought of himself as a pure thinker, an Auguste Dupin, but there was something of the adventurer in him, and even a little of the gambler" (1962, 76). The disjunctive sentence announces the poetics of failure: despite his auto-perception to be like his model, there is a flaw in Lönnrot that separates him from them. And what is interesting is that this flaw is a vice, gambling, which no longer grants the detective success (as cocaine would to Holmes, for example), but leads him to failure instead. Equally, being adventurous, another mythical attribute of the classic private eye, is what leads him to his own defeat. After all, Lönnrot gambles when he misreads the clues, taking them at face value, thus failing to really solve the crime and subsequently to restore the social fabric. This rupture with the Anglo-American tradition informs the configuration of Latin American private detectives for decades, signaling the unfeasibility of faithfully reproducing the traditional Anglo-American mythification of individualism in the region.

Just as Dupin had to outwit both G—and D—and Holmes had to beat Scotland Yard as well as Moriarty, Lönnrot has an analogous pair of antagonists: the police officer in addition to the criminal mastermind. Borges depicts of the policeman, an anodyne caricature named Inspector Treviranus, reproducing the tradition of the individualistic hero's hostility towards the state, insofar as he is unfamiliar with cerebral speculations, closer to force and alien to knowledge. He is not interested in Lönnrot's "rabbinical explanations," merely in "the capture of the man who stabbed this unknown person" (1962, 77). Unlike Treviranus, Lönnrot is constantly reading and (over)thinking to reveal the truth. Like his predecessors, Borges's sleuth relies on knowledge to solve the puzzle. By contrast, Treviranus acts, guided by his anti-intellectual motto "no need to look for a three-legged cat here" (1962, 77). There is an asymmetry in their degree of literacy.

Without reading, nonetheless, the symbolically illiterate Treviranus predicts what happens before Lönnrot does: he foretells the causes of the first crime as well as the possibility that the third one is a simulation, something that goes unnoticed by Lönnrot who, despite all his reading skills, is too earnest to understand the fictional contours of these murders. But it is still Lönnrot who, thanks to his ability to read, manages to "solve" the case when he shows up at the encounter with the criminal mastermind, where the fourth murder takes place. Treviranus, by contrast, remains imprisoned by the limitations of his role as a state officer. His name itself implies that he is unable to foresee this fourth murder: as Paiva Padrão reminds us, Treviranus's Latin etymology *"tres vir,"* three (not four) men, already points out to an insufficient series of three murders (27).

According to Cristina Parodi, one of the main narrative strategies that Borges follows in this short story is identifying the "intelligibility of the real" with "legibility" (2), i.e: reading reality as a text. This applies particularly to Lönnrot who is, first and foremost, a bookish hero, a holder of a high degree of literacy. In this sense, he reproduces Holmes's passion for knowledge but, as Parodi points out, Lönnrot goes a step further. He is not interested in the book's materiality, for instance, but strictly in its textuality. Whereas Holmes "would have been able to identify the type of paper and would have made an effort to locate the place where this paper is sold," Lönnrot's interest is purely meta-literary: "he is solely interested in the text as an object that refers to other texts" (Parodi 8). Lönnrot's interest in a higher degree of abstract knowledge seems to embody, even more than Holmes, the mythical attributes of the individualistic hero.

Yet at the same time it is because of his intellectual approach that Lönnrot falls into the trap laid by Scharlach. Lönnrot is outwitted because of the one thing that hitherto distinguished his forerunners: reading clues accurately. In other words, the private eye is defeated in his own realm, of knowledge and literacy. The private eye misreads Scharlach's signifiers until the end of the narrative, something that would be rare for Anglo-American detectives.

In detective fiction, signifiers, that is, the clues that the sleuth follows, refer to crucial meanings: life and death. Lönnrot's inferences, though, are nothing but the product of Scharlach's deception. Borges thus displaces successful individualism (traditionally ascribed to the private eye) onto a wittier criminal mastermind, while at the same time relocating failure (typically the outcome of state investigations) with the detective. In the same way that Dr. Shepperd commits suicide before Poirot can conclude that he is the murderer in Agatha Christie's *The Murder of Roger Ackroyd* (1926), Scharlach gets away with murder before Lönnrot can solve the puzzle. Both cases portray a private eye who fails to discover the murderer on time. The crucial difference is that in Christie's novel, the promise of the restoration of order remains intact as the detective is ultimately rewarded with the disclosure of truth. Borges, by contrast, subverts tradition by punishing Lönnrot with death, because of his misreading of Scharlach's deceptive hints. As Cristina Parodi concludes, "the dénouement does not reestablish order but imposes disorder" (10). Borges inverts the expectations of the genre concerning the success of the private eye and the soothing effect of conservative closure that the happy ending has in the genre's readers.

Scharlach assassinates Lönnrot in Triste-le-Roy, a fictional space located at the south of "an industrial suburb where, under the protection of a political boss from Barcelona, gunmen thrive" (Borges 1962, 82). Argentine critic Elisa Calabrese reads this passage of the story in dialogue with its historical background. She claims that Scharlach is a "distorted image of Ruggero [. . .] the most prominent sidekick of the conservative caudillo Alberto Barceló, who made it to the governorship of the province of Buenos Aires" (41). Calabrese reads this as Borges's political commentary against a corrupt government's attempt to restore conservative policies, after having ousted the elected president Hipólito Yrigoyen who was favored by the author in his youth. So, it could be argued that, to a certain extent, Scharlach, like Treviranus, also works as a metonymy of the state. Here, there is another rupture with tradition: Scharlach evokes a gesture that later Argentine detective fiction writers will often reproduce: the idea that crime impregnates the different layers of the state, canceling out the hitherto-flawless private detective's agency. Despite the knowledge that Lönnrot accumulates, literacy does not bestow on him any immunity to failure. Instead, his literacy is the cause of his downfall.

North American Medievalist Suzanne Akbari points out that "both vision and language are imperfect mediators, open to deception. Yet paradoxically [. . .] they represent the only possible approaches to knowledge" (qtd. in Frelick 6). As with any other detective, it is only through reading and seeing that Lönnrot may access the truth. Nevertheless, knowledge does not make him the successful hero he is supposed to be. The symbolic blindness and illiteracy, hitherto ascribed to the police, is now problematized in the body of the private detective: is it a lack or an excess of vision and literacy that ultimately leads to his loss of immunity?

Incapable of reading between Scharlach's lines, in the end Lönnrot fails because of his distorted relationship with language and knowledge, because reading is too much but at the same time not enough or not well done to have an effective impact on the world. "La muerte y la brújula" introduces the reader to a new world in which, as the Spanish critic Francisca Noguerol notes, it is the criminal, not the private eye, who is "conceived as an individual of extraordinary abilities" (3). By contrast, Lönnrot is a "failed hermeneut [. . .] the conventions of detective fiction are here inverted: the detective fails to imagine an explanation that leads him to death, turning him into the hunter hunted" (3). Scharlach's main "extraordinary ability," of course, is his superior literacy.

Originating in Lönnrot's flawed body, language, and knowledge act like a counterforce. Whereas knowledge and literacy traditionally bestowed success on the private eye, or inversely, it granted them immunity against failure; here it is this distorted relation with knowing and reading what destroys the sleuth's immunity. In his essay *Immunitas*, the Italian philosopher Roberto Esposito discusses the different aspects of immunity in contemporary politics. For him, "the immunitary paradigm does not present itself in terms of action, but rather in terms of *reaction*—rather than a force, it is a repercussion, a counterforce" (2011, 7). In "La muerte y la brújula," knowledge works as an autoimmune reaction that attacks the detective's immunity from within, eradicating his perennial flawlessness. If Esposito defines immunity as an exemption from paying tribute to the rest of society ("those who are immune owe nothing to anyone" [2011, 5]), here Lönnrot's has clearly lost his forerunner's privilege, because he pays for his failure with death.

Borges, thus, starts a tradition that proves to be very productive in Latin America, where the private detective is no longer an exception, radically different from the multitude that surrounds him in the urban environment in which he operates. Unlike Dupin, Holmes and the like, Lönnrot must obey the same rules that apply to the rest of society and has lost his status of a privileged unilateral autonomous agent towards the community. After all, a dead detective who can neither make his success public nor bring the criminal to justice is no hero at all; still less, when the criminal who has outwitted him is closely linked to the state apparatus, his classic rival. Lönnrot may not be blind or illiterate like Poe's G—, but his vision and his readings are no longer flawless. Borges inaugurates a trend that becomes more prominent in post-dictatorial detective stories: the loss of the private eye's immunity as well as the association between failure and symbolic disabilities, once ascribed exclusively to the state. And by "loss of immunity," I do not allude merely to Todorov's immunity to death (violated when Scharlach kills Lönnrot), but also the destruction of immunity to failure and to the state.

## REPORTING CRIME: THE END OF THE CHESS MATCH

Reading Borges's multilayered work on detective stories, the Uruguayan literary critic Ángel Rama traces the beginning of a genealogy that recovers such popular genres to elevate them into high culture. For Rama, Borges's main inheritor in Argentina is the journalist and non-fiction novelist Rodolfo Walsh (296), who considers "La muerte y la brújula" to be "the ideal of the genre" as well as "an essay on the ultimate possibilities of the detective story" (1953, 7). Written fifteen years after Borges's story, in the context of the "Revolución Libertadora," the dictatorship that overthrew Perón in 1955; Walsh's *Operación masacre* (1957) reconstructs the state-sponsored execution of a group of male citizens, through the testimony of the seven would-be victims that survive the event. Walsh examines how, the night of June 9, 1956, the Buenos Aires Provincial Police (locally known as *La Bonaerense*), illicitly shoot these men in the garbage dump of José León Suárez, on the outskirts of the city, under the premise that they were involved in the attempted Peronist countercoup. Most of the kidnapped men were workers who were not only not involved in the countercoup, but also not even implicated in political activism at all.

In the book's prologue, Walsh mentions that he first heard about the executions while he was playing chess (2013, 17), the same game that Dupin, Holmes, or Marlowe would play, when solving their own crimes. Walsh, an avid reader both of chess and detective stories, had partaken in the genre in his first books, such as *Variaciones en rojo* (1953), mimicking the style of the British mystery murder, "obeying respectfully to the genre's laws," as Rama puts it (298). On a literal and metaphorical level, *Operación massacre* starts with Walsh's abandonment of the chess match, interrupting the playful whodunit narration of crime to focus on denouncing its political implications. The mythical attribute of the detective, for Walsh, is more about successfully reporting the crime instead of revealing the criminal. Through this shift, Walsh contributes to the Argentine rewriting of the tensions that oppose the mythical individualistic private eye and the dictatorial state.

To a certain extent, the book partakes at once in literature and journalism, its legacy constituting, in the words of Argentine philosopher Horacio González, "the foundations of modern critical journalism in Argentina" (495). Beyond this hybridization, for Argentine scholar Rita De Grandis, Walsh's use of the first person conflates the figure of the journalist, narrator and character (307). With Rama, I would add that Walsh's first person incorporates the literary figure of the private detective as well. After all, as Rama mentions, "for a reader who is distant from the political events" the reading of *Operación massacre* "will preserve its validity [. . .] as an excellent detective story" (300) as the book builds on the genre's models. Against Walsh's own authorial intentions to not read his non-fictions novels as detective fiction (Rama 299), my close reading of *Operación massacre* favors the literary dimension of the text over its political intricacies, because although the political conflict at stake in the book, the tensions between Peronism and Anti-Peronism in Argentine politics, is still very much relevant sixty-five years later, the proper names and specific circumstances that crowd *Operación massacre* are not relevant for examining the tensions between individualism and the state.

As Argentine scholar Rita De Grandis notes, the book tells two stories (307). Walsh follows the typical narrative strategy of classic detective stories: to tell the story of the crime and its investigation, to which he adds a radically new political element: the vicissitudes to make both stories public. The stories are separated by their function in the book: the main text is made of how Walsh finds out about the execution and his interviews to the workers mentioned above. The paratextual elements (prologues, epilogues, appendixes), at the same time, give an account of the public disclosure of the event, where Walsh shares changing attitudes towards it through the different editions of the book: "on top of the execution's odyssey, there is that of the journalist who seeks the truth" (De Grandis 307). Walsh presents his quest, wandering "into increasingly remote outskirts of journalism" (Walsh 2013, 20), looking for a publisher who would take the risk of letting the testimonies go public during the dictatorship.

In this odyssey, there is already a rupture with the Anglo-American models, as the individualistic attributes that help Walsh "solve" the case are no longer related to wit but to prosaic persistence. Walsh's character works as an ordinary, stubborn investigator, closer to Don Isidro and Don Frutos than to Dupin, Holmes, and even Marlowe. This small portion of heroism, however, soon comes to an end, as he later admits that his story "gets more wrinkled every day in my pocket because I walk around all of Buenos Aires with it and hardly anyone wants to know about it, let alone publish it" (2013, 20). Nevertheless, Walsh's admission only reinforces the belief that publishing his work to bring the massacre into light will eventually reinstate justice to the public sphere. For Rama, Anglo-American detective stories, "without admitting it, hinge upon their trust in justice's impartiality and effectiveness" (2013, 301). As we concluded in Chapter 1, they implicitly operate presupposing the state's perfectibility and benevolence. In this initial admission, Walsh still shares his models' belief.

Walsh describes his quest as a heroic and individual triumph, as he eventually finds a man who would help him: "He is trembling [. . .] because he's no movie hero either, just a man who is willing to take the risk, and that's worth more than a movie hero" (2013, 20). Journalists, like him and the book's publisher, displace mythical individualism from a purely aesthetic dimension (the "movie hero") to a more flesh-and-bone hero, who turns out to be even more heroic for lacking supernatural attributes.

Through this prosaic heroism, Walsh exposes another underlying belief: if only the masses would know the truth, he could restore the social fabric. Like the presumption of state benevolence, this belief is short-lived. Whereas the initial appendix of *Operación masacre* opens "I wrote this book for it to be published, for it to act [. . .] to bring them to light in the fullest way possible, to provoke fear, to have them never happen again" (2013, 185), the second one (written in 1964) closes wondering "if it was worth it, if what I was chasing was not a fantasy, if the society we live in really needs to hear about these things" (2013, 222). Walsh's rhetoric of gradual disillusion is aimed both at the state and individualistic agency: "I may have lost some [. . .] faith in justice, in compensation, in democracy [. . .] and, finally, my trade" (222). Neither the dictatorial state applies the rule of law to imprison the executioners, nor the individualistic persistence cannot restore the social fabric.

To a certain extent, Walsh's initial belief in state's perfectibility is even stronger than in his Anglo-American models, as he expects that even dictatorial states should be lawful and just. Walsh fully loses his belief in state's perfectibility once his published book does not manage to make the state officers admit it had executed five workers, illegally, since they were arrested before the declaration of martial law. From a post-dictatorial perspective, this disappointment may sound naive. However, it is worth noting that capital punishment had rarely been legal in Argentina till then. In democratic times, Hipólito Yrigoyen's government violently suppressed a rural worker's strike in Santa Cruz, between 1920 and 1922, in an episode that historiography would call "Rebel Patagonia," where the Army executed around 1,500 workers. Apart from that, even before Argentina's formal independence from Spain, the death penalty had been abolished along with slavery in an assembly held in 1813. It was only during the 1950s that the Revolución Libertadora unilaterally reintroduced capital punishment and extra-judicially to execute its own citizens in a conflict other than war.

For this reason, these state executions and the subsequent cover up imply a historical loss of innocence. State-sponsored forced disappearance of bodies become in *Operación masacre* (as Osvaldo Bayer suggests in the book's prologue) a prelude to the 1976–1983 dictatorship that systematically and illegally executed tens of thousands of citizens, leaving no trace of their corpses or reliable register of their execution that would allow anyone to assess its magnitude. This historical trauma would result in the all-pervasive brutality and the prominence of violence in subsequent Argentine detective fiction, but, more importantly to this book, in the genre's representation of individualism and the state.

Besides disillusion, Walsh is obsessed with the illegality of the way in which the state captured and executed its victims: the martial law, that was supposed to justify these acts, only came into effect after midnight, an hour after the workers had been randomly arrested in their homes. What emerges from Walsh's text is that midnight is an arbitrary boundary. In short, there is no midnight: the chronological change of dates does not entail a substantial change in the way the Argentine dictatorial state treats its citizens. Walsh's obsession is reminiscent of Benjamin's adage that "the tradition of the oppressed teaches us that the 'state of exception' in which we live is the rule" (2003, 279). As Italian philosopher Giorgio Agamben comments in his *State of Exception*, following Benjamin, exception is an inherent possibility for modern states. In Esposito's terms, it could be argued that exception, in Argentine detective stories, features as an attribute that no longer belongs to the individual but to the state, because it owes nothing to anyone.

Argentine author Pilar Calveiro notes in her essay *Poder y desaparición*, that Argentine society often perceives the 1976 dictatorship as a sort of midnight, a "parenthesis," in national history. She goes on to say that "it is precisely in these periods of 'exception,' in these inconvenient and unpleasant moments that societies try to forget by putting them between parenthesis, it is then when the secrets of daily power emerge without mediation or attenuation" (28). Something similar happens in Walsh's lost midnight: a breach in the dictatorial state's narrative allows us to see its own true colors.

To sum up, Walsh rewrites the tension between state and individualism in the following ways. Like Borges, he transposes the traditional attributes and lacks assigned to individualistic heroes and the state. This transposition can be read following the notion of symbolic disabilities that were so prominent in classic detective fiction. To begin with, whereas the Anglo-American private eye was the voice of truth and science, Walsh has no voice at all, he is infected with the symbolic muteness that once was circumscribed to state officers (like Poe's G—) only.

Despite Walsh's persistence, his story displays a distinct failure: his knowledge and his thorough narration of the massacre do not grant him any kind of recognition from the dictatorial state that these arbitrary crimes were committed by its own agents. Not even one of them were punished or publicly acknowledged as criminals. Therefore, Walsh is not that different from Lönnrot: both identify the murderer thanks to their relationship with knowledge, but knowing is no longer enough, because it does not entail any kind of repercussion outside language. Walsh may be allowed to express himself in written form, as he eventually has the chance to get his story published under the dictatorship. His voice, nevertheless, is not heard.

In the Epilogue to *Operación masacre*, Walsh explicitly discusses how this symbolic muteness affects also the state: "three editions of this book, about forty published articles, a bill presented to Congress, and countless smaller initiatives have all served to pose the question to five successive governments over the course of twelve years. The response has always been silence" (2013, 173–174). This silencing, though, is asymmetrical: while it is imposed to individuals by disregarding the legitimacy of their voice, it is freely chosen by state officers to build their dictatorial narrative. Because it chooses not to listen, the Argentine state no longer merely displays symbolic muteness but deafness as well. Beyond having to deal with the classic obstacles, the detective is now competing against a deaf-mute body that does not speak because it no longer wants to hear or help in revealing the truth. Hammett's Noonan or Borges's Treviranus may be corrupt or simple minded, but they are still policemen invested in fighting crime, even if they occasionally benefit economically from it. Walsh's *Bonaerense* are closer to Borges's Scharlach, the gunman at the service of a state who no longer entails an inefficient group of officers, but a squad of murderers, not different at any point from the criminals that they are supposed to chase.

This asymmetry shows the extent to which immunity, in Argentine detective stories, is no longer an attribute of individualistic heroes, it belongs rather to the state. Snatched from the individual, the state now inherits the privilege of not owing nothing to anyone, in Esposito's term, it can proceed as it sees fit without having to pay anything in return. *Operación masacre* thus marks a milestone in Argentine history, that will allow the state under subsequent dictatorships not just to connive with crime but to practice systematic terror against its own population with the presumption that it will remain ever immune and unpunished. Both Borges and Walsh pave the way for the post-dictatorial poetics of failure, in which neither individuals nor benevolent state officers can restore social justice.

## THE POST-DICTATORIAL DETECTIVE AS A FAILED INTELLECTUAL

### From Parody to Memory

Following Argentine parodic tradition, Osvaldo Soriano wrote his first novel *Triste, solitario y final* (1973), right before the most recent Argentine dictatorship. Soriano plays with the limits of plausibility, by setting a homonymous *alter ego* in the streets of Los Angeles in order to solve cases with none other than Chandler's Marlowe. Tribute and parody are again present in the very title of the book, that paraphrases one of the final lines of Chandler's *The Long*

*Goodbye* (1953), when Marlowe bids farewell to his friend Terry Lennox: "I said it when it was sad and lonely and final" (1953, 378). Similarly, during the early 1980s, Juan Sasturain's private detective, Etchenike, corrects his clients saying that his surname must be pronounced "Etchenaik," not with a Spanish but with an English accent, reproducing the comedic tone of Argentine detective fiction.

As Borges foretold in his essay "Our Poor Individualism," the cultural abyss between Anglo and Latin America becomes explicit in detective fiction. With this abyss in mind, Sasturain writes in his first detective novel *Manual de perdedores* (1985): "But [private detectives] do not exist [. . .] it is a Yankee invention, pure literature, cinema and TV shows . . . Or do you think that guys like Marlowe [. . .] ever existed? [. . .] Have you gone mad like Don Quixote and believed that you could live in real life whatever you read in books?" (58). It is no coincidence that Sasturain evokes Don Quixote, one of Ian Watt's myths of modern individualism, to discuss the cultural distance that separates Anglo and Latin America. Sasturain dedicates his "losers' textbook" to his parents, because they did not teach him "to win," thus partaking in the poetics of failure. As Giardinelli notes, whereas the North American detective is a hero, "what matters in Latin America is the situation, not the individual merit, which is often ridiculed" (232). Already in the title of Sasturain's novel, there is a link between parody and failure, recovering Borges's precedent.

Using parody, then, Argentine detective stories constantly remind the reader: "do not take us seriously." But should we? After all, they do not use parody solely for the sake of entertainment. Parody is also a mechanism that expresses a different consciousness when compared with its models. Mexican detective fiction author Paco Taibo II puts it very clearly: "What can happen in San Francisco [. . .] cannot happen in La Habana, Mexico City or Madrid [. . .] It is not enough with changing the scenery; the stage itself must be different" (37). Similarly, Díaz Eterovic echoes Taibo, in that it seemed implausible that a Holmesian private eye could exist as such "in a filthy big house in Santiago or Valparaiso" (31). This change of stage is also necessary for detective stories that take place in Buenos Aires, Montevideo, Concepción or Rio de Janeiro; where it takes shape of a poetics of failure: one that acknowledges that it is impossible to reproduce successful individualistic myths in the region.

As I outlined in Chapter 1, Anglo-American tradition conceives detective stories taking at face value individualistic agency and state perfectibility to restore the social fabric. By contrast, as the Argentine detective fiction writer Carlos Gamerro claims, "a Marlowe, for our reality, would be as exotic or implausible as a Sherlock Holmes or a Miss Marple; and if it were possible, he would end up floating face down in the Riachuelo River in the middle of the first chapter" ("Disparen sobre el policial negro"). This quest for plausibility in Argentine fiction features not only in the construction of their parodic heroes, but also in the settings in which they move through, from Borges's allegorical setting in his "La muerte y la brújula" to Ayala Gauna's rural landscape and José León Suárez's garbage dumps in Walsh's non-fiction piece.

Parody gradually disintegrates, though, especially after Sasturain, from the late 1980s onwards. As parody becomes less prominent, a different kind of crime narrative emerges, focusing on memory instead. At least in this sense, it could be argued that Walsh's way of narrating crime triumphed over Borges's still playful one: once detective stories were no longer perceived to be an imported genre, once they were read as a local production with its own canonical authors (some of them even recognized internationally, such as Borges himself); subsequent generations of Argentine authors did not feel the need to resort to parody as their forerunners had.

However, like parody, memory creates a bridge with a genre that may now be more local, but ultimately still retains its foreign origin. An inheritor of both Borges and Walsh, Ricardo Piglia, along with other writers of his generation (born in the late 1930s and early 1940s), such as Miguel Bonasso, Juan José Saer, Luisa Valenzuela and Mempo Giardinelli, write their detective stories in the 1980s and 1990s, that is, from a different historical background: that of post-dictatorship. They hark back to the past, preferably to the 1970s, to come to terms with national traumas of genocide. Their stories are also in stark contrast with the Anglo-American canon, now for different reasons: as we have seen, English mystery stories only use crime as cerebral puzzles and most of North American hard-boiled talks about murder as a means of depicting society's corruption during Prohibition and the Great Depression. As Giardinelli says, "one of the most evident differential traits, between North and Latin American writers, lies in that the latter always include a political ingredient in their plots" (229). With the exception perhaps of Himes's Harlem detective series, the Anglo-American models were not ultimately interested in using crime to examine historical conflicts.

Does this use of political memory mean Piglia and his generation are somewhat unfaithful to their models? According to Argentine philosopher José Pablo Feinmann it does. For him, Argentine detective fiction has "not obeyed" the conventions of the genre. By contrast, it has operated in its edges, using the genre "as a metaphor or a parable of the political" (152). However, one of the main laws that Zohar and Lambert describe for poly-systems is precisely the "submission to the conventions of the importing literature" (252). In this sense, the Argentine appropriation of Anglo-American detective fiction works as a perfect example of what Zohar and Lambert label "imported genres": the submission of imported conventions could only be valid if these conventions are adapted to be plausible in their new geo-cultural context, perceived itself in a clear antithesis of its distant but ever captivating Anglo-American models.

If there is such a thing as a Southern Cone detective fiction, it can be traced in this poetics of failure that originates first in the Argentine reception and re-appropriation of the Anglo-American canon, and is later re-exported, South-South, to Brazilian and Chilean literatures. A common historical legacy marks these three national literatures: that of the transnational Operation Condor, which shapes the ways in which detective stories were conceived first as parody, then as memory.

Paraphrasing the German philosopher Theodor W. Adorno, Gamerro claims that the impossibility of producing local private detectives is inseparable from the dictatorial experience: "after El Olimpo clandestine detention center it is not possible to practice hard-boiled fiction" ("Disparen sobre el policial negro"). By equating the effects that Auschwitz had on Western culture with the impact that the dictatorship had on Argentine literature, Gamerro claims that the bloodiest of the country's twentieth-century experiences changes the paradigm in which state, individualism, and crime ought to be read. Unlike the United States, the United Kingdom, or Scandinavia, countries where detective fiction is profusely cultivated, the Argentine re-definition of the state after the dictatorial experience offers a singular historical framework. Building on Gamerro, I add that the impact of this context should not be solely circumscribed to Argentina, as it also features in the Brazilian and Chilean novels I examine in the following chapters.

Gamerro suggests that to make post-dictatorial detective stories plausible, a common narrative strategy is setting fictions far from Argentina. Certainly, there are examples that follow this prescription, such as Mempo Giardinelli's *Qué solos se quedan los muertos* (1985), Luisa Valenzuela's *Novela negra con argentinos* (1990), Juan José Saer's *La pesquisa* (1995), or Guillermo Martínez's *Crímenes imperceptibles* (2003), which take place in Zacatecas, New York, Paris, and Oxford, respectively. Yet there are contemporary detective fictions that do take place in South American cities, and they actively engage with post-dictatorial memory, as well. The stories and novels that I examine below are set in Buenos Aires, Montevideo, Concepción, and Rio de Janeiro. These narratives observe Gamerro's displacement not in geography but history, since they often take place in the past. In each of them, the detective, in one or way or another, fails to restore the social fabric at the hands of a brutal dictatorial apparatus.

With Feinmann, I may inquire how it is possible to depict a criminal state in a genre usually meant for mass entertainment: "What happens with detective stories when crime is not only in the streets, but it is there [. . .] because the state is the main responsible of its existence? What happens when the police, far from embodying the image of justice, personifies instead the image of terror?" (215). Feinmann never fully answers. He states that whereas North American hard-boiled fiction equates law with crime and portrays the police as unreliable, "in Argentina, the police, to be plausible, must still play the role of the villain" (220). Similarly, Giardinelli observes that whereas the Scotland Yard and the FBI enjoy a favorable reputation in their respective societies, there is no equivalent for these institutions in Latin America (236), where "the police not only inspire mistrust but also hatred and resentment" (235). For Giardinelli, this becomes increasingly "natural" during the 1980s, i.e.,: after the post-dictatorial transitions to democracy in the region (235). This is why Argentine police officers are not just villains: they are a personification of criminality itself. Furthermore, they feature as successful and immune criminals, often to the detriment of a defeated detective, a key aspect that rarely happens in such a prominent way outside of the Southern Cone.

Let us take as an example recent Scandinavian TV crime shows, such as *Forbrydelsen* (2007–2012) or *Bron* (2011–2018), and their North American remakes. They do depict policemen as murderers. Yet the individualistic investigator still catches them in the end and the personifications of evil get punished. In one way or another, the sense of social order still prevails. Instead, Southern Cone detective fiction's distinctive features are that detectives always fail to get the criminal policemen, their agency dismantled by the state against with which they compete. Both displacements, from present to past and success to failure, allow these authors to deal with the trauma of dictatorship, by intertwining the narration of crime with the exploration of memory.

## LABOR AND FAILURE

Emilio Renzi is the incarnation of the private detective in most of Piglia's novels and short stories from the 1970s to the 2010s. Argentine detective fiction scholar Jorge B. Rivera traces Renzi's genealogy to Borges's Lönnrot (101). Building on Rivera, I would like to offer a closer reading of this genealogy. Renzi features for the first time in the short story "La loca y el relato del crimen" (1975), a story that won a literary contest organized by the magazine *Siete días*. In fact, as Piglia mentions in *Los diarios de Emilio Renzi. Los años felices* (2016), Borges was among the jury members who gave him the prize (2016, 409). Piglia's story offers some interesting parallelisms, the most obvious of which is in the title, separated by a cumulative conjunction: "La muerte y la brújula" / "La loca y el relato del crimen." Piglia mirrors madness with death; and the story, with the compass, in that both organize facts. As I study in Chapters 4 and 5, madness is also prominent in Fonseca and Bolaño's detective stories.

A more subtle parallelism can be found in the way Piglia reproduces Borges's strategy of introducing the detective through the adversative conjunction "but": "Emilio Renzi was interested in linguistics, *but* he earned a living writing literary reviews in the newspaper *El Mundo*" (2000, 97, emphasis added). Borges, in turn, presents his detective as follows: "Lönnrot thought of himself as a pure thinker, an Auguste Dupin, *but* there was something of the adventurer in him, and even a little of the gambler" (1962, 76, emphasis added). Like in Borges, "but" works as an announcement of the detective's problematic personality, showing a disconnection between the way Renzi perceives himself and his actual role in society. For this reason, Renzi is a parodic character, too, as he is even more prosaic than his already mundane forerunners. Piglia takes one step further Borges's parodic downward displacement: Lönnrot sees himself as Dupin, yet he is but a gambler; Renzi wants to be as sophisticated as Lönnrot (someone with strong ties to language), yet he is a failed version of him: an amateur linguist turned into a wage-earning journalist.

Piglia reveals what Renzi is by saying what he is not: a detective disguised as a non-detective. Most of the private eye's embodiments in Argentine post-dictatorial detective fiction share this gesture: private detectives are always private but never detectives *per se*. For Feinmann, this is "an essential feature of Argentine detective stories: it does not display neither policemen nor detectives" (213). Why is it so? Colombian scholar Héctor Hoyos explains the absence of private detectives in Colombian detective fiction "not due to how realistic but how plausible this archetype can be" (63). Something similar happens with the Argentine case: with Borges and Bioy Casares's hairdresser as a parodic model, most of these authors envision anomalous detectives because they are more plausible than the Anglo-American sophisticated dandies. Whereas Ayala Gauna imagines a rural inspector, Walsh does the same with the investigative journalist. As Marcelo Gobbo mentions, Piglia's choice of turning his detective into a journalist is a direct homage to Walsh (46). But Piglia does something else: he displaces Walsh's journalist hero from a non-fictional realm to an auto-fictional one (in that Emilio and Renzi and Ricardo Piglia's second name and surname); bringing back the figure of the detective to a more literary realm.

During the 1970s and 1980s, other Argentine writers do the same as Piglia. In fact, according to Argentine scholar Nora Catelli, Soriano's *Triste, solitario y final* (1973) is the first to transform the author in a character in the Latin American literary field ("El laboratorio Bolaño"). Along with him, Giardinelli's *Qué solos se quedan los muertos* (1985) and Bonasso's *La memoria en donde ardía* (1990), embody auto-fictional journalists turned into one-time investigators. A later generation of writers (born in the 1960s) brings up even more heterogeneous incarnations, tied to the recent demilitarization of the Argentine democratic state, such as Tony Hope, the retired navy cadet of Carlos Feiling's *El agua electrizada* (1992), and Felipe Félix, the ex-combatant of the Falklands War turned into a hacker in Carlos Gamerro's *Las islas* (1998). More recently, the mathematician and novelist Guillermo Martínez recovered the auto-fictional tradition in *Crímenes imperceptibles* (2003), with a math graduate student playing the role of the sleuth. Eduardo Sacheri moves from the military to the judiciary, with his Inspector Chaparro, an attorney who inquires into an old crime in *La pregunta de sus ojos* (2005) and Claudia Piñeiro imagines for *Betibú* (2011) a female detective fiction novelist in charge of a real investigation.

Back to Piglia, by the time of his last novel, *Ida's Journey* (2013), Renzi has become a lonely middle-aged South American professor who, like his author, teaches literature at Princeton. Beyond the ways in which he engages with labor and the task of detection, Renzi shares with Lönnrot and Walsh that he is an intellectual who fails to solve his cases because of his intellectuality. Renzi's knowledge of neurolinguistics and his dexterity as a journalist are part of his detective's bookish attributes. But there is a sense of malfunction, and of implied failure, in the way Piglia constructs him right from his first appearance: trained in linguistics but compelled to work in something trivial and underpaid such as "writing short literary reviews on the devastated panorama of our national literature" (2000, 97). A precarized intellectual, Renzi is diametrically opposed to the upper-class detective. He is a sleuth who, like Parodi or Don Frutos, investigates from an underclass position, as his profession is somewhat below the symbolic capital he holds.

As Renzi himself admits in *Ida's Journey* (2013), successful sleuths are no longer of any use: "we detectives no longer solve crimes, but at least we can narrate them" (2013, 151). This is his function in most of the texts he appears in: organizing the narratives around crime and their aftermath. Unlike the classic detective, who would symbolize an endorsement of the limitless power of individualism, Renzi's individual agency is reduced to the task that once was reserved to sidekicks: narrating, instead of solving puzzles and restoring social order. In "La loca y el relato del crimen" and the novel *Plata quemada*, Renzi fictionalizes Walsh's role, namely, writing about a case he cannot really solve or even have an impact on. In political terms, the story of Lönnrot, Walsh, and Renzi, is the story of powerless heroes and their impossibility of holding sovereignty. Renzi becomes a chronicler who can merely accumulate facts to capture them through language.

In *Plata quemada,* Comisario Silva describes Renzi as "that disrespectful kid, with his glasses and curly hair, with his goose face, foreign to the real world and the danger of the situation" (2003, 134). Renzi "seemed a parachutist, a legal aid lawyer or the youngest brother of a convict that complains about the treatment that criminals suffer in police stations" (134). Here, Renzi shows the negative attributes that once belonged only to state officers like Silva himself, all associated with a lack of productivity and pragmatism. In short, Silva sees Renzi as an incompetent and oblivious crybaby, who lacks force and whose wit is unthreatening, not too different from inept policemen, such as Lestrade or Treviranus.

Charles Brownson claims in *The Figure of the Detective* (2013), that it is in this "contemporary problem of knowledge in naked reality, set in a world of political power, wealth, and cynicism" that "the detective detects nothing. In the end he is not even sure of his own identity" (157). Browson's definition of the postmodern detective applies to Renzi, whose account is committed "not to repair the torn fabric of society but to help tear it farther" (157). If, as Lacan saw, symbols helped Dupin to solve the purloined letter case, here they have an inverted outcome: they paralyze Renzi and condemn him to constant failure. In Lacanian terms, the post-dictatorial private detective remains a prisoner of symbols. Thus, Renzi inherits Lönnrot's distorted relation with language, as what once constituted the private eye's mythification is now the aspect that heads him towards failure: knowledge.

## FROM KNOWLEDGE TO FAILURE

Brazilian scholar Idelber Avelar (2000) and Venezuelan writer Rodrigo Blanco Calderón examine the issue of failure in Piglia's first two novels, *Respiración artificial* (1980) and *La ciudad ausente* (1987), respectively. Blanco Calderón notes how silence has shaped Piglia's entire career in the way he positioned himself in the Argentine literary field: in so far as he was often "silent," only publishing five novels from 1970s till the 2010s. He explains Piglia's scarce production (especially when compared with more prolific writers such as Puig, Saer, or Aira), by a strategy in which he "kept a distance from success and a silent vocation for failure" (27). I concur with their reading of failure in the sense of "defeat," but I also understand failure in terms of "malfunction," following the twofold translation that "failure" has in Spanish, as *derrota* and *falla*. Furthermore, failure is key not only to reading these two canonical first novels; it is also prominent in Renzi's first appearance, "La loca y el relato del crimen" (1975), which, according to Piglia, is the only "pure" detective story he has written (Mattalia 2006, 118).

Piglia publishes this short story a few months before the formalization of dictatorial rule in Argentina, which took place with the military coup of March 24, 1976. Nonetheless, the narrative portrays an oppressive atmosphere that was already very much present during the government of Isabel

Martínez de Perón, the widow of the then late General Juan Domingo. A short-lived government (July 1974–March 1976), this period worked as a prelude to the dictatorship that, despite being originally democratic, ended up getting involved with the ruthless persecution of citizens through the Argentine Anticommunist Alliance. The Triple A, a far-right death squad with close relations with the Argentine Police, engaged in state terrorism to an extent that showed a seamless continuum with the following dictatorial experience. Piglia portrays this oppressive context by focusing on the absent presence of the police institution. As Gobbo notes, "crimes, in Piglia's stories, are always (at least metaphorically) *political*" (46, emphasis in original). This is certainly the case for "La loca y el relato del crimen."

The story seems somewhat simple. A homeless and psychotic woman, named Angélica Etchevarne, speaks up the causes and the details of the murder of a prostitute. As Mattalia notes, Piglia tells two stories, much like Walsh, and the classic detective tradition he theorized so much about in his critical work (118): the story of the crime and its revelation, which is hidden in Etchevarne's words. Whereas the Madwoman happens to be the one holder of truth as she is the only witness; Renzi is the only one who has the symbolical literacy to understand her incoherent language. At first sight, all of this seems to reproduce the traditional endorsement of individualism that features in classic detective stories.

Renzi's reading of the Madwoman's speech is made of the typical digressions that boast knowledge and erudition, updated now to late twentieth-century neurolinguistics. Renzi explains to his supervisor his method of rendering legible the meaning behind madness: "The madman [. . .] is forced to repeat fixed verbal structures, as in a mold [. . .] that then gets filled with words [. . .] To examine this structure, there are thirty-six verbal categories that are named logical operators. [. . .] You arrange them in order, and you can realize that the delusion makes sense
[..] Whatever does not fit that order [. . .] is what the madman tries to say despite the repetitive compulsion" (2000, 100). With his method, Renzi deciphers triumphantly the madwoman's delirious speech: the excluded words point out that the assassin is not who the police say it is, but another suspect called fat Almada.

The knowledge of Piglia's detective stems from "five years at the university specializing in Trubetzkoi's [sic] phonology" (2000, 97). His high degree of literacy prepared him to decrypt Echevarne's broken speech. An "incomprehensible story" (97), the Madwoman's words offer a classic enigma, which the successful private eye can solve by decoding "a series of linguistic laws, a code that is used to analyze the language of a psychotic person" (100). Nonetheless, heroism, once more, is short-lived. The story opens with an endorsement of individualism that quickly vanishes into thin air by the end.

Like Lönnrot and Walsh, language distances Renzi from the world rather than truly enabling him to read it. For this reason, his supervisor old Luna has sent him to cover the story of the crime alluded to in the title, a crime involved with Buenos Aires's underworld, filled with prostitutes and pimps. We expect the contact and the exposure with the mean streets would transform the private eye in the successful tough guy of North American hard-boiled fiction stories. But what he gets, instead, is sheer failure.

If for Mattalia, "in the 1940s, Borges and Bioy questioned [. . .] the classic detective story's faith in generic and state legality," Piglia, in this story, "goes a step forward by questioning rationality and investigation as guarantors of public truth" (117–118). Equally, Piglia also deepens Walsh's social futility of revealing the truth of a crime. In the dialogue that closes the short story, old Luna warns Renzi that solving the case will only be a mere anecdote in his career: "Have you learnt this at the university? [. . .] What are you going to do with all these papers now? A dissertation? [. . .] Calm down, kid. Or did you think that we care about semantics in this newspaper?" (2000, 101). Renzi insists, but old Luna refuses. After his supervisor's ban, Renzi writes "The story of the crime," which is no other than Piglia's story that we are reading.

Díaz Eterovic defines Latin American detective fiction as a way of "establishing (if only within the realm of fiction) the justice denied by dictatorial governments, corrupt judges, and the mendacious media that was an expert in hiding the horror" (38). In short, Renzi is "a researcher that will solve the mystery but will never be able to make it public, except through literary speech" (Gobbo 46). The fact that Piglia uses the same paragraph to open and conclude his story suggests that the only outlet for truth is reserved not to journalism (if we can understand journalism as a pristine narration of facts) but to literature.

However, like Walsh's, Renzi's writing does not truly lead to justice not even in a literary dimension, because the punishment of the murderers remains circumscribed to an inoffensive text. The delirious speech, "repeating the same for the past ten hours without saying anything" (2000, 100), may have a meaning for Renzi, but that does not imply anything in the actual restoration of the social order, it signifies nothing for the world, as identifying the murderer verbally does not lead to their punishment.

Like Lönnrot and Walsh, Renzi endures symbolic muteness, since the readers of the newspaper will never get to hear or read his voice, only Old Luna does. The real murderer, fat Almada, is shielded from the top (2000, 98), which the story connects to the Argentine state. Once more, the sleuth's symbolic muteness and failure is caused by something that was but no longer is enough to restore social order: knowledge. The detective's powers of observation are useless in the face of state power. Renzi solves the case (he identifies the murderer), but fails to restitute justice. So, what distinguishes Piglia from Borges or Walsh? The fact that Renzi's hopes to have an impact in the world by revealing a truth are destroyed from the beginning. Unlike Walsh, Piglia writes absorbed in skepticism: once revolution has been defeated by a counter-revolutionary dictatorial state, Piglia is no longer able to believe that restoration is even available and condemns his detective to symbolic muteness from earlier on.

Piglia depicts knowledge (dominated to state force) as a sterile game, divested from the traditional effect it once may have had. Old Luna tells Renzi: "All this play on words looks great but let's stop here [. . .] Don't get into trouble. If you mess with the police, I will fire you" (2000, 101). His warning somehow foretells the *leitmotiv* of the soon-to-come dictatorship: do not get involved, do not dare to alter the social order or to interfere with the state. Blaming state officers out loud for its crimes against civilians will not affect social justice at all.

The Hungarian researcher Ágnes Cselik highlights the prominence of failure in the story: as she points out, in the end, everyone fails (126). Brownson believes that, when failure prevails because cases remain unpunished or unsolved, detective stories engage in a bitter social comment, which precisely states this "impossibility of knowledge" (84). But the unsolved case of the Madwoman expresses something different. It is not so much that knowledge is no longer possible but that it is not useful, as Mattalia notes (119): when knowledge is uttered outside of the state apparatus, without force, it is as useless as burnt money. Piglia's poetics of failure entails that knowledge does not pay. Renzi's symbolic muteness leads to a futile literary mythification. Speechless, the detective's knowledge is restricted only to his privileged use of literacy: writing.

## THE ARGENTINE STATE: A DEAF-MUTE BODY

### Money and Failure

In "La loca y el relato del crimen," the Argentine state and its police are deliberately silent and indifferent—much like in *Operación Masacre*. As we said, the police is absent, in that there are no characters fully embodying it. We start to see here a crisis of representation that will become more and more prominent in Latin America detective fiction. The gradual lack of policemen as metonymies of the state shows an abandonment of the narrative strategy that is central to the classic detective tradition: using characters as personification of ideas. Instead, as Mattalia mentions, it is journalists who replace the role traditionally assigned to the police (118). Piglia writes this short story in the mid-1970s, a time in which, as British economic geographer David

Harvey explains in his *Brief History of Neoliberalism* (2005), neoliberalism was being dictatorially enforced as a test in Latin America, especially in Argentina and Chile.

One of the key aspects of neoliberalism is the privatization of state's assets, such as public companies, for example. This was the case for Argentina, during the 1970s dictatorship, and even more sharply in the 1990s during the democratic government of Carlos Saúl Menem (See Jofré). As British theorist Jon Beasley-Murray explains, however, neoliberalism should be understood not simply as a process for shrinking the state's agency, but rather a "radical reconstruction of the state's contours" (102), in which states may "relinquish direct control of the economy but are highly interventionist in other areas" (102). During the emergence of neoliberalism, Piglia sees this shift of the state's boundaries, when he imagines this privatization of the state's personification.

Piglia outsources the state's muteness in the figure of Old Luna, who does not even need any of state coercion to restrain himself from publishing subversive information. As Luna tells Renzi: "You don't mess with the police. If they told you that the Virgin Mary was the murderer, you just write that" (2000, 101). In this sense, Cselik defines the police in the story as "an organization that feeds and verifies fictions" (123). Because of its connivance with organized crime, the police can only create fictions and then administer them: impose them to the press, which in turn spreads it following thoroughly the requirements of censorship. In short, Piglia represents the state, through journalism, as selectively deaf-mute body. In his own definition, the state, "on the one hand, does not say and on the other hand forces to say" (qtd. in Pellicer 97). And this can be read both as systematic torture and the enforcement of the state's own narratives. It is a state that has no real competitors: the idea of any private eye who could stand up against it seems not only implausible but also ludicrous.

For this reason, Renzi does not compete with a policeman to reveal the truth. He lacks a G—, an Inspector Lestrade, or a Treviranus to contend against. Instead, his rivals belong to the private sector itself: on the one hand, Luna, his own supervisor, who has absorbed (normativized in Foucaldian terms) the criminal nature of the police and internalized the authoritarian rule of the state as his own. On the other hand, Mattalia's idea that journalism inherits the police role becomes crystal clear in characters such as Rinaldi, a police reporter from *La Prensa,* the competition of *El Mundo,* "an incompetent character who considers a wrong and all too obvious hypothesis" (Mattalia 118). Piglia, then, outsources not only state's muteness, but also its incompetence.

Rinaldi inherits the same monstrous attributes that once were ascribed to the state: his "skin was fluffy, as if he were just emerged from the water" (Piglia 2000, 98). He boasts about being "able to smell a criminal a block away" (98) and contends with Renzi in terms of knowledge, when he states that the Madwoman's broken speech "seems a parody of Macbeth [. . .] The story told by a madman signifying nothing" (99). At which Renzi responds: "By an idiot, not by a madman [. . .]. And who told you that it means nothing?" (99). Renzi's display or bookish erudition, by the end of the story, would prove to be the futile rectification of a powerless savant, who is defeated by power structures he cannot control.

In *Plata quemada*, we have a slightly different scenario. Published in 1997, at the end of 1990s Menemismo, but written through more than three decades, Piglia's third novel narrates a crime that took place in the 1950s: it is the story of two homosexual criminals, el Gaucho Dorda and el Nene Brignone, and other accomplices, who raided a bank in downtown Buenos Aires and escaped with three million of pesos in cash to Montevideo. After six weeks, the criminals found themselves surrounded by three hundred military policemen both from Argentina and Uruguay. Once the thieves have lost all hope to escape, they surprisingly decide to burn the money. After the conflagration, the police end up executing them.

In this novel, the police seem to be more present and embodied in specific characters, such as the Superintendent of the Buenos Aires Police, Comisario Silva, who "does not investigate, simply tortures and uses the accusation as his method," as Renzi describes him (2003, 60). Conversely, individualism and hostility towards the state appear now, not exclusively in the Renzi's voice, but in that of the criminals, who, more than the private eye, are the real protagonists of the novel. While Piglia defines "La loca y el relato del crimen" as his purest rendition of the genre, with a well-defined detective who solves a crime, *Plata quemada* is a more heterodox take on detective fiction, especially for the gradual disintegration of the figure of the detective. As American scholar Michelle Clayton notes, Renzi opens the novel "by erasing himself" (137), vanishing in other character's voices. In a similar vein, Argentine critic Julio Premat talks about how the polyphonic ensemble of voices exhibits a sense of "depersonalization" (128). All these tendencies, as we will see, are even more pronounced in Bolaño's detective fiction.

In any case, some of the loudest voices belong to the thieves. For Premat, even if he is a criminal, el Gaucho Dorda inherits the *hard-boiled* detective's toughness (130). Let us hear Dorda's voice: "Policemen [. . .] do it all just for a little salary, for their pension" (Piglia 2003, 110), he rants in *Plata quemada*'s final scene. They "have their woman at home complaining because the cop earns too little, spends all the night out, under the rain" (110). Dorda goes on to wonder "who could even think to be a policeman, only a sick guy [. . .]

a 'pusillanimous' dude (he had learnt that word in jail and he liked it because it made him think on someone without a soul)" (110–111). Entrenched in the Liberaij, an emblematic building of Montevideo, along with his lover, Dorda contrives against the officers while he resists their massive shooting, for fifteen hours. They have been ambushed and besieged after a long persecution, for committing one of the most impressive bank robberies in Buenos Aires. But Dorda's rant reproduces not so much a conventional thief's speech. It rather sounds much like a private entrepreneur's underestimating the lives of public functionaries, these sick and pusillanimous wage-earners who take no risks in life and prefer the security of permanent employment that public administration has to offer. Individualistic hostility towards the state, once funneled through the private detective, pervades the schizophrenic speech of Dorda, a criminal who is also a madman, like Etchevarne.

Full of delusions and paranoia addressed against the state, Dorda's speech can be read in the light of Foucault's notion of "state-phobia," which he coins after art historian Berenson's reflections on the state, that read as follows: "'God knows I fear the destruction of the world by the atomic bomb, but there is at least one thing I fear as much, and that is the invasion of humanity by the state" (2008, 76). For Foucault, this example is the "clearest expression of a state-phobia" (76). The French philosopher, who develops this idea in the late 1970s, clarifies that state-phobia "is not that recent since Berenson expressed it around 1950–1952" (76). Instead, it spectrally reappears in different political forms, from the left and the right, throughout the first half of the twentieth century, in "the Soviet experience of the 1920s, the German experience of Nazism, English post-war planning" (76). "State-phobia," then, is a multicausal and reactionary phenomenon aimed at the state, as the Post-War dominant liberal trend (the one that ultimately won the Second World War in the West) regards authoritarian sovereignty with fear.

Foucault sees earlier traces of state-phobia. He understands it to be "one of the signs of the crises of governmentability" (76), whose embryonic manifestations hark back as early as the sixteenth century, to reappear in the "second half of eighteenth century, which manifest itself in that immense, difficult, and tangled criticism of despotism, tyranny, and arbitrariness" (76). State-phobia is ambivalent, as it exhibits, at once, disdain but also fascination towards state power, through multiple "agents and promoters, from economics professors inspired by Austrian neo-marginalism to political exiles who, from 1920 to 1925 have certainly played a major role in the formation of contemporary political consciousness" (76). What Foucault outlines here is the international trajectory followed by the origins of neoliberalism, a traveling economic school arising in Vienna, (by Ludwig von Mises and Friedrich von Hayek, fathers of Austrian Neo-marginalism), and moving via England to Chicago, where it will be further elaborated. As I mention above, according to Harvey, from Chicago, neoliberalism (and state-phobia) is exported as a dictatorial test in the global south. In the 1980s, it later returns to the north under Reagan, Mulroney and Thatcher' democratic administration, eventually becoming the mainstream way of doing politics, especially after the Soviet Union's collapse.

Neoliberal state-phobia, or "anti-statism" as Foucault also calls it (76), impregnates Gaucho Dorda's rant. When, besieged in the Liberaij, he shows mistrust towards the police's speech: despite they insistently "guarantee the life of delinquents before the very Judge," Dorda gives them only "new and worse insults" (Piglia 2003, 125) in return. Renzi, once again, a journalist in charge of compiling and narrating the events for *El Mundo*, depicts the criminals in the same light of anti-statist individualism: while policemen are starving in the middle of the night, standing guard next to the Liberaij, Dorda and his sidekicks flaunt their ephemeral wealth, enjoying chicken and getting drunk on whisky, always surrounded by the stolen money. This is a clear reproduction of the old asymmetrical rivalry that once place the private detective and the state face to face. Except that now, the criminals, as Pellicer and Premat put it, have eclipsed the private eye.[3]

Renzi highlights how anti-statist individualism operate in the criminals' discourse: "And you, how much do you earn? You'll be killing each other over small change" (126) brags Dorda's partner, el Nene, whose delusion of grandeur rectifies or rather transiently solves class resentment. As Giardinelli notes, whereas the obsession for money lies the at the core of North American detective fiction writers, their Latin American counterparts focus instead on the ways in which money produces social distinction (222). Usually an outcast who must steal to earn an income, el Nene now perceives himself to be above the wage-earning policemen, thanks to the bank robbery. The loot makes him, if for but one night (and even if it will be his last one), into an updated version of the myth of individualism: the self-made man, who is able to enjoy good food and alcohol, to look down on the police, those working-class officers suffering through the cold Montevideo night, who, if anything, are risking their lives for a scant wage, while enforcing the state's standpoint.

Obviously, the criminals' phobic suspicion is entirely well founded: after all, the ruthless state from which they are running certainly looks no different from Foucault's description of despotic, tyrannical, and arbitrary states. Beneath the apparent benevolence of the police to ensure their human rights, el Nene knows they had other intentions: to execute them. Piglia's choice of using an execution as literary material is another explicit tribute to Walsh. But the state-sponsored execution we see in *Plata quemada* is slightly different to *Operación masacre*'s: what triggers the shooting is not the suspicion of a political conspiracy but, as Gamerro notes, the conflagration of the stolen money. Burning the loot implies that "this time the burglars rebelled and refused to make a deal with the police" (Gamerro 2006, 79). In other words, the extra-judiciary state punishment has more individualistic reasons: as Renzi infers, the police favor the execution over an arrest because, once the money is gone, they will not be able to get their share, as it had been agreed (Piglia 2003, 97). Killing the criminals keeps the police's immunity intact, as they avoid incrimination.

Max Weber's notion of fear of the state in the form of obedience resonates with Foucault's state phobia. Alongside his famous definition of the state as the one holder of the community which "(successfully) claims the monopoly of the legitimate use of physical force within a given territory," Weber points out that obedience to the state "is determined by highly robust motives of fear and hope" (2005, 79). What is robust, then, is not the state body itself, but its powerful effects upon the people who must obey them.

When Piglia describes the Argentine state as sick, he imagines it as a body that far from being robust is weak and soulless, finding its incarnation in these policemen "without a soul," a characterization that resonates both with Weber and with Foucault's definition of the state as a body that "has no heart, as we all know, but not just in the sense that it has no feelings, either good or bad, but [. . .] in the sense that it has no interior" (Foucault 2008, 77). This empty body can be traced in Renzi's description of the policemen's voice, ordering their capitulation. The voice "arrived in a distorted way, in *falsetto*, a typical voice of a guanaco, devious and arrogant, emptied of any feeling different from humiliation" (Piglia 2003, 102). In the police, Piglia reproduces the old symbolic disabilities of the state, a monstrous body whose voice is either too loud or out of tune, filled with different sorts of distortion and deformities, but it is essentially void.

Because by itself the state's voice is weak, it needs technology to amplify and multiply its violence, "through the loudspeaker in the cells, in the corridors of hospitals, in the patrol cars that carry inmates in the middle of the night through the empty city to the basements of police stations" (102). But beyond the reproduction of these traditional flaws, there is here something new: Piglia underlines that the voice of power is a voice that has been "emptied," much like the nocturnal city that serves as a background for the patrol cars. It is a hollow voice, whose oppressive effect relies precisely in its hollowness. The representation of the Argentine state differs from its Anglo-American counterpart, as the main state's flaw is not simply that its officers cannot speak nor that they do not know how to operate efficiently. The main symbolic disability of the state, Piglia reveals, is that it lacks content, it is a vacuous silhouette.

In *Plata quemada*, more than in "La loca y el relato del crimen," Piglia engages with personification to depict the state, by embodying it in the figure of "el Comisario Silva," whose presence Dorda demands in an equally derogatory way, invariably comparing him to repulsive animals: "If the fag swine of Silva is around, tell him to come himself to negotiate, tell him not to chicken out" (110). Premat notes how the narrator describes Silva in terms of femininity (131–132), (which Dorda addresses here when he calls Silva a "fag"). The state officer's mirrors the criminal's homosexuality. Piglia touches upon another genre convention, the equation between state and criminality, but in an original way: authority's hollow voice is inseparable from the masculine DNA that Segato observes in the configuration of the state, made of "men that yell, confident that the other will obey or sink" (Piglia 2003, 102). As I briefly mention in Chapter 1, according to Segato, the state's sovereign is inextricably linked to masculinity but not necessarily to heterosexuality (see p. 41). Here, Piglia explicitly imagines the Argentine state's hollowness in terms of queerness.

Colombian journalist John William Archbold claims that the presence of homosexuality in *Plata quemada* is understudied, even claiming that Premat "evades completely the issue" (109–110). However, this is true only partially, as both Rodríguez Pérsico and Premat do discuss the criminal's queerness in relation to state power. Rodríguez Pérsico cites Lévi-Strauss's *Myth and Meaning*, to argue that Piglia offers a myth that "contradicts the exemplary pedagogy of myths while at the same time offering a turn of the screw to detective fiction's conventions, as the heroes are murderers, homosexual and drug addicts" (115). Premat mentions how homosexuality acts as a marginal form of sexuality that signified a counter-discourse against the state, in mid twentieth-century Argentina (131). This was also true twenty-five years ago, in 1997, when Piglia publishes his novel, a historical period that is worlds away from the present. But, as Archbold notes, even though Dorda and el Nene are gay, they are still extremely masculinized: "through the relationship between 'el Gaucho' and 'el Nene'" Piglia exhibits "the hegemony of patriarchal and heterosexist blueprints, whose influence is so deep that it [. . .] affects even an opposed sexual expression" (Archbold 111). Ultimately, both criminals are like Silva in that their tough masculinity shows a slippage between what they are, and what they are supposed to be.

The physical dismemberments of the state's body find in this slippage its symbolic counterpart: the absence of a soul, a heart, a voice or even a human constitution; not only masculine cruelty, as Foucault warns us, but also vacuity. Through mere nihilist force, the policemen will eventually shoot to death the three criminals after their Numantine resistance. But since they have soulless bodies—i.e.,: bodies lacking among others the ability of literacy—they fail to read the situation well enough to recover the money, to reinstate it to the financial system. Piglia himself mentions in an interview that burnt money is no different than counterfeit money (qtd. in Carrión 435). As Bruce and Wagner point out, the destruction of the money entails an even more severe failure as, once it is turned to ashes, it is non-productive and hence non-rational: "As the bills metamorphose into ash, money is gradually divested of its function of guarantor of rationality" (4).

Even laundered money, despite its origins stained with crime, can still be of use to the market. But once incinerated, the bank notes are suddenly located at the opposite side of the spectrum of the space of fluidity where they are supposed to be. It is not a coincidence that the aquatic metaphors alluding to cash are very prolific in economics: "liquidity," "flow," "circulation," "laundering," "leaks," "waves," "stagnation," "splattering,"[4] all of which are reminiscent of Harvey's concept of "fluidity" as central to Marx's conception of capitalism (2010, 34). As long as money keeps circulating, it fulfills its utilitarian purpose. By contrast, "burnt, money is reduced to its ultimate materiality, ashes, the illusion of its intrinsic value shattered end and with it its referential status with regard to all that it measures (time, work, commodities)" (Bruce and Wagner 5). Once the flow is interrupted and water cannot extinguish the fire, the logic of money and its meaning are cancelled.

As the siege drags on, a curious multitude gathers outside the Liberaij building and starts clamoring for punishment. The fact that they are burning money makes Dorda and his sidekicks look more criminal than mere thieves, deserving an even worse sentence. The press, the media and the witnesses of the siege see their conflagration as "a nihilist act and an example of pure terrorism" (Piglia 2003, 103). Like Bruce and Wagner claim, as it dissipates in the smoke, "money appears to be what is most valuable in society, representing, beyond its exchange value, the values upheld by society and even the sheer fact that society has such values" (4). The destruction of the bank notes "exceeds their material existence, and affects the entire imaginary make-up of the crowd, its actual perception of what is 'the real'" (4–5). For this reason, it is so relevant to look to the relationship between the criminal's extra-judiciary punishment and Piglia's re-elaboration of Argentina's recent traumatic past.

## MONEY AND HISTORY

As he discloses in his epilogue, Piglia began working on *Plata quemada* during the late 1960s, (just a few years after the crime took place), to publish it only during the late-1990s. What began as a non-fiction journalistic account of a contemporary crime, in Walsh's style, trying to stay loyal to the facts, ends up as a reconstruction of the past with a far from negligible dose of literary invention. Piglia quickly corrects himself elsewhere stating that he tried to "stick to the facts just like I imagined that their protagonists have lived them" (qtd. in Fresán 305). In this regard, *Plata quemada* became one of the many post-dictatorial detective fiction novels written in the Southern Cone that hark back to past events to deal with trauma and memory. As Piglia acknowledges, "the events were now so distant and closed, that they seemed the lost memory of a lived experience" (2003, 171) This chronological distance, he says, helped him to write the story "as if it were the account of a dream" (171) and dreams are unavoidably filled with subjectivity and invention. As Premat notes, "a simple close reading" of the novel "shows the lack of plausibility in the text," as it goes "constantly from source documents" to imagined scenes (127).

In "Useless to Revolt?" Foucault claims that "revolts belong to history. But, in a certain way, they escape from it. The impulse by which a single individual, a group, a minority, or an entire people says, 'I will no longer obey,' and throws the risk of their life in the face of an authority they consider unjust seems to me to be something irreducible" (1979, 5). Foucault is thinking here of the Iranian Revolution, but Piglia's gang of criminals, "who will no longer obey" either, surely displays this same desire to revolt, by resisting in a besieged building and subsequently burning their stolen money, thus momentarily interrupting rationality, productivity, and history. For Foucault, there is always the chance to resist power, "because no authority is capable of making it utterly impossible: Warsaw will always have its ghetto in revolt and its sewers crowded with rebels. And because the man who rebels is finally inexplicable; it takes a wrenching-away that interrupts the flow of history, and its long chains of reasons, for a man to be able, 'really,' to prefer the risk of death to the certainty of having to obey" (5).

While for Foucault this Benjaminian interruption of history leads to religion, Piglia's escape from history, from the 1960s to the 1990s, results in literary mythification, as he unabashedly admits when he describes the writing process of the novel, as "an Argentine version of a Greek tragedy [where] the heroes decide to face the impossible and resist, choosing death as their fate" (2003, 170). In a way, it could be argued that they succeed because they fail, they become myths because, having failed to escape with the money, they resist the state's rule, burning it. They invert the fate of Borges's Lönnrot, who fails because he succeeds.

The most prominent metaphor of this mythification is encapsulated in their Numantine resistance, when el Nene and el Gaucho look at themselves on TV news, that broadcast live the siege: "they were trapped in a sort of capsule, lost in space, a submarine [. . .] that ran out of gas and lies on the rocks in the bottom of the sea" (2003, 108). But as in "La loca y el relato del crimen," the myth no longer works. Their death by execution makes them tragic myths, as Renzi wants, in the sense that they die out of *hubris*. But they are very far from Watt's myths, in the sense that they are punished at the end of the story because of their individualism, as they unilaterally breach the state's will.

So, what is Piglia's bitter "social comment" in Brownson's terms? After all, *Plata quemada* offers the traditional resolution of detective stories: we know from the beginning who robbed the bank, and there is even punishment as all the criminals are executed in cold blood. But is there restoration? What is the book's take on failure? For Rodríguez Pérsico there is no failure: whereas in "'La loca y el relato del crimen,' [. . .] the resolution of the crime offers a certitude and a failure," i.e.,: a case is lost but a story is gained (118); in *Plata quemada* "failure feels like success, as heroes (in their decline) refuse to surrender" (115). Despite the "positive" outcomes of failure (literature and resistance), the burnt money breaks with the happy ending that Mandel ascribes to the genre, as there is no restitution of bourgeois values: the ashes of the carbonized banknotes will never return where they once belonged, that is, the Provincial Bank of Buenos Aires, and thus, to the fluid circulation of the market.

This absence of restoration and the reaction this absence provoke in the press, the media and the witnesses of the conflagration, resonate with a historical absence of restoration: that of post-dictatorship. Premat sees the different utterances of violence and the verbal punishment towards the criminals, as a breeding ground for the brutal 1970s dictatorship, which "is already hinted, even justified in the 1965 lexical explosion" (126). Piglia, of course, imagines this from the 1990s. During the 1980s, Raúl Alfonsín's administration (the first democratic experience in Argentina after the dictatorial rule) made sure to trial and punish the military *junta*. By the time when Piglia finishes his novel, 1990s Menem's government has pardoned the dictators, in a series of legal measures that would neutralize all dissent from the left, helping to impose the neoliberal post-Soviet world's *pensée unique*, which the dictatorship itself had previously paved the way for.

In this sense, it is difficult not to think of "burnt money" as an inversion of "sweet money," the popular name for the result of the implementation of monetarism during Videla's administration (1976–1981). The dictatorial state's endorsement of neoliberal policies aimed to generate foreign investment through the purchase of cheap American dollars. The result was the social perception of "sweet (as in easy) money." Like Argentine private detectives, however, the policy failed, solely generating unprecedented debt (escalating from $7,8 to $45 billions of dollars in only just seven years), structural unemployment, and hyperinflation.

While Piglia finishes his novel, an updated monetarist *doxa* returned in the 1990s during Menem's administration in a much more effective way, legitimized by the IMF and the Washington Consensus. The convertibility of the Argentine peso to the US dollar reversed the recession (if temporarily) and ended the sky-high inflation (for most of the 1990s) that had haunted the Argentine economy for decades. Amidst this apparently triumphant monetarist *doxa*, Piglia puts center stage his poetics of failure, disintegrating money, divesting it of its utilitarianism. If in Hammett and Chandler, money made it possible to investigate crime and resolve social problems; in *Plata quemada* it has the opposite effect: money ensures that crime remains truly impune, much like the military *junta*, pardoned by Menem.

Similarly, if hard-boiled fiction posited a state that was corrupt but still perfectible, the image of burnt money enables Piglia to imagine the state as a body that cannot be perfected because it does not have any content. To a certain extent, Piglia has learnt Chandler's lesson and taken seriously the idea that the state, (which in *Farewell, My Lovely* is personified in the Lieutenant Nulty), is a null body. Menemismo, during the 1990s, spread monetarist policies that fostered middle-class individualism (at the detriment of collectivism) as its highest drive for economic growth: the public delegitimization of unions, the favoring of the private versus the public sector, the promotion of individual capitalization system for retirement plans, the deep deregulation of collective bargaining agreements and the systematic dismantling of most social achievements that have been protecting the working class since Perón's administration during decades are only some examples. At its peak, Piglia anathematizes and condemns individualism to failure.

What Avelar claims about *La ciudad ausente* applies even more for *Plata quemada*: "if in the exactitude of representation, appropriated by the State, our narrations have become archival citation in the bureaucratic machine, the only way is to invent false and apocryphal stories" (2000, 1). In short, since the 1990s neoliberal state has coopted public memory through the systematic misrepresentations of facts (for instance, by pardoning the military junta, contributing to negationist absolution), all that remains is literary mythification against history, a falsification of historiography's narration. Echoing Avelar, in the "Preface" of their edited collection *Diseños de nuevas geografías en la novela y el cine negros de Argentina y Chile* (2013), Schmitz and Verdú Schumann note how Southern Cone detective fiction aims to challenge and to go against the official memory imposed in the region, working as the literary amendment of historical processes (16). If burnt money, as Piglia says, is as useless as fake money, the novel's content informs its writing: ultimately, *Plata quemada* stays loyal to literary representation, more than to the historical facts, because the latter had been seized by the state's official narrative.

Premat understands Piglia's relation with failure in terms of falsification, too. According to him, Piglia here is following the Argentine literary tradition, especially the influence of Roberto Arlt, as a "failed writer." Premat traces the idea of writing as failure, in that Piglia was obsessed with "the difficulty of making stories" (127). Premat cites "Homenaje a Roberto Arlt," another short story by Piglia, about a failed writer, a "guy who cannot write anything original, who steals without even knowing it [. . .] All the writers in this country are like this [. . .]. Everything is false, forgery of forgeries" (Piglia 1988, 171).

Failure and falsification, nevertheless, are not only literary, but also political. Dorda and his gang see themselves as political subjects who evoke another resistance, a historical movement that was fundamental for Piglia's constitution as a writer: the 1950s Peronist resistance that Walsh portrays in *Operación massacre*. "We are political exiled who struggle for the return of Perón" (2003, 111), they say. British critic Jason Wilson reads this passage as evidence that the novel "sentimentalizes these thugs," establishing parallels between these 1960s criminals and the 1970s political "urban guerrillas who raided banks and were decimated by the police and military in orgies of violence" ("The Tragic, Seamy Underbelly of Buenos Aires"). *Plata quemada*'s Peronist tradition encapsulates a symbol of resistance against the post-dictatorial state, under Menemismo, which subverted the laborist agenda of the Peronist movement to adapt it to neoliberalism.

However, it would be far-fetched to interpret this as Piglia's nostalgia for the guerrilla. The police in *Plata quemada* execute a group of men, but although they declare themselves to be "followers of Perón," they are not killed on the presumption that they were involved in politics. The men here have clearly committed a crime and the state does not chase them arbitrarily. It executes them extra-judicially not because of what they are thought to believe in, but because of what they do. Therefore, Piglia's literary mythification is not a nostalgic celebration of the pre-dictatorial past: instead, it takes part in a counter-discourse. In his own words, that is what literary speech must create: "a sort of imaginary counter-economy that conveys well whatever is not being said in society's dominant collective imagination" (qtd. in Carrión 435). It is a counter-discourse made of a different understanding of what "money" means.

As Premat puts it, this is a fictional counter-discourse that is "rooted in a way of saying things which resists dominant narratives, that are equally fictional" (125). Premat cites as an example the scene that I previously discussed, when Dorda invents a meaning for the word "pusillanimous," equating it with the wage-earning policemen. The very act of burning the money, for Premat, is way of introducing another counter-narrative (126), mainly, because, unlike the official narrative of the state, it does not claim to purport meaning.

This counter-discourse, then, rewrites the traditional rivalry between individualism and the state to confront the 1990s individualistic rhetoric, negating what neoliberal *doxa* promises: the almighty aura of individualism. The state phobia displayed in *Plata quemada* is not necessarily an endorsement of individualism, like we see in Piglia's models: Renzi's chronicle of the siege cites Piglia's own work, namely "La loca y el relato del crimen," in that both are narratives about defeats that affect mainly individuals. According to the horizon of expectations of the genre, after all, individualism is expected to perform a constructive task: restoring the social fabric. By contrast, here, they engage in a destructive one. Dorda and el Nene may succeed in burning the money, but they do not manage to escape alive with it.

In *Plata quemada* there may be myths, but its heroes are defeated and there is room only for paranoia, fear, and failure both on the part of individualism and the state in providing social justice, which remains circumscribed to literature precisely because it has been banished from history and politics. As Piglia claims: "history is written by the victors and narrated by the defeated" (1986, 212). Literature, thus, emerges as a response to a state discourse whose failure is captured in fiction, only to "escape," in Foucaldian terms, from its victory in history. Both "La loca" and *Plata quemada* partake in what Piglia himself considers to be "a narrative that flows underneath, tied with the defeat of society's segments that have been dominated and defeated by the state" (1986, 212). Putting failure and defeat center stage, through literary mythification, offers a counter-narrative that aims to defy the triumphant narratives of the post-dictatorial state.

## FROM INCOMPETENCE TO ARBITRARINESS

The Argentine detective stories examined above subvert but still rely and linger on the reproduction of the classic rivalry between an individualistic hero against a state that is still linked to incompetence and corruption. These attributes are rewritten in multiple ways. The most interesting of them is in Walsh, when the typical state policemen's ineptitude is displaced to their inability not to solve crime but to commit it. Walsh's *Bonaerense* appears indeed as cruel but not exclusively so: they are also useless when they must execute, since they actually fail to accomplish their plan. After all, seven of the twelve men manage to escape their execution.

Even more interestingly, incompetence is reshaped in the form of arbitrariness: Walsh concludes that "the government did not have the slightest idea who its victims were" (2013, 112), because most of them were not really involved in the rebellion against the dictatorship that prompted the repression. In fact, the police were not even aware that some of them were not even activists. From the survivors' testimonies, Walsh manages to reveal that "the prisoners don't know where they are going or why" (64). The absence of martial law allows Walsh to re-read the workers' arrest as their arbitrary kidnapping; and, ultimately, their state execution as sheer murder.

Nevertheless, these facts do not change the state's legitimacy and its symbolic domination of individuals, which we can see in its officers' sense of entitlement to illicitly punish workers and remain unpunished themselves. As Beasley-Murray points out, it is precisely arbitrariness which is key to understand the very symbolic domination of the state to its subjects. This, he says, "is legitimated and arbitrated by institutions and officials who need not be aware of what they are doing" (192). This broad theoretical definition tallies thoroughly with Walsh's policemen: despite arbitrariness, or perhaps because of it, Walsh is defeated by the dictatorship's deaf muteness because "power is most effective when it is symbolic" (Beasley-Murray 191). It is the selective absence and silence of the state what produces its aura of might, in Michael Taussig's terms. Through its deaf muteness, the state appears to act with a calculated motivation that does not necessarily correspond with the arbitrary nature it actually operates with.

The symbolic muteness of the Argentine state is powerful and persuasive, because as Bourdieu points out "what is essential goes without saying because it comes without saying" (1977, 157). Silence allows the state to mask its arbitrariness with the illusion of control of the social order. In *Los años setenta de la gente común* (2014), the Argentine historian Sebastián Carassai addresses the social perception of authority on the dictatorial state, in middle-class' speech. He finds in language the foundations of this perception, especially in "the maxims 'it must be because of something' or 'he must have done something'" (186) that were (and still are) common in Argentine society, to justify military cruelty against its own population: if someone was punished, it must have been because of something they did, otherwise they would be safe.

Carassai reads these maxims from a different perspective, "as something more [. . .] than mere complicity or ignorance." Instead, they exhibit the societal "belief that the state had returned" (186) after troublesome times, the 1970s, in which urban guerrillas were gaining power and thus producing the perception of the state's silence and absence. In turn, people "attributed an ultimate, unknown, and even unattainable rationality to the representatives of a power that at the same time was imposed on them, but at least [. . .] sheltered them from a greater chaos" (186). Carassai goes on to say that if we observe these maxims from the standpoint of the "the state agent who exercises it," then the issues of assuming criminality or terrorist activity loses its importance over "the knowledge of the agent that represses" In short, "the state, to exist efficiently, needs that its citizens suppose in it an unlimited, occult and even secret knowledge" (186). He defines this "secret knowledge" as "a civil superstition" (187) that bestows an omniscient dimension on the state.

Far from the state's incompetence and arbitrariness that emerges in Walsh, Carassai describes the perception of the state as a competent all-knowing entity, because as he himself notes "one thing is what power is, and another thing, often different, is how it is perceived" (184). Carassai supports his claims through a notion coined by Taussig, which can be read as a supplement to Foucault and Weber understanding of the state: the idea of "state fetishism," "the sacred and erotic attraction, even thralldom, combined with disgust, which the State holds for its subjects" (Taussig 111). Despite its apparently robust constitution, the state is nothing but a fiction or a mask. Piglia knew this very well and for this reason he imagines the police through an emptied voice that conceals something else. Policemen may look incompetent to commit or conceal crime and may fail to do so in secret, but their reasons are never questioned by civil society because of the assumption of the state's omniscience.

Feinmann's claims about the absence of "police nor detectives" (213) in Argentine detective stories can be seen now in a more nuanced light. It is not so much that there are no characters embodying the police. For in fact, there are some policemen, such as Borges's Treviranus, Walsh's *Bonaerense* and Piglia's Silva. Their "absence" resides in that the state, through the organized criminal institution of the police, remains silent and impervious to individuals. Taussig observed this connection between silence and criminality in Colombia's dirty war, which is "above all [. . .] a war of silencing. There is no officially declared war. No prisoners. No torture. No disappearing. Just silence consuming terror's talk for the main part, scaring people into saying nothing in public that could be construed as critical of the Armed Forces" (26). A similar case could be made about the Argentine dictatorial state, except that its silence has a counterpart in a selective absence. Despite its neoliberal rhetoric of a lighter state, it takes a strong present apparatus to implement systematic state terrorism or neoliberal policies that go against the multitudes, as Beasley-Murray notes in the radical reshaping of the state's contours, mentioned above. Even when it seems absent (or especially when it does), the state is all-pervasive, as Foucault insists in several passages of his lectures on the *Birth of Biopolitics*.

Taussig's reflection on the state builds on the English anthropologist Alfred Radcliffe Brown, for whom "there is no such thing as the power of the State; there are only, in reality, powers of individuals—kings, prime ministers, magistrates, policemen" (qtd. in Taussig 112). What Taussig names the "fetishism of the state" is what conceals this overlapping between concrete individuals and an abstract depersonalized entity, which brings a new light to Carassai's idea of the superstition towards the state's power: "if the state is a fetish, if it does not exist [. . .] but rather in small doses [. . .] the subjects need to believe in its real existence as the only way of not feeling themselves abandoned" (184).

Perhaps this is the main point that Argentine detective stories share: they all aim to unmask the state's fetish. The clearest example is Walsh himself who reveals the extent to which the state becomes a blank space at the service of constituted power, specific citizens made of flesh and bone, enabling them to impose their interests upon constituent power through sheer arbitrary force. Bearing in mind this selective absence and fictional nature of the state, Argentine detective stories could be read through a common denominator: whereas their Anglo-American models (despite their criticism of the state) still relied heavily in its Hobbesian fictions of benevolence, (its constitutions, its social contract, its separation of powers), all the cases examined in this chapter seem to agree that the state's hollowness and its mute-deafness are structural. In a nutshell, they all seem to say: there is no such thing as a benevolent state.

## FINAL THOUGHTS: CONNIVANCE AND SOVEREIGNTY

Following Marx and Freud, the Argentine essayist Josefina Ludmer claims that crime "founds cultures" (14). This equation between crimes and not only cultures but also democratic states is neither original nor particular to Argentine literature. German author Hans Magnus Enzensberger claims in *Politics and Crime* (1964) that "even the more 'progressive,' 'civilized' constitutions allow for the killing of people and permit it" (23). The state, by definition, is inseparable from crime and its most characteristic expression: murder. For Enzensberger, "an ancient, intimate, and dark connection exists between murder and politics, and it is retained in the basic structure of all sovereignty to date. For power is exercised by those who can have their underlings killed" (22).

In turn, Foucault historicizes this "dark connection" of sovereignty along with the origins of detective stories in 1840s, when "the long cohabitation of the police and criminality began" (1980, 45). Born out of a failure, since the French society realized that prison did not really reform prisoners, "but on the contrary manufactured criminals and criminality," this cohabitation emerged in that "criminals can be put to good use, if only to keep other criminals under surveillance" (45). Foucault uses the term "cohabitation" instead of "marriage" to define the unconventional relationship between the police and criminals, thus reflecting the illegitimate albeit institutional nature of the tie. In the original French text, Foucault uses the term "concubinage": *concubinatus,* an institution practiced in Ancient Rome, that allowed men to enter in an informal but legally recognized relationship with women other than their legal spouse (Grimal 111). This relationship between state and crime is somewhat not formal as marriage but nevertheless inherent to one another because of its *de facto* institutionalization.

Poe's G—and Gaboriau's Lecoq are based on Vidocq, a historical figure that Foucault sees as the ultimate personification of this concubinage: a former criminal who is integrated into the state as the first head of the SÛreté Nationale, the French National Police, he condenses the connivance of state and crime. The state uses him to better manage criminality because he knows it from the inside. He "was for a while a smuggler, a pimp, and then a deserter," who "became absorbed into the system. Sent to forced labor, he emerged as an informer, became a policeman, and ended up as head of a detective force. [. . .] He is the first great criminal to have been used by the apparatus of power" (Foucault 1980, 45). The modern police, born from a failure (that of the prison) that permeated the modern state with criminality, nurture its force with "rehabilitated" criminals whose destructive agency is used to manage crime in a more efficient way.

If Enzensberger and Foucault have a point when they claim that connivance is inherent to any modern state, what is the particularity of the Argentine case? I concur with Calveiro in that, even though almost all types of political power are criminal and murderous, not all of them funnel state violence through concentration camps, as is the case of Argentina (28). Feinmann, in turn, notes how "in Hammet and Chandler, the police as an institution does not present more moral attributes than the criminals. Corruption and violence are their constant features" (215). What is different in Borges, Walsh and Piglia is that their policemen are not merely "violent and corrupt." As Gamerro points out, "in Argentina, there are no corrupt policemen: the police, as an institution, is inherently corrupt" (2006, 48); so, it is impossible not to imagine the state as murderous. Argentine detective fiction enables a re-reading of its models, unmasking the criminal, arbitrary, and fictional nature of the state, that was always there but remained concealed within them. The detective stories read in this chapter allow a re-interpretation of how Anglo-American detective stories imagine the state. Beyond their differences, English mystery stories and American hard-boiled fiction make a similar critique of the state: if only it were not so lethargic or corrupt, the state would function. Despite (or even because of) its ineptitude, they treat the state as perfectible. And, they all simultaneously endorse individualism because the two are inseparable. As Giardinelli observes, it is precisely because of the state's perfectibility that individualism is such a valued notion: after all, if the state is malleable and has the potential to become benevolent, then all the power to improve it falls on individualistic agency (223–224).

In the essay "Teoría del complot," Piglia hints explicitly at the mirage of state perfectibility, when he claims that "the capitalist society is not what is says it is: when it denounces its presumed malfunctions (corruption, fraud, political misdemeanors), it also reinforces the idea that these are only anomalies" (2002, 5). Argentine detective fiction exhibits these malfunctions, not as sporadic deviations but as the norm, it portrays the state's lacks not as actual lacks but as an inherent part of its irreversible criminal and empty nature. Beasley-Murray notes that, according to Italian philosopher Antonio Negri, Contractualism is an apology for constituted power (128). Seen through the lens of their Argentine counterpart, Anglo-American detective stories, far from criticizing the state, participate in this feature of Contractualism: what according to Poe, Doyle, and Chandler appears to be a critique of the state, from the point of view of Borges, Walsh, and Piglia, can be read as its blatant apology.

*Chapter 3*

# Chile

## *Individualism within the State*

*Y el cielo escucha el paso de las estrellas que se alejan*

Vicente Huidobro, *Altazor* (1931)

### FROM SOUTH TO NORTH: BOLAÑO NARRATING CHILE FROM EUROPE

"Graham Greenwood [. . .] like a true North American [. . .] had a firm and militant belief in the existence of evil" (2004a, 102), says the narrator of *Estrella distante* about a minor character in the book. The Chilean Roberto Bolaño defines his novel, published in 1996, as "a very modest approximation to absolute evil" (Manzoni 201).[1] The story partakes in the detective fiction genre, by rewriting the traditional tension between individualism and state.

According to Díaz Eterovic, "Chile is not a country with a solid tradition of detective fiction" (38). He argues that Chile shares with the Argentine tradition a prominent trait in its origins: they are both rooted in a "strong inclination to imitation" (32), i.e.,: a parody of the Anglo-American models. Díaz Eterovic quickly clarifies that detective fiction acquired in Argentina a larger literary quality (32), that was absent in Chile for most of the twentieth century, at least until the 1980s (39). Similarly, Franken Kurzen notes in *Crimen y verdad en la novela policial chilena actual*, that Chilean detective fiction authors absorb Anglo-American classics at the same level as Argentine models (16). This is certainly the case of Bolaño, who, in the 1990s, equates the post-dictatorial state with crime, following Borges, Walsh and Piglia's tradition.

Bolaño himself once declared the centrality of the Argentine literary tradition in the region, when he wrote to the Mexican writer Carmen Boullosa that in Latin America there were "only two countries with an authentic literary tradition, namely Argentina and Mexico" (Manzoni 106). Building on them, Bolaño portrays the Chilean dictatorial experience in an original manner: although equated, the state and the criminal relationship in the novel is no longer transparent but problematized instead. Thus, the ways in which Bolaño represents "absolute evil," far from being "firm and militant," are opaquer and more nuanced.

In his study on Chilean detective fiction, Franken Kurzen notes about Bolaño's approach to detective fiction that "he actually writes at the outskirts of the genre, not only parodying it, but also disputing its conventions" (253). Franken Kurzen classifies Chilean detective novels into two groups: one that deals primarily with state-sponsored criminal violence and the other that, always according to him, engages with "private crime of passions," focusing on how "violence features in marital and parental relationships" (9–10). Perhaps, because he pays more attention to *La pista de hielo* (1993) than to *Estrella distante* (1996), Franken Kurzen makes the questionable decision of locating Bolaño in the second group of his classification.

Franken Kurzen believes that studying this novel "only from the conventions of detective fiction, is practically impossible because it would involve degrading [it] to a certain extent" (244). Against this underlying and outdated assumption which continues to underestimate the literary importance of detective fiction, I hope to show in this chapter that Bolaño's novel is far from being a story that somehow favors the literary exploration of private lives over political and historical matters. In fact, much like Franken Kurzen's first group, *Estrella distante*, too, "puts center stage how the dictatorial and post-dictatorial Chilean states wield violence against its population" (9–10). Reimagining Latin American history, Bolaño harks back his narrative to the recent past to deal with the trauma of genocide, setting his novel in the context of the 1973 Chilean coup d'état that deposed Salvador Allende's democratic government, and the first years of Pinochet's subsequent dictatorship.

As Bolaño himself warns the reader in its preface, *Estrella distante* is in fact a rewriting of "El Infame Ramírez Hoffman," the last chapter of his previous novel *La literatura Nazi en América* (1996). An expanded retelling of his own work, the novel tells the story of a character who has multiple identities, names, and roles. Alberto Ruiz-Tagle a.k.a. Carlos Wieder is an air force pilot, a spy infiltrated among literature students at the Universidad de Concepción, who subsequently becomes the assassin of two of them—the Garmendia sisters. He is also an avant-garde poet, a performance artist who writes visual poems with his aircraft.

Tagle/Wieder is a character defined by his Latin American origins. His look is typical of "Latin Americans over the age of forty, quite different from the hardness you see in Europeans or North Americans" (2004a, 144–145). This distinction resonates with the way Argentine detective fiction distinguishes itself from its Anglo-American models to represent the political differences of Latin American history. An anonymous narrator tells Tagle/Wieder's story, which, following the narrative strategies of detective fiction, traces the whereabouts of the poet/pilot over two decades, from the 1970s to the 1990s. In the final section, a private detective, Abel Romero, hires the narrator to help identify Tagle/Wieder's whereabouts, to get him ultimately executed in Blanes, on the outskirts of Barcelona, Spain, from where Bolaño (reimagining Chile's dictatorship from Europe) wrote and published most of his prize-winning work with the Catalan publishing house Anagrama.

Whereas in his later *Los detectives salvajes* (1999) or *2666* (2004), Bolaño chooses to portray Mexican cities, *Estrella distante* is one of his "Chilean novels" (along with *Nocturno de Chile*) and is mainly set in Concepción. There is here again the use of the genre to talk about something other than the specific crimes portrayed in the plot. In Chapter 2, I discuss how the only way to reconcile the abyss between Anglo and Latin American detective stories was parody. Bolaño, instead, manages to do what no other Argentine novelist from his generation (Piglia, Saer, Giardinelli) did: he bridges South and North through memory, while at the same time becoming an author whose career was launched and promoted in Europe and North America. Bolaño re-appropriates and re-exports a genre that had already acquired canonical status in Latin American literature. And it is thanks to this that he would later become a best-selling author in Europe and Anglo-America, his work translated into multiple languages, often marketed as the new post-boom novelist that came to represent Latin America in the genre of "world literature," a position once held by García Márquez and Vargas Llosa.

It is not a coincidence that most of Bolaño's novels take place in different corners of Latin America, going comfortably from Chilean Patagonia and the Argentine Pampas to the Sonora desert and the Mexican American border, passing through Acapulco or Mexico City: this narrative strategy reaches more potential readers, who are interpellated by a re-appropriation of what Zizek calls "eccentric locales."[2] In the late 1990s, the Argentine translator and writer Marcelo Cohen wrote: "the European publishing industry needs a new Latin American star [. . .] Bolaño [. . .] seems like a good candidate for the position" (Manzoni 34). This is one of the many novelties that appears with *Estrella distante*: the fact that memory can also be absorbed by the market as a coveted commodity. Two decades after Cohen's prediction, Bolaño indeed has fulfilled this position, confirming at the same time Idelber Avelar's claim that "the erasure of the past as past is the cornerstone of all commodification, even when the past becomes yet another commodity for sale in the present" (2000, 1). Bolaño tackles the region's dictatorial experience by re-imagining memory in order to transform it into a literary product that successfully circulates in literary systems and is quickly absorbed by its market.

*Estrella distante*'s relationship with its models is therefore more complex than the Argentine case studies, since the book contrasts its elaboration of Latin American history not only with the United States, but also, Europe—particularly Spain, where the novel ends. This twofold axis is not merely related to literary but also more broadly to political history, namely Operation Condor. On the one hand, the United States appears alluded as the specter behind it. As Harvey points out in his *Brief History of Neoliberalism* (2005), Chile was relevant to the United States: after all, Pinochet's dictatorship in the 1970s was "the first experiment with neoliberal state formation" and the fact that it was "backed by US corporations, the CIA, and US Secretary of State Henry Kissinger" (Harvey 2005, 7) is not a marginal anecdote. Instead, it "provided helpful evidence to support the subsequent turn to neoliberalism" in the United States and the United Kingdom (9). On the other hand, Europe appears as a space generated by the dictatorship: the Chilean diaspora affecting the main characters, problematic embodiments of individualism and the (dictatorial) state: Romero, the anonymous narrator, and Tagle/Wieder; the private detectives and the criminal mastermind that works for the state. These tensions, between literature, history and politics, are mirrored in the ways Bolaño redefines in his novel the borders between individualism and the state, destabilizing (even more than his Argentine models) the traditional *ego contra mundum*.

## DICTATORSHIP AND NEOLIBERALISM

Tagle/Wieder performs his most important flight/poem from the Military Airport El Cóndor. There, he exhibits his aerial poetry before a "democratic crowd milling among festive marquees" (2004a, 31), made of generals and civilians. Bolaño's choice of this airport, of course, is neither innocent nor arbitrary, since its name references a vulture that holds a prominent symbolic place not only in the Southern Cone imaginary but also in the Andean countries, Chile being at the intersection of both groups. Both the condor and the aircraft that resembles it work as metonymies of Tagle/Wieder (and therefore, the Chilean dictatorial state that he is expected to personify), as well as his preying predisposition towards his defenseless victims. The Andean condor has its counterpart in a paratextual element: the quintessential avant-garde American artist Andy Warhol's *Bald Eagle* (1983). A reproduction of this painting of the national bird of the United States, featured on its seal, appears on the cover of the original 1996 Anagrama edition. Both the Andean Condor and the American Bald Eagle are birds of prey that constitute founding myths symbolizing different regions of the Americas. Yet they are merged in a transnational political event that encapsulates both of them: Operation Condor.

For Santiago Quintero, Tagle/Wieder's "use of aircraft, under the dictatorial context, could also be read [. . .] as an oppressive act of force [. . .] that evoked images such as the bombing of the the Palace of La Moneda in 1973" (166), the seat of the President of the Republic of Chile where Salvador Allende was ousted. Because Operation Condor was transnational, the image of this vulture aircraft, and its flights, nonetheless, should not be reduced to national borders. Instead, there is here a veiled mention to a specific type of traveling that goes beyond Pinochet's dictatorship, namely: death flights.

One of the many extrajudicial systematic execution practices implemented by military aircraft, death flights were imported from Europe to Latin America, where they later circulated transnationally. Invented in the 1950s by the French state during the Algerian War, against urban guerrilla, death flights were profusely practiced both in Chile and Argentina during the 1970s. Although there is no direct representation of Tagle/Wieder dropping any of his victims from a plane, it is not a coincidence that he is a military pilot. This ellipsis can be read in terms of a crisis of representation that is fundamental to understand Southern Cone detective fiction. A crisis of representation that relies, first and foremost, in the problem of personification: it is a crisis to represent politically and literarily. There is no explicit portrayal of other murders, yet the narrator (and everyone in the novel) knows that the poet/pilot committed them. This is not the only significant elliptical scene, since the difficulty of representing the dictatorial experience is one of the main topics of *Estrella distante*.

The resistance to representation points to another transnational practice implemented by Southern Cone dictatorships: the void left by disappeared bodies. As Calveiro notes, without corpses, there is not only no evidence but also no autopsies, there is no real testimony of the crime (26). Thus, the state, maintaining its immunity, dodges the possibility of an accurate account of what happened. Tagle/Wieder's aerial performances can then be read as deferred death flights in which the deaths have already taken place but are reincorporated in language through the poet/pilot's hermetic verses. Only few realized that he was "conjuring up the shades of dead women" (Bolaño 2004a, 33). Here the book prepares us for one of its key problems: being able to surmount illiteracy is what in the end restores the certainty of the victims' death, only "an informed, attentive reader" could have deciphered that these women had already been killed (32). For this reason, Romero hires the anonymous narrator: after all, like any good detective, he has this ability to read.

A paramount case of what Esposito, following Derrida and Plato, names *pharmakon*, Operation Condor, with its systematic disappearing of bodies, must be understood as a joint effort, a transnational "vaccine" (state terrorism) that presented itself as a neutralization of an equally international "poison" (urban and rural guerrilla warfare). As Esposito mentions, "nothing reinforces the host body politic better than an ill that has been dominated and turned against itself" (2011, 124). According to him "the point of intersection between political knowledge and medical knowledge," i.e.,: the core of biopolitics, "is the common problem of preserving the body" (121–122). The ways that Southern Cone dictatorships claimed to preserve the state body are closely linked to this notion of a self-inflicted poison, aiming to eradicate a foreign agent (Soviet influence) that was disturbing, as a "cancer," an imaginary equilibrium of an otherwise "healthy" region.[3]

In the 1970s, equating communism with cancer was a commonplace often revisited by constituted power. But evidently, beyond cold war slogans, what was guiding these dictatorships to operate beyond state borders was precisely the selective reassembling of their external and internal contours. Far from being an anti-revolutionary transnational movement (as their slogans promoted), these regimes triggered instead what Italian philosopher Paolo Virno calls the "counter-revolution of the New Right" (1996, 241): namely, the implementation of neoliberal practices without dissent. Virno focuses on the ways Italian parties paved the way for this New Right to emerge in the Italian democratic context during the 1970s and 1980s; but during that same period, after having brought down Allende's government in 1973, the Chilean military dictatorship absorbed the possibility of a revolution from the left with a similar counter-revolution.

In Jean Franco's words, after Pinochet's regime, dissent from the left "was decimated" ("Preface," Richard viii). Despite being functional to reassure constituted power, this counter-revolution was a revolution, nonetheless. A conservative "revolution in reverse [. . .] an impetuous innovation of modes of production" (Virno 1996, 241) that generates a new order which, in turn, produces new subjectivities. In *Estrella distante,* we can see this "new order" paradoxically encapsulated in one of the few traditional cornerstones of the engaged Latin American left (from Neruda to Gelman): the poetic word. Tagle/Wieder's aerial poetry is perceived to be "the New Chilean poetry," an aesthetic response carrying the Chicago Boys' slogans of neoliberalism.

However, knowledge cannot be enforced without violence. A counterpart of the academic Chicago Boys, the Chilean military, such as Raúl Iturriaga, Manuel Contreras, or Miguel Krassnoff were also trained on American soil, far from University think tanks, at the U.S. Army School of the Americas. The narrator of *Estrella distante* says that Tagle/Wieder flies sponsored by various corporations (2004a, 43). From the beginning of the novel, the pilot's origins are linked to the Chilean oligarchy, as his ancestors owned a *hacienda* in Puerto Montt. Tagle/Wieder, whose performance flights were not only attended but also funded by financial powers and the social class he represents, encapsulates both the pen and the sword, the two arms of the Chilean dictatorship, problematizing, at the same time, its boundaries.

## A CRUMBLING RIVALRY

For Argentine scholar Ezequiel De Rosso, "a purist would hardly see in Bolaño an author of detective novels; what seems clearer is that he is a *reader* of detective novels that writes about a generic matrix producing a narrative that can be read from the genre but that does not satisfy its basic premises" (135). One of these unsatisfied "basic premises" is related to how Bolaño engages in the traditional tension between individualism and the state. The main difference resides in that here the rivalry starts to crumble, its borders gradually seeming more blurred. At first glance, Tagle/Wieder, a military pilot for Pinochet's regime and a criminal mastermind, appears to be the usual metonymy of the dictatorial state. We have then our usual personification of sovereignty in a concrete public officer. But what Bolaño does is more complex as the poet/pilot's relationship with the state is more problematic: he may temporarily represent the state but ultimately does not fully embody it. Though he works for the state willingly, he displays a resistance to personification. In short, the state tries but fails to make him stand in for it.

On the other pole of the rivalry, *Estrella distante* does not feature any singular private detective to take all the credit in solving the puzzle. What's more, there is really no puzzle to be solved (as in Borges) or denounced (as in Walsh or Piglia). Neither Romero nor the anonymous narrator are responsible for revealing or reporting who is the murderer, they are only hired to track Tagle/Wieder down. From early on, the narrator discloses that the poet/pilot is the murderer of the Garmendia sisters, two of the narrator's university friends. The whodunit logic is entirely absent: it is not a matter of *who* but of *where*. Establishing Tagle/Wieder's whereabouts alludes to and mirrors the unknown whereabouts of his own adversaries: the narrator, but also his friends from Concepción, the *desaparecidos*, the missing ones of Pinochet's dictatorship.

All these narrative strategies are ways through which Bolaño displays the gradual disintegration of personified individualism, dismembered in fragmentary identities. Whereas the state criminal can no longer fully embody the state; the private detective can no longer synthesize all the mythical attributes, discussed in the first chapter, having instead to share them. Far from being unified and undivided heroes and villains ("individual," etymologically means, "indivisible," i.e., that which cannot be divided [*Online Etymology Dictionary*]), they are fragmentary. As examined in Chapter 1, whereas successful Anglo-American private detectives often outwit the state, Argentine writers invert the outcome of this tension by producing multiple failing detectives against a successful murderer state. In both cases the nature of the rivalry, clearly embodied in respective singularized characters, was never questioned and remained stable.

In this novel, there is something new: the personification of these abstract ideas and entities (individualism and the dictatorial state) still exists but is now fragmentary and reticent, its characters resisting in one way or another to reproduce their incarnations, respectively, of *ego* and *mundus*. The resistance is multi-causal: it can either be because of their problematic individualism, their multiple identity or even their passiveness. This fragmentariness does not solely affect the *mundus* but also the *ego*; it is all-pervasive.

In one of the final scenes of the novel, the encounter between the narrator and Tagle/Wieder, the two are explicitly mirrored: he sat only "three tables away. For a nauseating moment I could see myself almost joined to him, like a vile Siamese twin [. . .], so close he couldn't fail to notice." However, the poet/pilot does not recognize his investigator. "He had aged. Like me, I suppose," says the narrator, emphasizing the reflection between them (2004a, 144). Tagle/Wieder's lack of recognition introduces a blurriness to the scene. The blending of the two characters points to the traditional boundaries that here starts crumble: the borders between individualism and the state examined in Chapter 1; the borders between crime and the state clearly demarcated in Chapter 2. The dissolution of these traditional boundaries exposes a displacement, where an individualistic self is no longer opposed but gets intertwined with the state, by fragmenting its identity into a multiplicity of selves: the *Doppelgänger*, that features not only in Tagle/Wieder but also between him and his adversaries.

When the narrator starts his job as an investigator for Romero, he has an eloquent nightmare about a shipwreck, that puts center stage the issue of the *Doppelgänger*: "the galleon began to sink, and all the survivors were cast adrift on the sea. I saw Carlos Wieder, clinging to a barrel of brandy" (2004a, 122). The dream allows the narrator to realize that he and Tagle/Wieder have been "travelling in the same boat; he may have conspired to sink it, but I had done little or nothing to stop it going down" (122). As Chilean scholar Arenas Oyarce notices, the novel's beginning had already hinted at the shipwrecking image, tying it to the downfall of Allende's administration and, as a result, to the idea of the twofold political sides involved in the debacle—left and right (57). The literary trope of the *Doppelgänger*, then, allows Bolaño to expose an equation between oppressor and oppressed, between culprit and victim(s), that is absent in the Argentine detective stories. Equally, as Catelli notes, the *Doppelgänger* (specifically the double of an artist) puts center stage the matter of fragmentariness ("El laboratorio Bolaño"), pulverizing the uniqueness of the individualized hero/villain.

## THE POST-DICTATORIAL DETECTIVE AS A HITMAN

### From Individualism to Fragmentariness

Abel Romero is the character the resembles the conventional detective the most. He quickly fulfills the genre's horizon of expectations and its requirements of personification—a traditional embodiment of individualism in the figure of the sleuth. What is interesting about Romero is that he has a past that belongs to the state (having worked in the police force during Allende's administration) but owes his reputation to having successfully solved a case much like a private investigator: in only one day, before Pinochet's coup, the case is reminiscent of Dupin's Rue Morgue case, since it is a locked room mystery crime, at a house in Valparaíso. Romero, also, evokes Poirot, as both are former state policemen who become private investigators. But whereas Poirot's work as state policeman in Belgium is less relevant than his endeavors as a private investigator in the English countryside; Bolaño historicizes and delves into Romero's belonging to a specific kind of state: a socialist democratic one.

Once a state officer who received an award by Allende, Romero's leap to the market is not merely an allusion to the mythical individualism of the private detective. It is also a comment on one of the main factors that neoliberal doctrine promotes and that we mention in Chapter 2: the selective privatization of the public sector that has taken place systematically under neoliberal administrations. After Allende's defeat, bereft of the state power and the authority his former position held, Romero becomes an exiled who is only interested in money. Tagle/Wieder's case is going to allow him to come back to Chile. As the narrator notes, Romero cares less about his one task (solving the case), than about its generous reward (2004a, 124). He is reduced to exchange value, expelled from the state to the market, his skills and services outsourced to a mysterious and anonymous client who hired him to find the poet/pilot's whereabouts in Europe.

Like any classic private investigator, Romero does not work alone. He is helped by the story's narrator who recounts the adventures of both Tagle/Wieder and Romero. At first sight, the narrator seems to inherit the task that Anglo-American detective stories had originally assigned to the sidekick. But he goes further than Watson ever could have, because it is only thanks to him that Romero can find Tagle/Wieder. Romero's obsession with money is present even when he hires the narrator, since he inspects his sidekick's apartment "as if he were calculating my price" (2004a, 117). Whereas the classic detective would hold the monopoly of literacy in the face of his less witty sidekick, Romero has to delegate (or better, to purchase or subcontract) the ultimate task of detection, which traditionally has been linked to reading clues. Like Piglia's Renzi, the narrator is hired because of his ability to read.

*Estrella distante*'s novelty resides in the fact that reading is reformulated through more original types of language and signifiers. Romero justifies his decision of hiring the narrator because of the latter's knowledge on poetry: "Wieder was a poet, I was a poet, he was not. To find a poet, he needed the help of another poet" (2004a, 117), says the narrator. In terms of Russian linguist Roman Jakobson's communication theory, what Romero wants from the narrator is his ability to decode the poetic function of Tagle/Wieder's messages. Like Lönnrot or Renzi, the narrator is bookish, so his literacy is more literal than symbolic, since it applies to a direct contact with letters, that is, he is good at reading texts, not situations. But ultimately, it is not exactly classic symbolic literacy what helps the narrator to succeed in his detective task. Instead, he discovers the poet/pilot's artistic signature not through sophisticated texts but by way of images, while watching Tagle/Wieder's snuff movies and pornography. What the narrator does is then a different act of reading, since he traces Tagle/Wieder's authorial footprint behind the frame.

What is also interesting about the narrator is that he accepts this task so passively, to a certain extent, much like Romero. When the narrator gets paid, he denies having earned anything and claims he does not need that amount of money (2004a, 148–149). This is considerably different from the attitude towards money that we have seen in Chapter 1. After having identified Tagle/Wieder in Blanes, the narrator accepts the money only reluctantly: he takes it without acknowledging the merit of his task. He becomes a reluctant detective, thus crashing all the expectations of private initiative, wit, and pride. Whereas Holmes and Watson held clearly delineated personalities, (we could easily discern the detective from the sidekick), here the undivided entity of the private detective crumbles into an undistinguishable and problematic entity, where fragmented individualism can no longer be embodied accurately and in a unified way.

## FROM PERSONIFICATION TO DEPERSONALIZATION

This attenuation of individualism also affects the murderer in an original way, since Tagle/Wieder has multiple identities, that go beyond Stevenson's Dr. Jekyll/Mr. Hyde. For the sake of clarity and in order to respect his

*Doppelgänger* nature, I am referring to him as Tagle/Wieder, even where the text names him otherwise, and even though he goes under many more names: Tagle/Wieder is a poet who, much like Fernando Pessoa (also a conservative avant-garde poet), has sundry heteronyms, such as Jules Defoe and R.P. English. Each name is linked to a different moment and occupation in Tagle/ Wieder's life: he is Ruiz-Tagle when he works as a disguised self-taught poet among the left-wing literature students of Universidad de Concepción. Jules Defoe is his pseudonym when he signs literary articles in far-right-wing French magazines, once he is exiled in Europe. R.P. English is his name when working as a cameraman in the European porn industry. Finally, the narrator starts referring to him as Wieder only from the moment at which he murders his first victims (the only murder that the narrator describes explicitly), to later become an air force pilot.

The *Doppelgänger*'s combination of surnames (indicating paternal and maternal affiliations), mixing Spanish (Ruiz-Tagle) and German (Wieder), cites historical meanings that go beyond the novel. While the doubled surname is a common practice in Spain, in the Hispanic Southern Cone it traditionally implies Peninsular lineage of ancient (often wealthier) settlers, especially when compared with Italian or Jewish single surnames. Ruiz-Tagle, then, cites *criollo* aristocracy and old money that contrasts with the origin of other migrants and subalterns (*mestizos*, indigenous, slaves). The German part, Wieder, cites the Nazi presence in Chilean (and Argentine) Patagonia. Bolaño explores the genealogy and multiple connections between German and Southern Cone dictatorial experiences in a great deal of his work. Bibiano, one of the narrator's friend, offers different etymologies for Wieder, that point to several monstrous attributes (2004a, 41), but the narrator mocks all of them, as no etymon really says much about Tagle/Wieder's identity.

Tagle/Wieder is not only ambivalent (a pilot and a poet, with an avant-garde tradition that belongs both to the left and to the right) but also polysemic. Not only because of Wieder's polyhedral etymology but also because of "Tagle," which is reminiscent of the Chilean presidency: in the nineteenth century, Francisco Ruiz-Tagle's brief 1830 administration and, in the twentieth century, María Ruiz-Tagle's husband Eduardo Frei Montalva (1964–1970) and their son, one of the first post-dictatorial presidents, Eduardo Frei Ruiz-Tagle (1994–2000). Despite the recent Chilean history being "pitted with discontinuities" (Beasley-Murray 276), "Tagle" cites a seamless political elite, a lineage of statesmen. The two more recent presidents belong to the Christian Democratic Party: Eduardo Frei Montalva preceded and later opposed the Salvador Allende's socialist administration. In turn, his son Eduardo Frei Ruiz-Tagle was the Chilean president when Bolaño publishes *Estrella distante*.

Austrian literary critic Leo Spitzer examined in *Don Quixote* "a peculiar aspect of Cervantes's novel [...] namely, the instability and variety of names given to certain characters—and the variety of etymological explanations of those names" (135). Spitzer coins the terms "polionomasy" and "polietymology" to describe this onomastic and etymologic instability. He notes that Cervantes refuses to pin down Don Quixote's name, introducing instead a myriad nicknames and epithets. He records at least eleven variations: Quijada, Quesada, Quijana, el ingenioso hidalgo, Alonso Quixano, pastor Quijotiz, Don Azote, Don Jigote, Quijotísimo, El Caballero de la Triste Figura, and El Caballero de los Leones.

Whereas Cervantes's choice is related to individualism, conveyed in a "glorification of the artist" (Spitzer 136); in Bolaño, Tagle/Wieder's onomastic, semantic and etymological instability point to depersonalization. After all, who is Tagle/Wieder? Is he a poet, a literary critic, a spy, a porn/snuff videographer, a pilot, a murderer? Is he all of them simultaneously? Or are neither Tagle nor Wieder the real him? Is there a real him? These different forms of resistance to personification seem to claim that there is no authenticity nor any possibility of a coherent individualistic narrative. Bolaño's use of "polionomasy" and "polietymology" can be read, then, not only as a sparkle of depersonalization, but as a response to the detective story tradition and its endorsement of individualism: although Tagle/Wieder reproduces the criminal mastermind, his fragmented self is hardly a solid personification of evil.

This sparkle of depersonalization is prominent when the narrator identifies the murderer in Blanes, by describing him in terms of negation: he does not seem a poet, nor a pilot, nor a killer (2004a, 145). The narrator, unable to outline Tagle/Wieder's personality, must resort to anaphoric negations to articulate his depersonalized entity. In the first pages of the novel, Tagle/Wieder's poems are also defined by negation, as if they were not his (11). When the poet/pilot becomes a missing exiled in Europe, one of the main challenges that the detectives face in the search is that he almost seems not to have existed at all. Romero travels through Italy showing a picture of the murderer, but no one recognizes him, "as if he had never existed or had no face to remember" (125). Tagle/Wieder, with his forgotten, almost inexistent face seems to have here no real (id)entity. This picture shows him like a ghost that resembles many other ones. The blurry portrait mirrors his multiple names: here, too, Tagle/Wieder is fragmented, his phenotype resembling "thousands of men in Europe" (136) but also "many other figures, other faces, other phantom pilots who had flown from Chile to Antarctica and back" (46).

As many critics have pointed out (Paz Soldán & Winks, Carini), *Estrella distante* draws not only from the detective genre but also from the Latin American dictator novel. It is significant, then, that instead of representing the

Chilean dictatorial state with its supreme representative, Augusto Pinochet, Bolaño chooses an obscure Eichmann-like middle-ranking public officer to perform that task. This is how the Chilean author problematizes personification: making it opaquer and more fragmented. This fragmentation exhibits a gradual tendency towards the complete absence of personification, i.e.,: depersonalization, that is fundamental to understand Bolaño's *2666*, his response to his own literary project, that I examine in Chapter 5.

## FROM IMPUNITY TO VIGILANTISM: SUCCESS OR FAILURE?

In *Immunitas*, Esposito develops the notion of *compensatio*, a prominent concept in modern legality, defined by him as a "counterforce to a [. . .] force to be neutralized in such a way as to restore the original equilibrium" (2011, 81). Criminals are often punished on this basis, which "has a consolatory function" (82) for the rest of society, especially for their victims: before the impossibility of restituting the damages caused by crime, the law acts in order to bring "back to equilibrium the pans of the balance scale tipped to one side by the 'weight' of a debt, a deficiency, or a lack" (81).

*Compensatio*, "the reinstatement of a shattered order" (81), is fundamental for detective story dénouements, that since Poe has repeatedly posed "the idea that social fragmentation could suture through imagination by means of the figure of the detective and the knowledge of truth" (De Rosso 18). *Estrella distante* portrays an act of vigilantism. The detectives never take Tagle/Wieder to court to receive judiciary punishment for his crimes against humanity. After vigilantism, is there *Compensatio*? Can the equilibrium be restored, or social order and justice reestablished? Is vigilantism an expression of collective popular justice or is it an enhancement of individualism in the form of personal revenge? For Díaz Eterovic, "Chilean detective novels are crowded with antiheroes who investigate what the real police ignore and who restore justice in situations where the judiciary has remained blind, mute, complicit" (34). But does *Estrella distante* truly offer a restoration of justice like other Chilean detective novels?

Bolaño does not offer a simple answer to these questions. Instead, he makes the issue of restoration through detective stories more problematic. Because, in fact, as the Argentine sociologist Juan Carlos Marín points out, "crime is not an 'abnormality' but the other way around; what is normal, what is dominant as a means of social normalization, is crime" (qtd. in Ludmer 17). Or, as Esposito puts it, the law does not "have the task of protecting the community *from* conflicts, but, on the contrary, *through* them" (2011, 49), mainly because there is no order without conflict, rather "conflict *is* order"

(Esposito's italics, 50). Detective stories presuppose an ideal order, whose conflicts are perfectly demarcated as exterior and accessory. As established in the first chapter, Mandel defines the genre precisely as "the realm of happy ending," where "the criminal is always caught" and "justice is always done" (47). Happy endings are the return to the fantasy of order that precedes the detective story: everything goes back to normal.

It is when conflicts (crimes) arise that the detective needs to perform *compensatio*. But, as Hoyos claims, "the dénouement of detective stories in Latin America doesn't come with a restauration of order" (61). It is in this sense that the poetics of failure is a symptom of the political and the historical: as Hoyos says, this "narrative resolution represents the impossibility of establishing an order" (61). Diametrically opposed to what he calls "the promise of the traditional detective story, which ultimately order prevails over chaos" (61), Latin American detective stories fail to meet the genre's horizon of expectations. It is in this regard that Giardinelli explains how Latin American detective novels do not resort to the restitution of order, because "the order that the police preserve is an unfair order: it is the order of the elites," i.e.,: of constituted power (236).

Building on Hoyos and Giardinelli, I read this absence of order as the impossibility of representing triumphalist individualism and state benevolence. But how does *Estrella distante* engage with this problem? As in the Argentine detective stories, if the state is equated with the criminal, there is no possibility of restoration in the first place. Categories of success or failure, in terms of happy endings or their absence, become obsolete as such but pave the way instead for a different categorical dimension.

Several critics have noted the extent to which failure is one of the main issues that Bolaño, like Piglia, tackles in his work. Peruvian scholar and detective fiction writer Diego Trelles Paz, for instance, claims the Bolaño's "adventures around perpetual quests [. . .] often lead to failure or end up tragically" (276). For him, Bolaño's *Los detectives salvajes* features "the existential anxiety of a whole generation doomed to failure" (368). Similarly, although he claims it is difficult to "define Bolaño's generation" (244), Franken Kurzen notes that most of his characters (not only in *Los detectives salvajes*, but also in *La pista de hielo* and *Estrella distante*) are *fracasados*, i.e.,: a failure (246). Arenas Oyarce also sees the prominence of failure in *Estrella distante* as "a product of socio-political transformations" (51). However, he emphasizes the ontological dimension of failure, relating it rather to loss, nostalgia and decadence. Finally, De Rosso, too, speaks about failure in the Chilean's detective stories, which display "an investigation [. . .] doomed to failure, because these narratives do not assume truth (a soothing mechanism of detective stories) but its appearance as the only possible verifiable variable when the account ends" (141). De Rosso equates success with the social closure that these detective stories lack, as "a typical procedure" in Bolaño is "the systematic disappointment of the expectations of a reader who is specialized in the genre" (135).

For De Rosso, "failure" is solely formal, i.e.,: tied to the betrayal of the genre's conventions. But what is the political nature of this failure beyond literature? What has Bolaño's generation failed to do exactly? Closer to Trelles Paz's claim, Spanish novelist Enrique Vila-Matas cites Bolaño's own words in his novel *Los detectives salvajes,* in terms of generational failure as "the story of a generation, mine and Bolaño's and that [. . .] we could name 'the May 68 generation,' a catastrophic generation [. . .] that has left its survivors—us—'confused in the same failure'" (102). Failure, in this sense, has to be something more than just a quest for literary originality.

Failure, a literary topic that exceeds detective stories and even the modern novel, is particularly emphasized in these detective stories to funnel a common political post-Cold-War sentiment. In *Entre paréntesis,* the Chilean author himself discloses the generational element of his own work, which he defines as "a farewell or a love letter to my own generation, who was born in the fifties" (2004b, 37). Of course, what Bolaño refers to here as his generation is not a de-historicized chronological group of people but a historical and political one: "Those who have chosen in a given moment to become activists to give the little we had (which was also a lot): our youth. And we gave it to a cause that we believed to be the most generous of the world and to a certain extent it was, but also wasn't" (2004b, 37). In brief, Bolaño is alluding to the Latin American left, that grow up with the shadow of the Cuban revolution and who, in their twenties, were protagonists of political activism and armed struggle in the 1970s. A political generation that failed to constitute power in front of the dictatorial states that would subsequently defeat them with a neoliberal counter-revolution aimed to reassure constituted power instead.

This lack of narrative closure, the denial to succumb to the horizon of expectations, amounts to the refusal of reproducing once again "the triumph of bourgeois legality" (Mandel 47). Nevertheless, it is crucial to ask a question that is both formal and political, both literary and historical. A question that lies at the foundation of the detective story tradition: In *Estrella distante,* who has done it? Who wants to take revenge with Tagle/Wieder's death? Yes, Tagle/Wieder is a murderer, but who wants to murder him? Who is Romero working for? Romero never discloses the identity of his mysterious client. He only reveals that the latter is wealthy enough to afford him (2004a, 140). The intellectual author of vigilantism is someone who "has real money" (140). This ellipsis leaves a vacant agent, an implied subject of an impersonal sentence. Who in the story has both reasons to get rid of him and the resources to do it other than the Chilean post-dictatorial state itself? To investigate this mystery (a mystery that the book itself leaves open), it is important to examine how the novel portrays the Chilean state, through Tagle/Wieder and beyond him, in terms of a series of symbolic disabilities that were inherent in the Anglo-American and Argentine counterparts: muteness, illiteracy, and paralysis.

## THE CHILEAN STATE: A LISTENING BODY WITH SELECTIVE MUTENESS

### Muteness and Literacy

Some critical readings of *Estrella distante* have noted the powerful presence of silence in the text. Mazoni and Bruña Bragado, to name a few, understand it as an allusion to the complicity between Chilean society and state-sponsored crimes (Manzoni 47). However, none of them examine how structural silence operates in the novel in a selective way, nor they pay much attention to something even more relevant: the scene in which the state's silence has been breached. Silence, a chosen forbearance from speech, should be understood as symbolic muteness because, in the Chilean dictatorial state, it is not subjected to choice, it is rather forced.

From the novel's first page, Bolaño draws attention to the state's symbolic muteness, encapsulated in Tagle/Wieder, who, following the horizon of expectations, "wasn't particularly talkative" (2004a, 3). Whereas the poet/pilot does not speak much, his victims are verbose. Like Dupin, the narrator, Bibiano, the Garmendia sisters, and others talk profusely and discuss passionately among many things about "travel (little did we know what our travels would be like)" (3). This unimagined and unimaginable future of traveling condenses an ambivalent allusion: the above-mentioned flights of death and the diaspora, both of which are inseparable from silence. The book, then, opposes the state's muteness with the verbosity of its victims. The narrator constantly highlights Tagle/Wieder's succinct speech: when he would occasionally speak, the poet/pilot does it "as if he were living inside a cloud" (4). As Arenas Oyarce observes, the novel "blurs the boundaries that were previously established for people and social roles, dissolving binary logics" (52). The image of the cloud evokes this blurriness (through which the plane flies) to mutate into symbolic unintelligibility: whereas he seldom intervenes, when he does, his voice obfuscates rather than reveals meaning.

Despite his lack of clarity, Tagle/Wieder's speech sounds more "neutral" than his victims' and that is another trait that distinguishes them. Whereas the latter's speech is filled with Marxist jargon, the former spoke Spanish (6). Because he is the only one to disregard political vocabulary, the poet/pilot is the only one who manages to do what any of his politicized left-wing victims would dream of: affecting successfully the other's behavior with his speech. His house is a space of sheer symbolic muteness: "Rather than breaking the close silence of the flat, [his] words accentuated it" (9). Amid this all-pervasive muteness, his house lacks "something unnamable" (7). Whatever cannot be named (i.e., spoken) points to an absence of signifiers, which in turn alludes to the impossibility of signifying, echoed in the many ellipses of the novel that engage with a crisis of representation.

As Manzoni claims the all-pervasiveness of *Doppelgängers* ought to be read as a rectification of history: "the illusion of becoming another person, of displacing to another space and time whatever cannot be explained, to put it differently, the horror that resists speech, the indescribable, works as an imagination game that enables the construction of a world in which history could rewind, in which death is not definitive" (41). Whatever is lacking in Tagle/Wieder's depersonalized and mute house is the horror that resists being transformed into speech. A horror that cannot overcome symbolic muteness and unintelligibility; the real that is not susceptible of being symbolized. The silence of the poet/pilot's house are nothing but an extension of his own symbolic muteness, which obviously goes beyond the simple impossibility of vocal speech: when Tagle/Wieder drives to kill the Garmendia sisters, his victims cannot hear even his car lurking outside their house, "because they're playing the piano or stacking firewood at the back of the house" (2004a, 19). When he does speak or even when he drives, the poet/pilot is subjected first and foremost to the protection of the state's symbolic muteness.

As De Rosso points out, voice is the cornerstone that distinguishes "the investigator from the force of the state and the criminal" (134). The private detective is known for his "ability to hold the word that organizes the narrative" (134), which is contrasted to the symbolic muteness of his adversaries—be it the state or the criminal. The verbose narrator and the silent Tagle/Wieder, then, reproduce the traditional conventions of the genre. However, Bolaño offers us something new: unlike the deaf-mute Argentine state, *Estrella distante* imagines the Chilean as a state which hears its own citizenry very thoroughly. Tagle/Wieder is an extremely good listener (2004a, 12) and he is receptive to the student's criticism of his poems, accepting them without pushing back. He gives careful attention to his female victims, when they recite poems ("closing his eyes the better to listen" [20]) before he murders them.

Moreover, Tagle/Wieder discusses the enforcement of silence as a theme in his own declarations after his performances: "Silence is like leprosy [. . .] silence is like communism; silence is like a blank screen that must be filled. If you fill it, nothing bad can happen to you" (45). This cryptic equation between silence and communism, (which Tagle/Wieder understands to be as contagious as a disease), seems to introduce a paradox: the dictatorial Chilean state can only overcome its own symbolic muteness by a different form of language, rendering words opaque enough so that its recipients would hear that something important is being said without fully grasping its content. Thus, the Chilean dictatorial state distinguishes itself from whomever dares to contend its authority by means of exposing them to symbolic unintelligibility. Tagle/Wieder "speaks" by filling white screens (be it paper or the sky where he writes his poems) with undecipherable written words, compensating (and funnels) the entirety of his oral muteness.

Before killing the Garmendia sisters, Tagle/Wieder hesitates to read his own poetry out loud to them. In other words, he is reticent about transforming text into speech. Again, he temporarily remains mute, entangling the state's symbolic muteness with writing. More specifically, there is here a link between muteness and illiteracy, the inability to understand writing: after a few minutes of resistance, Tagle/Wieder ends up reading his poems and only after that, does he murder his victims. Before dying, they endure symbolic illiteracy: the sisters "*think* they understand, but they don't understand at all" (Bolaño's italics 20). Their aunt equally claims that her own nieces' poems remain beyond her ability to read (20). Bolaño circumscribes symbolic illiteracy to the victims only. By contrast, Tagle/Wieder knows. In the Garmendias' house, he holds the monopoly of literacy. He understands the meaning of his own poems: he is aware that they encapsulate his subsequent actions, i.e.,: the killings and disappearance of his victims' bodies. The poet/pilot does understand the political implications and the underlying meaning of "the New Chilean Poetry" that he once discussed with the Garmendia.

In the beginning of the story, before the coup, the narrator and Bibiano are compiling poems in order to publish them. They consider Tagle/Wieder for the anthology, but his poems are short. Ironically, the narrator describes the poet/pilot's writing as too Japanese, alluding to the short nature of haikus. Even when he funnels his voice in written form, his speech is sparse. Furthermore, "it's as if they weren't his poems" (14): even in his writing, his meager voice is not his. Tagle/Wieder does not own his speech. The depersonalization of his voice amounts to a twofold reason: on the one hand, the fact that he does not speak but instead is spoken by the state's narrative; on the other hand, that his hermetic poems respond to the logic of avant-garde aesthetics.

Whereas for Russian literary theorist Viktor Shklovsky, "the technique of art is to make objects 'unfamiliar,' to make forms difficult to increase the difficulty and length of perception" (9), the mandate of avant-garde poetry was to enhance as much as possible this sense of unfamiliarity. In the pilot's poems, form informs form: the increase of unfamiliar signifiers is in direct relation with the decrease of the text's length. Despite his fragmentary personality and his selective muteness, the narrator tells us that there is a force or "the reflection of a monolithic will" in Tagle/Wieder's speech (Bolaño 2004a, 44). But why is his poetry, speech, and performances so succinct? Perhaps it is because his force does not reside in the content of his enunciation but in their avant-gardist shock effect. In political terms, this shock could be read through the oppressive impact that brevity and muteness generate. Again, this is reminiscent of Weber's definition of the "obedience" towards the state as something that "is determined by highly robust motives of fear and hope" (2005, 79). What is robust in the state is not the content of its voice but the effects it generates.

But as mentioned above, there is an even more significant passage of the novel that must be addressed: when the symbolic muteness of the state is breached. Tagle/Wieder displays a rupture with symbolic muteness only once and that will cost him his position in the military and even his ability to stay in Chile. This rupture expresses a slippage: his resistance to fully embody the state. Once he becomes famous, during the first years of Pinochet's dictatorship, when Chile was formally under a state of exception (1973–1979), the poet/pilot organizes a party, where he exhibits pictures of his own. These pictures are portraits of females, seemingly dead, looking like disjointed manikins (2004a, 88), including the Garmendia sisters and other *desaparecidos*. There is here another significant ellipsis of the book: the reader never learns who these women are because the photos lack quality. Despite this, they make an impression in the audience. The room where the pictures are displayed does not meet the requirements of the space. Their poor quality hinders an accurate visualization of them. As with the skywriting, obscured by clouds, wind and storms, the quality of the reception of the photos is poor. Perhaps precisely because of that, they have all the more impact: the blurriness (the difficulty to read the poems or to see the pictures) is a direct cause of its force.

Whatever remains under symbolic illiteracy, whatever privileges the prominence of form over the clarity of content, or better, whatever funnels content through form is functional to the speaker's power over the recipient. It is in this symbolic illiteracy that the dictatorial practice resides: not coincidentally Southern Cone dictatorial states never fully acknowledged to society who (and how many) were its victims or the treatment they have received. After seeing Tagle/Wieder's portraits, one of the guests invited to the party reacts with muteness and illiteracy: she fails to find words and she vomits before making it to the bathroom (86–87). The guest, unable to convey her repugnance with words, has a silent reaction, vomiting instead. At the party, symbolic muteness is all-pervasive: "There was hardly any talking" (87). At first an ephemeral tumult, "everyone fell silent" (89). If this exhibition is an act of (non)verbal communication, it is as if the speaker (Wieder) infects the recipient (his audience) with symbolic muteness; or better, what the speaker communicates to his recipients is essentially the prominence of imposed silence.

There is, nonetheless, a moment when silence ends. At midnight, Tagle/Wieder takes the floor. Paradoxically, he interrupts symbolic muteness by asking for silence. The poet/pilot opens the door to the bedroom where the pictures are exhibited and then, and only then, does he truly "speak" through his pictures, revealing the authentic nature of the new art, the "new Chilean poetry": he intervenes in the public discussion about what is going on in the dictatorship. He manages to do so without words but with images, a more explicit representation of state terrorism, in spite of their blurriness. The pictures reveal the true nature of the dictatorship: disappearance, torture, and genocide.

When the state intelligence realizes that Tagle/Wieder is disclosing its genocide practices to an audience that may be small but still is not supposed to explicitly know about them, its agents burst in on the party and confiscate the exhibited pictures under a mute atmosphere, leaving "as quietly as they had arrived" (91). The narrator emphasizes that the officers of the Dirección de Inteligencia Nacional (DINA) operate without uttering a single word in public. After they admonish Tagle/Wieder, only muteness remains: "only silence" (91). If they stop the exhibition, it is because of the poet/pilot's rupture with the state.

The pact of silence is breached by the very same instrument that once ensured it: revolutionary poetry. After all, dictatorial states do not like avant-garde poetry. As Catherine Belsey reminds us, "both Nazism and Stalinism deplored the avant-garde" (104). Whereas Hitler "endorsed Classicism and pronounced modern art decadent; Stalin promoted Socialist Realism at the expense of the experimental forms that had developed immediately after the Revolution" (104). In a way, the DINA officers replace Tagle/Wieder because he relinquished the personification of the state, becoming themselves its surrogate (more reliable) incarnation. They cover with more symbolic muteness what failed to be silenced. When discussing substitution in politics, Esposito asks himself "what else is a surrogate [. . .] if not a device that substitutes a presence, thereby reaffirming its absence?" (2011, 82). This is exactly what the DINA officers do: replacing Tagle/Wieder accentuates the resistance to embody the state. Even better, the replacement questions the very possibility of reproducing the traditional strategies of personification that may once have worked in the Anglo-American tradition but remain implausible in the Southern Cone.

Through the exhibition, Tagle/Wieder displays the reassurance of his force in the same way as he does with his flight-performances. At the same time, he ends up contradicting the state's silence on genocide and exposing a misunderstanding: he breaks an unspoken contract, which should not be surprising since despite engaging with symbolic muteness in a thorough manner, he nonetheless had condemned silence explicitly when he equated it with leprosy. In a nutshell, Tagle/Wieder himself becomes a victim of symbolic illiteracy, since the state punishes him for speaking unrestrictedly, for betraying a fundamental premise of the dictatorship: that the state may speak only elliptically and selectively, never relinquishing its own immunity nor publicly acknowledging its responsibility in the crimes against humanity. It is by violating symbolic muteness that he not only betrays the state but also one of the most important genre's conventions: personification.

## ILLITERACY AND FORCE

The length of Wieder's writing is directly linked to its hermeticism. Like the objects that accompany the exhibited pictures, his verses "were few but telling" (89). An avant-garde author, Tagle/Wieder starts his aerial writing with cryptic biblical verses in Latin, an unintelligible language for most of his audience. Critics have often pointed out the extent to which *Estrella distante* (1996) draws on the Chilean lyrical poetry tradition. Among many others, Quintero and Arenas Oyarce have found Tagle/Wieder to be an inverted far right-wing parody of leftist intellectuals such as the Chilean poet Raúl Zurita, who as Diego Trelles Paz recalls "made someone write his verses in the sky of New York" (297). Gareth Williams himself cites Zurita's poem "The New Life," which was "transcribed by five airplanes over the skies of Manhattan" (2009, 133) in the 1980s. Zurita's anaphoric verses equate God with different elements in upper case: "MY GOD IS HUNGER / MY GOD IS SNOW [. . .] MY GOD IS PAMPA / MY GOD IS PAIN" (qtd. in Williams, 2009, 134). Indeed, these verses inform one of Tagle/Wieder's poem that also includes five different definitions of "death" as "friendship," "Chile," "responsibility," "love," and "growth."

As he will in *2666*, Bolaño invokes here a literary tradition that goes well beyond that of detective stories, even that of the modern novel. But Tagle/Wieder's anaphoric verses go beyond the Chilean literary field, too. For instance, European and North American modernist authors whose commitment to fascism was explicit, such as the English Wyndham Lewis, the Italians Filippo Marinetti and Gabriele d'Annunzio, the Spanish Manuel Machado, the North American Ezra Pound and, in the Southern Cone literary tradition, the Argentine Leopoldo Lugones. Ascribing death to concepts that are usually their antithesis, after all, was one of Francoism's *leitmotivs,* as in founder and first commander of the Spanish Foreign Legion Millán-Astray's motto "Long Live Death."

One of the main elements of fascism that exerted an influence in modernism and avant-garde movements amounts to two juxtaposing obsessions: between the old and the new and between action and thought. As American scholar

Juliet Lynd mentions, Tagle/Wieder's performance "reminds the reader that the public avant-garde *happening* [. . .] is susceptible of being appropriated both by the right and the left" (178). After all, the revolutionary inauguration of a new era is an element shared by the most prominent avant-garde political and cultural movements of the twentieth century: fascism and communism, the new man in the new world.

However, something that most of the critic loses sight of is that, if the narrator expresses Tagle/Wieder's literary work as revolutionary, it is also because it points to another prominent and more recent political movement: neoliberalism. Of course, this tension between the old and the new does not belong exclusively to fascism. As the Chilean cultural theorist Nelly Richard underlines, the Chilean "neoliberal democracy is divided" (9). On the one hand, there is the new, which amounts to "the exacerbated rhythms of capitalist globalization, whose promiscuous regime of commercialization dissolves hierarchies of values and transcendent meanings" (10). On the other hand, there is the old, which is related to "the moral conservatism of sectors that need to oppose, in the cultural sphere, this dissolving force of the same market that they so clearly uphold economically, seeking a [. . .] refuge [. . .] in a retrograde defense of the purity and integrity of national traditions" (10). This contradiction between past and future is one of the many elements shared by fascism and neoliberalism. Neither quite solve this contradiction, remaining actually located in the utmost core practices of its regimes.

"Revolution," in *Estrella distante*, does not imply what is often understood as Leftist uprisings. Instead, it means its opposite: counter-revolution. The verb "revolutionize," assigned to Tagle/Wieder's poems, is an ironical reference to the failure of socialist parties at the hands of conservative dictatorships. As Virno claims, it is important to understand "counterrevolution" neither merely as "violent repression [. . .]" nor simply as "the reestablishment of the social order that had been torn by conflicts and revolt" (1996, 141). "Counterrevolution" also means "literally revolution in reverse [. . .] an impetuous innovation of modes of production, forms of life, and social relations that, however, consolidate and again set in motion capitalist command" (141). Counter-revolution instrumentalizes the new to secure the old.

When the narrator and Bibiano consider including Tagle/Wieder in the anthology they prepare, another female character says that the pilot's poems take part in the new Chilean poetry. Bibiano asks if she means the ones he is going to write for the anthology, to which this character replies: "That he's going to *perform*" (Bolaño's italics, 25). Like Pinochet's counterrevolution, the poet/pilot's New Chilean poetry "actively makes its own 'new order,' forging new mentalities, cultural habits, tastes, and customs—in short, a new common sense" (Virno 1996, 241). As an avant-garde writer, Tagle/Wieder does not merely write but "makes" his poems, through a happening that blends visual and experimental poetry with verses from the *Vulgata*, (the new and the old, the technology of the aircraft, and the antiquity of the bible), as a performative expression of neoliberal force.

Even more broadly, Tagle/Wieder goes beyond contemporary literature, citing a more ancient literary trope: the rivalry between arms and letters, the sword and the pen. In Williams's words, "poetry" is established in *Estrella distante* "as a relation, forged in violence, to the exceptional status of sovereign command" (2009, 129). Wieder's poems, then, epitomize the individual intellectual's knowledge and state's depersonalized force all in one. This trope, that harks back as far as the Middle Ages and the Spanish Golden Age period, features in works by the Marquis of Santillana or Garcilaso de la Vega, both military officers who devoted their time to writing poems themselves. It is even thematized in the thirty-eighth chapter of Cervantes's *Don Quixote*, where the knight errant pronounces a speech arguing in favor of the superiority of arms—ironically, in a literary text. It is not a coincidence that Bolaño himself cites this chapter in his "Speech of Caracas," read at the Rómulo Gallegos Award in 1999 for *Los detectives salvajes*.

Trelles-Paz believes that it does not matter if Zurita was a representative of the left resistance to Pinochet's dictatorship; for him, he still informs Tagle/Wieder because "the fake biographies of Nazi writers resound with real facts of real writers that [...] are not far-right winged" (296). Similarly, for Quintero the equation between the narrator's and Tagle/Wieder's diasporic biographies is a sign of Bolaño's "monstrous criticism against the double standards of the Chilean left as well as the systematic impunity that they conceded to many of the authors and leaders of the regime, such as Manuel Contreras and Augusto Pinochet" (172). Tagle/Wieder's ambivalence, according to De Rosso, makes him "both a devilish character and a symbol of a whole generation" (136). By contrast, I believe that Bolaño is doing something more complex than a unidimensional critique, or at least one that is not solely enclosed in national issues. The keys to understand *Estrella distante* go beyond the Chilean literary field and its recent history. They point instead to a broader literary tradition: Don Quixote (presaged in Bolaño's retelling of his own work, as he mentions in the preface of the novel, under the influence of Borges's Pierre Ménard [2004a, 1]), a quintessential myth of individualism fighting against the world, informs Tagle/Wieder more than Zurita.

Whereas in Anglo-American and Argentine detective stories, private investigators embody individualism, in Bolaño individualism affects their rival: the officer of the state. Because even if he works at the service of the state, Tagle/Wieder is essentially an individualist, who is susceptible to literary mythification, his mythic stature equated with Jonah's (79). In the Scriptures, the Jewish prophet travels to Nineveh to warn its residents to repent of their sins: he carries and conveys the message of the sovereign will to the multitude. Similarly, the poet/pilot's flights warn Chileans through aerial poems that they should subject themselves to what seems to be the state's narrative. But these texts (despite representing the state's neoliberal narrative) still carry his signature.

Moreover, unlike his victims (who are sheltered middle-class literature students), Tagle/Wieder calls himself a self-taught poet, who erases with force what they have or could have written. Ultimately, there is yet another significant difference between the fictional poet/pilot and Zurita: whereas the latter made someone else put his aerial poems in writing; the former, instead, performs himself his own text. He acts and writes simultaneously. Read from the twenty-first century, the merging of the poet and the soldier, of literacy and force, of individualism and the state, may seem counterintuitive. Especially after decades influenced by Sartre's *littérature engagée*, the Latin American literary field often presupposes writers' political commitment with left-wing struggles—from human rights movement to *indigenismo* and *testimonio*.

Tagle/Wieder, as a poet, does not seem plausible, then. However, despite the emancipatory and democratic dimension that writing appears to have nowadays, since its appearance, writing seemed to "favor rather the exploitation than the enlightenment of mankind" (1961, 292), as Claude Lévi-Strauss claims in his *Tristes Tropiques*. The French anthropologist's conclusion, drawn after his research among Brazilian illiterate indigenous civilizations, can be easily illustrated in the Latin American literary field, especially in the figure of the sentinels of its constituted power: the traditional trope of the sword and the pen, although inaugurated in the Middle Ages, has been rewritten and reformulated in twentieth-century literature. In 1924, Argentine Leopoldo Lugones, for instance, advocated for the coming of "the hour of the sword," in a speech commemorating the centennial anniversary of the Battle of Ayacucho, a motto that was used by the first Argentine dictatorship, only six years later, in 1930. Over the past few decades, Mario Vargas Llosa has frequently intervened in the public debate in favor of constituted power. To sum up, many Latin American authors have promoted conservatism (either in the shape of a fascist state or the all-pervasiveness of the free market), by fighting emancipation with their *words* as if they were their *swords*.

Against English author Edward Bulwer-Lytton's metonymic adage, which claimed that "the pen is mightier than the sword," Wieder's pen (the ink left by his aircraft in the sky after him) is as mighty as his force, mainly because his skywriting performances expose the uneven distribution of literacy between him and his victims. As Lévi-Strauss claims, writing is a technology of power that works mainly through contrast, by "enhancing the prestige and authority of one individual—or one function—at the expense of the rest of the party" (1961, 290). This authority, in ancient civilizations, was conferred on the scribe, who was "rarely a functionary or an employee of the group as a whole" (291). In brief, despite his collective duty, the scribe was an individualistic agent who emerged above the multitude. Of course, Lévi-Strauss works with a Brazilian indigenous population whose illiteracy was literal, not symbolic. This is what he is alluding to when he remarks that "for thousands of years [. . .] and still today in a great part of the world, writing has existed as an institution in societies in which the vast majority of people are quite unable to write" (290). Instead Tagle/Wieder, a symbolic scribe, defamiliarizes language by rewriting it such that his readers (despite perfectly mastering the Spanish alphabet) cannot read in a symbolic level.

The poet/pilot's hermeticism is not merely yet another characteristic that defines him as an avant-garde poet, it also imbues his audience with a paralyzing illiteracy that freezes their eyes (Bolaño 2004a, 25). He writes the state's narrative in Latin, which immobilizes the inmates who happen to be readers of the poem. Whereas most readers would identify the meaning of the verses if translated to Spanish, the performance still manages to obscure the meaning. The multitude's symbolic illiteracy is a means of reaffirming constituted power's force: the dictatorial state can only preserve its constitution not through speech (its representative barely speaking) but through its systematic and multidimensional (oral and written) denial.

Tagle/Wieder is reminiscent of what Lévi-Strauss calls "the primary function of writing, as a means of communication," namely, "to facilitate the enslavement of other human beings" (1961, 292). The biblical verses' lack of legibility inflicts "an unintelligible murmur" in the multitude (Bolaño 2004a, 29). Not even the narrator, then an inmate who happens to be in one of the concentration camps of Concepción in front of which Tagle/Wieder performs, understands the biblical aerial poems (30). An educated poet, Tagle/Wieder's knowledge provides a contrast with the multitude's ignorance. And it is precisely through this ignorance, this symbolic illiteracy, that he subjugates them to constituted power.

Later, once the aerial text fully switched to Spanish, Tagle/Wieder writes a disciplinary command, "LEARN," aimed at all these left dissidents watching him. For Williams, "LEARN

[. . .] is a contentless command" (2009, 137). Divested of meaning, in the end this Spanish imperative verb is no different than Latin. The threat "does nothing more than guarantee the witness's exclusion from the true content of sovereign will" (137). The witness, the multitude watching below, remain benighted before this order, "a command that commands its own commandment. It is sovereign command in force but without significance or specific content" (137). Again, the concision of the message's form is far more eloquent than its content: the state, through Tagle/Wieder, says more by saying less. It reassures its constitution by selectively refraining from conveying explicit meaning. And this reassurance is directly linked with the inability of the state's victims to "decipher the language of sovereign will" (136). Here, too, the constitution of the dictatorial state can only be founded on its victims' symbolic illiteracy.

As Williams points out, "Wieder's poem calls attention to the inauguration in Chile of a new divine kingdom—the return of the commanding God of the Old Testament hand in hand with the on-going history of Nazism" (2009, 136). The tension between the new and the old are reminiscent of the rupture with tradition and what Mexican writer Octavio Paz calls "the tradition of the rupture," the avant-garde movements, such as the one created by another Chilean poet, Vicente Huidobro, in 1931, that of "creationism." The *Vulgata* verses belonging to the *Genesis* (i.e., the creation of a new world) should be read as an allegory of the new conservative era, the emergent constituted power under Pinochet's dictatorship. After all, Huidobro's "Altazor," like a Condor, is also an aerial biblical fallen angel. Tagle/Wieder is "the new era's major poet" (Bolaño 2004a, 35) and his poems, "heralded a new age of iron for the Chilean race" (43). But what is really "new" about these times? Where Bolaño ironically writes "new times" and "iron age," it must be read the times in which Latin America, according to neoliberal rhetoric is "modernized," "freed" from "anachronistic" communism. This new revolutionary poetry works, in Richard's terms, as "a denarrativization of memory orchestrated by voiding its historical reference" (9). The creation of a new world, a new order, a new poetry, annihilates the memory of whatever may have come before that inception.

In a later aerial happening at La Moneda, Tagle/Wieder performs only in Spanish. Even then, his speech remains unintelligible. Only few were able to decode his words, this time because "the wind effaced them almost straight away" (Bolaño 2004a, 80). When he writes his sixth verse, none of the generals or their families can read it, now because "an electric storm was building in the sky" (81). In this scene, the state (personified briefly in the military) appears already detached from Tagle/Wieder—watching his performance from below. Here, signifiers remain not only unreadable but also unread. What is the difference? The answer can be found in one of William Faulkner's poems collected in *The Marble Faun and A Green Bough* that works as the epigraph of *Estrella distante*: "What star is there that falls, with none to watch it?" Speech is social: if meanings cannot circulate, if words cannot be uttered or read, if symbolic muteness prevails, meaning cannot exist either.

Nevertheless, as in Piglia, meaning remains irrelevant. For Agamben the absence of meaning is inherent in the state of exception, defined precisely as "a law that is in force but does not signify anything" (Williams 2009, 137). It is important to ask again the question once made by Lévi Strauss and later recovered by Derrida: "What links writing to violence?" (Derrida 1997, 102).

In the case of Tagle/Wieder, performative force, much more than meaning. This is clear for instance in the scene where he delays the writing of his poems in the sky, flying away. The multitude waits for him, puzzled by his absence. Most of the audience starts to engage in futile conversation. They finally speak, but their speech is shallow and, as a result, it becomes divested of meaning as well. His temporary absence and its corresponding silence speak for themselves.

If Tagle/Wieder resists becoming a personification of the dictatorship, is he really a metonymy of the state or of individualism? When he betrays the state's silent pact, he becomes an individualistic rogue, who follows his will only. Rephrasing Watt's idea of *ego contra mundum*, Tagle/Wieder, beneath his depersonalizing heteronyms, also becomes *mundus*, which here no longer amounts to the state but to the multitude. After all, the state he once represented ends up punishing him. In short, Tagle/Wieder shows that this opposition between *ego* and *mundus* starts to collapse. Through him, the individualistic hero merges into a *mundus* that is also ambivalent, polysemic and susceptible of symbolic paralysis.

## FORCE AND PARALYSIS

Whereas Tagle/Wieder's force stems from the multitude's illiteracy, it also produces a ricochet effect of symbolic paralysis in everything that surrounds him. In the beginning of the novel, this paralyzing effect is presaged when Bibiano surprises Tagle/Wieder with an unexpected visit. In the encounter, the criminal's speech produces an affective paralysis in Bibiano, "prolonging the conversation [. . .] to keep him there" (9). Paralysis later reappears in another encounter, when the narrator and the poet/pilot meet (without fully meeting) in a silent bar. The imminence of the criminal's presence provokes a generalized set of symbolic disabilities in the detective. Before Tagle/Wieder even shows up, the narrator, who originally was hired because of his literacy, is unable to read, remaining prisoner of unintelligibility: "the words went scuttling past like beetles, busy at incomprehensible tasks" (143). Illiteracy, unintelligibility and muteness are merged with paralysis: "Nobody came into the bar; nobody moved. Time seemed to be standing still" (143). The poet/pilot (a problematic metonymy of Pinochet's dictatorial state, unknowingly disturbing the Chilean diaspora in Europe) briefly cancels motion even before he is present. As a contagious disease, his imminence affects the narrator even physically, causing him to feel sick (143), and to almost faint, once he enters the bar. After he leaves, the narrator tries to resume his reading but, once more, fails (146). Even after having identified him, he cannot surmount symbolic illiteracy.

We do not witness the moment in which Romero executes Tagle/Wieder. There is only another failed attempt by the narrator now not to read, but to write, to picture the scene, to imagine him by himself, "in his flat, an anonymous dwelling [. . .] on [. . .] an empty eight-floor building, as Romero's shadow glided steadily towards him [. . .] but I couldn't" (147). This significant last ellipsis works as an extra-textual symbolic paralysis: Bolaño's own inability to represent the murder itself with words and his subsequent choice to do it with silence instead, one of the many instances of the crisis of representation that hovers over the novel.

We can only surmise that the execution has taken place because the detectives endure the same symbolic disabilities that once were reserved for the state only. After having identified the poet/pilot, the narrator carries this set of symbolic disabilities with him out of the bar and projects them into the detective Romero, who "gestured in reply, but it was too dark to see what he meant" (147). Whereas during the dictatorship, it was only the state whose messages remain under comprehension; after dictatorship, the private eye, too, is unintelligible. The narrator claims that he cannot see Romero's face. He can only discern from his speech "that he was making an effort to be convincing" (147). Romero is here trying to legitimize to the narrator his act of vigilantism, but his body suffers from paralysis, which is mirrored in the narrator. Unable to see the detective's face, he also suffers from symbolic blindness. Both the fact that Romero's body is utterly immersed in immobility and his resilient symbolic muteness, (only partially overcome with an unconvincing narrative), are in direct relation with the narrator's inability to see clearly. While Romero leaves the scene allegedly to murder Tagle/Wieder, the narrator waits for him and tries once more to think but fails again (147). In this last elliptic scene, thus, symbolic paralysis and failure affect not only action but even thought and overflows the text, expanding to the crisis of literary representation above mentioned.

Williams notes that *La literatura nazi en América* "ends with a sense of paralysis that derives from the inability to truly measure distribution for past action" (2009, 132). The same could be argued about these final pages of *Estrella distante*. Both stories are set "in a context in which the democratic/revolutionary horizon of collective politics has been reduced to the utmost individualism of identifying one's former enemy, and nothing else" (132). Both stories portray individualism and vigilantism with an ambivalent meaning. The vengeful outcome is nothing but bittersweet. On the one hand, Tagle/Wieder's alleged execution creates the mirage of individualistic success: Romero and the narrator end up getting paid for their assignment and their enemy gets his comeuppance.

What Esposito names *compensatio* seems to take place only superficially: with the murderer's execution, post-dictatorial democratic order appears to be restored. Romero (an officer who worked for Allende's regime in the 1970s) regains his symbolic and material capital, and the narrator avenges the murders of his youth friends and colleagues. But the problem is that neither Romero nor the narrator seem particularly satisfied with nor convinced by this outcome. Neither of them believes in the mythical dimension of individualism any longer, their individualistic speech remaining ages away from being persuasive. In fact, killing the poet/pilot has not healed their symbolic muteness to the slightest degree: after the implied execution, the detectives leave Blanes for Barcelona, and muteness and paralysis still define their trip. Their scant conversation is interrupted only by monosyllables as they "didn't feel like talking" (Bolaño 2004a, 148). Right after Romero comes back from Tagle/Wieder's house, the narrator describes him paying attention to quintessential features of the traditional private detective: his sight and knowledge.

But knowledge points to failure, since Romero's eyes are "ready to believe that anything is possible but *knowing* [. . .] that nothing can be undone" (148 Bolaño's italics). The impossibility of *compensation* crushes the male fantasies of individualistic power. In the original Spanish text, Bolaño uses the word *remedio*: Romero's eyes know that nothing has a solution, a remedy. This word here is not innocent, as it reminds us of Esposito's re-elaboration of the *pharmakon* concept above mentioned: "Disease and antidote, poison and cure, potion and counter-potion: the *pharmakon* is not a substance but rather a non-substance, a non-identity, a non-essence" (2011 127). Vigilantism, a depersonalized remedy/poison, seems to be not enough: there is a sense that somebody has "won," that someone's force prevailed. And it is neither Romero's nor the narrator's. Before turning the poet/pilot in to Romero, the narrator emphasizes that the criminal has more entity that the multitude: "He was more self-possessed than the rest of us in that sleepy bar" (Bolaño 2004a, 145). In the end, Tagle/Wieder's individualistic entity, despite his fragmentariness and depersonalization, prevails even over his own death.

After finishing the silent trip, away from the murder scene, the detectives talk one last time. It is only when their train ride finishes, that symbolic paralysis and muteness recede temporarily. The narrator asks Romero about the murder. "Like these things always are, he said. Difficult" (148). The euphemistic response is more eloquent than an explicit account of the murder could ever have been. Romero has just avenged his nemesis. Nevertheless, he describes it not as a satisfying but as a difficult task. When they are about to bid farewell, the detective's symbolic paralysis and muteness ultimately recur. They "stood there for a while on the edge of the pavement waiting for a taxi, not knowing what to say" (149). The euphemism "difficult" conveys their dissatisfaction: despite having accomplished their task, they remain paralytic and silent, ages away of becoming the embodiments of successful individualism they are expected to be.

## FINAL THOUGHTS: NEOLIBERALISM AND STATE TERRORISM

Because Bolaño deliberately choses an elliptical dénouement, the reader will never know the cause of this dissatisfaction. Perhaps the answer should be found in the issue of *whodunit* above mentioned. If somebody from the Chilean administration is Romero's wealthy client, then what prevailed, through its violent use of symbolic muteness, illiteracy and paralysis, is the conservative force of the post-dictatorial state. Thus, the state ensures its transition to democracy by eradicating the possible threats (like Tagle/Wieder) that could sully its criminal past, while at the same time it secures symbolic muteness with its brand-new capital, accumulated after two decades of neoliberalism (Romero, the Chilean who made it abroad and is ready to bring back his wealth to Chile). After all, muteness is essential during the transition to democracy, which was founded as Jean Franco claims on "the restructuring of the economy on neoliberal principle" which "promoted a business class that is impatient of reminders of the past" ("Preface," Richard: viii). Muteness is inextricably linked to the suppression of any possible reminiscing voice that could question the democratic nature of this transition. If this were the case, then *Estrella distante* does not portray a case of vigilantism, but of state terrorism in democratic times.

As Esposito points out, the enactment of state laws follows an immunitary paradigm before vigilantism. If according to him "immunization" is "a protective response in the face of a risk" (2011, 1), here the Chilean state, then, would not only mirror its risk. After all, an ex-hitman at the service of a dictatorial state, that had banished him for insubordination, is a risk for the silent pact of the transition. Following Esposito, it could be argued that the Chilean state's immunization neutralizes this risk while at the same time it improves the mechanisms that it once created during the dictatorship: the now democratic state, through (un)lawful means, "not only takes [revenge] into its own hands but actually perfects into a form that connects prevention and cure" (Esposito, 2011, 40). This ability to improve the mechanisms of its domination is inextricably connected to the systematic use of symbolic muteness, as Romero never discloses the identity of his client.

Derrida, who wrote extensively about the prominence of the voice in the figure of the verbose Dupin, establishes that one of the main causes for the preeminence of voice (the opposite of muteness) over writing is in direct relation to Saussure's classic opposition between meaning and signifiers. Because "voice is the closest to the signified" (1997, 12), phonic articulations dominate writing, which in turn is closer to signifiers. If phono-centrism points to the subjugation of the sound over the mute letter, *Estrella distante* portrays an inversion, where voices seem subsumed to meaningless signifiers. To put it differently, Bolaño's novel builds a world in which this very verbosity is now subjugated by the silent literacy of the murderer (post)dictatorial state. Whereas the connotation of the state officer's silence in "The Murders of the Rue Morgue," as Derrida shows, is there as a foil to extol Dupin's loquacity, here silence takes on new connotations that, as we have seen, are less naïve and are related to the impunity of criminal practices performed by the state itself. Selective silence, in *Estrella distante*, cannot be separated from censorship, torture and the transition to democracy.

Writing, according to Derrida, refers to the "dead letter [. . .] a carrier of death" (1997, 17). The poet/pilot, with his selective and ambivalent use both of literacy and symbolic muteness (sometimes at the service of the dictatorial state, sometimes at the service of his own individualistic interests), wields that domination personally until its own depersonalized mechanisms end up dominating himself. For Derrida, along with this preeminence of voice comes the superiority of presence over absence, because the present voice is always perceived to be more reliable. By contrast, writing remains always "degraded" for having been produced in absence. It is in this sense that Romero and the narrator are instruments of these depersonalized mechanisms as well. Ultimately, that is what the most important ellipsis of the book points to: the fact that an anonymous client, who is both silent and absent, ends up holding much more agency and power than anyone else in the plot. This way, Bolaño exacerbates what he had read in Borges, Walsh and Piglia: the failure of the individualistic *ego(es)* in front of a and crumbling but still persistent *mundus*.

*Chapter 4*

# Brazil

## *The State against the State*

### REWRITING INDIVIDUALISM AND THE STATE AFTER THE BRAZILIAN DICTATORSHIP

#### Individualism within the State

"All authority contains, in a way, something corrupt and immoral" (207): this is how Inspector Mattos, the main character of Rubem Fonseca's masterpiece *Agosto* (1990), defines the Rio de Janeiro police, for whom he works.[1] Whereas in Argentine and Chilean stories, the detective is often private but rarely a detective per se; in this Brazilian novel, the sleuth is a more conventional inspector who instead belongs to the public sector. Nevertheless, this distinction does not stop Fonseca from reproducing the traditional tensions between mythical individualism and the post-dictatorial state. Even though Mattos is an officer who works within the state apparatus, ultimately, he is not significantly different from a private eye working against it.

Narrating crime investigations from the perspective of a public detective is not Fonseca's recent invention: Mattos partakes in an old Anglo-French tradition that re-signified the state as a space that was capable not only of hindering individualism but also of including and containing its heroic dimension. This tradition starts with 1930s writers, such as New Zealand Ngaio Marsh and French Georges Simenon. Marsh's Alleyn (an officer in London's Metropolitan Police) and Simenon's Maigret (the commissioner of the Paris *Brigade Criminelle*) forgo the model of state policemen as incompetent that Lestrade or Japp once embodied. Alleyn and Maigret, working within the state, are as witty as their private models. Like Dupin or Holmes, they solve

123

cases successfully despite working not for themselves or for private companies but for a bureaucratic entity.

This Anglo-French tradition was imported to the Southern Cone, especially to Brazil. It appears ever since the first detective novel written and published in the country: *O mistério* (1920). Printed as a serialized novel in the newspaper *A Folha*, four different writers authored the story: Afrânio Peixoto, Coelho Neto, Viriato Corrêa and Medeiros e Albuquerque. In this novel, the detective Major Mello Bandeira reproduces and parodies the figure of Sherlock Holmes (much like the tradition of imitation that we have seen in Argentina and Chile) but with the novelty that the investigator works for the Rio de Janeiro police (Tavares dos Santos 19).

More recently, this tradition of the public detective re-appears in Fonseca and even more prominently in Luis Alfredo García-Roza's novels devoted to his Inspector Espinoza (1996–2014). This import, like the ones previously examined, is nothing but problematic. In a region marked by the Operation Condor, where the state was consistently portrayed as ineffective and criminal, Fonseca imagines a policeman who works for a post-dictatorial government whose main constitutive elements are corruption and abuse of authority. The fact that Mattos works for the state may give the impression that their agencies are aligned, but this alignment is only apparent and does not imply an absence of tensions between individualism and state, but rather its rewriting.

Brazilian detective stories share many elements with their Southern Cone counterparts. To begin with, they also equate crime and state. Both in Fonseca's and García-Roza's works, as well as in Bernardo Kucinski's *K* (2011), the investigated murderers are either policemen or agents who belong, in one way or another, to the state. Equally, regardless of their position in the private or the public realm, detectives often fail to restore the social fabric, leaving their cases ultimately open or unpunished. It is in this sense that it is possible to understand a common poetics of failure between national literatures that are tend to be as parallel literary fields, oblivious to one another, often because of the language barrier.

The Brazilian tradition also shares a similar trajectory to the Argentine, as both oscillate from parody to memory, during the transition from dictatorship to democracy. In the 1970s, for instance, Luis Fernando Veríssimo's *Ed Mort* (1979) short stories (influenced by Borges and Bioy's parodic tone) reproduced the figure of a precarious investigator. "Mort, Ed Mort": this is how this parodic detective from Copacabana, the popular neighborhood of Rio de Janeiro, introduces himself. An obvious allusion to "Bond, James Bond," this is also a pun: his last name sounding like an Anglicized version of the Portuguese word "morte," i.e., "death," which is what any professional sleuth is supposed to know how to be immune to. Ed Mort, the narrator reiterates in a comic tone, is a detective so poor that he must pawn his gun to pay the rent on an office that has no chairs, tables or even clients, just a few cockroaches and a mouse named Voltaire. As in Parodi, humor reappears in playful names: Voltaire, the rodent, is the only one that always *volta* (i.e.,: "returns" in Portuguese) to Mort's office, to compensate for the absence of customers. Mort's cases are often ludicrous, making him yet another under-employed worker from a South American country. Veríssimo's urban stories are still reminiscent of Don Frutos, whose dismantled rural office is devoid of fingerprinting techniques, among poor gauchos in the Pampa.

Like in post-1983 Argentina, these parodic expressions gave way to more serious narratives after the last Brazilian dictatorship (1964–1985), frequently harking back to the past to explore the dictatorial experience. Fonseca's *Agosto* constitutes a paradigmatic example. What distinguishes this Brazilian detective novel is that the exploration of memory is not only carried out through a narration of a crime set in the past, but also in the retelling of the historical events and political personalities that preceded and even provoked the 1964 dictatorship. This novel relies not so much on the melancholic examination of memory but on a more detached rewriting of history. What is also distinctive in Fonseca is that the state representatives are not synthesized in a singular villain. They remain, instead, in a more amorphous and multitudinous dimension, that explicitly includes the heroic detective himself, his colleagues as well as the politicians and their accomplices.

Chapter 2 examined the ways in which Argentine detective stories depict a state that was deliberately absent, silent and deaf to its citizens. Chapter 3 explored how Bolaño's *Estrella distante* portrays the Chilean state as selectively silent, though thoroughly hearing (spying on) its citizens through a concrete (albeit resistant) embodiment. In this chapter, I look at how this Brazilian detective story represents the state as an inescapable presence, that, paradoxically, mirrors the Argentine absent state, allowing a common transnational reading.

## PERSONIFICATION AND PERSONALISM

The fact that Brazilian detective stories have more ties to Argentina than to the Chilean tradition could be explained in historical terms. Chile's longest-serving head of state, the dictator Augusto Pinochet, lasted in power for almost twenty years, after decades of democratic governments. By contrast, Argentines and Brazilians have witnessed sundry dictatorships interrupting their democracies more often and with different military officers in power (Videla, Viola, Galtieri, Castelo Branco, Geisel, Figueiredo, to name a few), succeeding each other sometimes in a matter of months. This distinction can be read in the ways political representation has produced a type of individualism at the service of the state, a sort of personification of sovereignty: personalism.

Whereas Chile funneled the cult of personality through one person, Pinochet, in Argentina and Brazil, personalism was not funneled through dictatorial regimes but through populist democracy. We need only think of Juan Domingo Perón's (1946–1955, 1973–1974), and Getúlio Vargas's (1930–1945, 1951–1954) administrations, which created an idealized and heroic image of their controversial leaders. This powerful image permeated and conditioned the history of their countries, polarizing its political spectrum ever since. Perón and Vargas shared a common dictatorial past: whereas Perón was an Army general who worked as a Minister of Labor for the dictatorship (1943–1946) that preceded his own democratic government; Vargas provoked a self-coup to stay in power, extending his first four-year term under a dictatorial regime named the *Estado Novo* (1937–1945) and returned to power as a democratically elected president in 1951.

The abrupt interruption of both administrations in the mid-1950s (in Brazil, with Vargas's suicide in 1954; in Argentina, with a military coup that overthrew Perón in 1955) only reinforced this Argentine-Brazilian personalist tradition. Personalist politics was even more pronounced in Argentina than in Brazil, as Perón (an exile in Spain for almost twenty years) had a tremendous impact in domestic politics, returning dramatically in 1973 to win an election for the third and last time, amidst civil unrest and social chaos. More recently, personalism reappeared in the presidencies of Lula Inácio da Silva (2002–2010) and Néstor and Cristina Kirchner (2003–2015), who carried the laborist legacy of their forerunners, now bereft of the military past that their models once held, while still preserving a strong personalist aura.

Fonseca's *Agosto* tackles this peculiar Southern Cone personalist tradition by blending a detective story with a historical account of the collapse of Vargas's final term as president, which ended in his suicide and, with it, the defeat of Brazilian populism at the hands of constituted power, encapsulated in the military. Fonseca, a former policeman who became a novelist in the early 1970s, published *Agosto* in 1990, five years after the end of the last Brazilian dictatorship. Like his *alter ego* Mattos, the novelist was a law student turned into a police inspector during the 1950s.

*Agosto* harks back not to the last dictatorship but to August of 1954, during the final turbulent days of Vargas's presidency, to delve into several agents belonging to the political sphere who would play a leading role during the subsequent decades: from Vargas's unstable democratic successors (Café Filho, Juscelino Kubitschek, João Goulart) to the civil and military leaders who would oust them only ten years later (the then journalist and later governor Carlos Lacerda, or the marshal Castelo Branco, among others). Fonseca stages the political scenario that not only preceded but also enabled the longest and bloodiest dictatorship in the country's history. Thus, he juxtaposes two different post-dictatorial moments: the one he is writing about and the one he is writing from. In French linguist Émile Benveniste terms, he places side by side the *énoncé* (the past, what is said) and the *énonciation* (the present, the act of saying). In *Agosto*, the *énoncé* informs the *énonciation*: Fonseca, writing about Vargas's post-dictatorial government in the mid-1950s, is also alluding to his own post-dictatorial context in the late 1980s.

## LITERATURE AND HISTORY

To juxtapose these two historical moments, Fonseca blends history with literature. All the historical figures who feature in the novel share their prominence with a singular fictional detective: the Inspector Alberto Mattos, who tries (and fails) to solve a conventional crime that is loosely connected with a state crime. On the one hand, Mattos investigates the fictional murder of Paulo Gomez Aguiar, a businessman, involved in import goods. On the other, he incidentally ends up following a political crime that becomes crucial for Brazilian history in the twentieth century: the "Crime da Rua Tonelero," the failed assassination attempt against Carlos Lacerda, a staunch anticommunist and conservative journalist and politician. Lacerda was Vargas's main adversary and, after the president's suicide, a participant in the coup d'état that in 1964 ousted João Goulart, the Minister of Labor during Vargas's administration. Although Lacerda survived the attack, Rubens Vaz, a major who happened to be with him, was inadvertently killed.

Regarding this magnicide, the horizon of expectations of a reader that may be acquainted with these facts and proper nouns does not hold any major surprises. As Sue Wasserman notes, each crime "works inversely": the fictional murder "has already taken place and the reader accompanies a police detective investigating the crime"; instead, in the historical murder, "the reader is privileged with knowing" (165) that the main instigator (or "intellectual author") of the assassination attempt against Lacerda was Vargas's personal bodyguard, an Afro-Brazilian named Gregório Fortunato, also known as the "Black Angel" ("Anjo Negro"). Fonseca recaptures the first twenty-four days of August 1954, in which the military disclose the involvement of Fortunato (and hence Vargas's administration, i.e., the state), in the attack. The scandal, capitalized on by this lurking military who then even toyed with the idea of a *coup*, would stain the president's reputation to the extent that it would eventually result in his suicide.

What breaks with the horizon of expectations is both the effects that the personalist leader's suicide elicits in the fictional hero of the novel (Inspector

Mattos) and the literary re-elaboration of the political proper nouns above mentioned. One of the conclusions that can be drawn after reading *Agosto* is that these literary effects inform the reader about history with an eloquence that is often absent in historiographic accounts. A few hours before Vargas takes his own life, for instance, his brother Benjamin remembers the speech of Gustavo Capanema, a pro-government politician, defending the president against the pressure that the military and the opposition have imposed to achieve the leader's resignation. The speech stated that president Vargas "could not abandon his post [. . .] in face of the exigencies of the political majority that supported him" (265). Vargas's duty to stay in power seems to be tied to something even more sacred than electoral accountability. Furthermore, Vargas had another duty: to his own sacred name. Equating the presidency with monarchy, Capanema believes that the name of the president (much like a king's or a prince's) was something holy (265). According to the personalist and hyper-presidentialist speech, what matters is something inherent not to a contract with the leader's constituency but with his personality, something inherent to his personhood: his name.

This is one of the main problems that the novel addresses: the functions of proper names in novels. Blending a fictional detective story with political proper nouns is one of the aspects that distinguishes Fonseca, when compared with his counterparts: none of the Argentine detective stories examined in Chapter 2 feature the proper names of Videla or Galtieri, for instance. Piglia's *Plata quemada* does mention Perón, but only in passing, in a brief paragraph, when Dorda mentions him with a euphemistic allusion to his military rank (*el General*). In *Estrella distante*, a novel that is first and foremost about Pinochet's dictatorship, Bolaño names the dictator only twice.

Yet the fact that politicians are explicitly mentioned in *Agosto* does not necessarily mean that they are the only ones who embody the state. Even if the novel constantly alludes to Vargas, it is only the final pages that are devoted explicitly to him. In fact, the reader barely hears him speak. Except when he pronounces his last words to his barber that "it doesn't matter" (266), that he does not want to shave; Vargas is an absent presence that haunts the novel by displaying the selective symbolic muteness of the state. The scenes portraying his suicide have an impact on a fictional character who is actually much more important for the plot: the detective Mattos. His name is charged with symbolic meaning that sheds more light on the historical events and tensions than the myriad of politicians' surnames (like Capanema or Vargas himself), that history would make either irrelevant or crucial. All of them, fictional and real proper names, share a problematic and multitudinous embodiment of the state.

Despite his resistance to embodying the Chilean dictatorial state, Tagle/ Wieder is portrayed as the only one who personifies constituted power, paralleling Pinochet's personalism. He encapsulates all the force of the state in his individual figure. Fonseca's representation of the Brazilian state is less concentrated in a single character. Like Tagle/Wieder, Mattos merges *ego* and *mundus*, but in different ways. To begin with, Mattos, a law student who becomes a policeman, follows an inverse trajectory: instead of fleeing the state, he goes towards it. But more importantly, Mattos is not the sole metonymy of the state, since he shares this embodiment with politicians and with his own colleagues. Although Mattos is indeed the protagonist of the novel, Fonseca delves into all these other agents of the state bestowing them a more even prominence: politicians like Vargas and Fortunato, policemen like Mattos's colleagues, Rosalvo and Pádua, personify the state in an even way. The presence of proper names, eclipsed by and entangled with fictional ones, thus, obfuscates more than it reveals facts about the past.

In *Agosto*, as in most of the detective stories here examined, literary representation mirrors political representation; personification reflects personalism, fiction echoes history. Díaz Eterovic regards detective fiction following the image of the mirror, in that the genre "reflects the perplexity of men facing a reality which is more and more aggressive and strange, a reality that puts them face to face to a violent world" (38). Yet these specular reflections, due to their literary nature, are not transparent, but distorted ones. In any mirror, obviously, everything is flipped: all images are portrayed in the opposite way. A historical and detective novel, *Agosto* works as a curved mirror, whose convex or concave regions generate altered images. Despite their distortions (or precisely because of them), these images express things that historiographic accounts often fail to. In short, Fonseca does not provide a pristine reflection but a critical commentary on history. Whereas political debates either censure or endorse personalism in a monolithic way, a literary re-elaboration of its mechanisms provides more nuances to understand how it affects history in a critical way, namely, as inseparable from the anonymous multitude it convokes.

## AN INDIVIDUALISTIC DETECTIVE WORKING FOR A POST-DICTATORIAL STATE

### Sickness and Politics

Fonseca's *Agosto* displays two *leitmotifs* that mirror each other: the traditional hostility towards the police and its officer's mental and physical uneasiness. These *leitmotifs* are located in Mattos's speech and body. As with the previous problematic personifications of the state, the policeman rarely speaks, and decides to do it only selectively. His sidekick Rosalvo describes him as a laconic person, only to nuance afterwards that he did become verbose when angry (167). Mattos talks only when he gets (becomes) mad. "Silence" says the narrator seven times in just a few paragraphs (153–155): that is Mattos's reaction when he learns that Alice (his ex-girlfriend and the current wife of a suspect in the case he is investigating) has been diagnosed with bipolar disorder. He fears contagion of what he perceives to be his own potential psychotic nature, rooted in his genetic background: As "there were several crazy people in his own family," Mattos is daunted by the possibility of suffering himself a psychotic episode (155). This is the way he "talks": not so much through words as through non-verbal infectious symptoms.

One of the figures that constantly reappears in his words is his awareness of the police's negative reputation in Brazilian society, "another unpleasant thing about being a cop: when people didn't hate him, they feared him" (10). The bad image of the police obsesses Mattos to the point that when trying to charge a husband with domestic violence, one of his colleagues describes him as "more Catholic than the pope" (26) to later add that even the wife will be against the police if they proceed with the case. Disregarding his colleague's warnings, he insists that "everybody's against us, always" (26), and takes the case to the end, only to witness how the husband is quickly absolved after paying a small bail. Whereas Bolaño depicts reluctant detectives, Mattos is closer to Borges's Lönnrot or Piglia's Renzi, sleuths that take themselves too seriously, a feature that contributes to their ultimate failure.

After this episode, the detective questions his ability to suture the social fabric by applying the law: "Mattos took an antacid from his pocket, stuck it in his mouth, chewed, [. . .] and swallowed. He had complied with the law. Had he made the world any better?" (27). The intake of antacids points to the second *leitmotif*: the state officer's mental and physical uneasiness (even more transparent than his own words) tied to his individualistic drive to "make the world a better place." To begin with, "Mattos," a conventional surname in Brazil, has (like Tagle/Wieder's) an eloquent and polysemic etymology: it comes from the Italian *matto* and *malato* and the German *mat*, meaning, respectively, "mad," "sick," and "tired" (*Dizionario Etimologico*). His surname anticipates and synthesizes the policeman's mental and physical sicknesses: his chronic fatigue and his growing duodenal ulcer perceived as tangible symptoms of madness. Ultimately, the German *mat* comes from Eastern languages (from Arabic, Persian and Sanskrit), which brought to the West the lexicon of chess, a game that is extremely prominent in detective stories from Poe to Walsh. Specifically, the word "checkmate." Not coincidentally, the Portuguese word for "chess" is *xadrez*, the very same slang word that Fonseca uses to refer to jail, because of the gridded vision that prisoners used to have of the outdoors from their cell windows. Mattos, the ever tired, ill, and mad detective, will checkmate and be checkmated at the same time when he opens the doors of the "xadrez."

Most critics who have written about *Agosto* (Wassermann, Schnaiderman, Waldemer, among many others) have noted the prominence of Mattos's ulcer, but there is hardly any close reading of the moments in which it features as a symptom of unsolved political tensions. The interiority of Mattos's body informs its exteriority: the pain recurs when the state hinders the detective's will. Through the ulcer, a metonymic sickness, Fonseca reproduces the symbolic disabilities of the state to rewrite the tensions between individualism and the post-dictatorial state. Thus, he displays the transference of figurative mutilations (such as muteness or paralysis) traditionally ascribed to the state, now endured by individual heroes such as Mattos, but not because he works for the state: because he goes against it. Both symptoms manage to overcome his immunity, that fails to protect him from corruption and politics.

Mattos's twofold immunity is on the one hand tied to the classic feature of hard-boiled fiction defined by Piglia as the "immunity to corruption" that I discussed in Chapter 1: the detective's imperviousness to crooked activities. Even if he works for the Brazilian state, Mattos functions against (or in spite of) its criminal acts. The policeman's individualism resides in his autonomy before the state's oppressive rule: an honest but controversial officer, Mattos never accepts dirty money unlike his colleagues, he frequently discharges suspects that he considers to be innocent and organizes strikes to complain about the overpopulation of Rio de Janeiro's jails.

On the other hand, he displays an original and somewhat more interesting type of immunity: against politics. At the end of the novel, almost as an affective reaction after he encounters Vargas's corpse, Mattos releases all the inmates from the police station holding cells, where they once were crowded together. Until that very moment, the state policeman constantly defines himself as indifferent to the major political events that are narrated in the background. Even if the characters are supposed to be witnessing one of the most important moments of the twentieth century, Mattos does not care about anything beyond his own performance as a policeman. If he is concerned about the poor state of the Rio de Janeiro's jails, he firstly does not justify it in ideological terms, but because it affects his own performance. In short, "the only thing that worries me is doing my job well" (207), he says. Mattos perceives himself as just a simple employee who cares only about doing the right thing.

Mattos' physical uneasiness is tied to his speech. Specifically, his ulcer first features when he is introduced early on in the novel, and it is closely linked with his symbolic muteness. The scene depicts Mattos obliviously and silently listening to Lacerda's speech, to which he does not react with any opinions nor words. The narrator presents the officer as "tired and feeling pain in his stomach" (3). To alleviate his pain, Mattos "popped two antacid tablets in his mouth," as if that were his bodily reaction to Lacerda's speech, i.e.,: to politics (3). His sickness acts as an immunitary counterforce that responds without words to what he considers the nauseating state of Brazilian politics. The ulcer shows his repugnance against *mundum*, the world he wants to make better but cannot. The internecine conflicts of Brazilian history, then, are echoed in his ulcerated body. If Gregório, Vargas's bodyguard, defines "Lacerdism" as an infectious sexually transmitted disease "worse than gonorrhea or syphilis" (6), Mattos's body responds to this infectious disease with another one: his own ulcer.

Like Tagle/Wieder, who overcomes his own symbolic muteness with alternative forms of signifiers (the ink of his aircraft or the blurred portraits of his victims); Mattos's ulcer speaks for itself and on behalf of him, thus compensating for his selective silence. The sickness of "lacerdismo" reappears later on, when Mattos's crooked colleague Rosalvo shows up at the police station with newspapers funded by Lacerda, filled with corruption stories involving Lutero Vargas (the president's oldest son) and "Jango" Goulart. Rosalvo comments on each of these stories and asks Mattos if he wants to hear more, to which he refuses monosyllabically, or succinctly, that he is not interested. Facing Mattos's lack of verbosity, Rosalvo insists, obtaining in return his colleague's symbolic muteness: "The inspector remained silent" (23). When cornered to answer if he sides with Vargas or Lacerda, Mattos asks back without really answering: "Do I have to be one kind of shit or another?" (23). His elusive answer is rather a question that eschews actually saying something on the matter. Mattos seems to put himself above and beyond the public debates of the moment. His reaction exhibits a resistance to get involved in the *res publica,* an ambivalent attitude towards politics. Mattos seems to side with Vargas rather than with Lacerda, but before the leader's final downfall, he does not express a public opinion on the subject.

These diversions remain constant until the climax of the novel: the moment of the jail evacuation. But should Mattos's act be read as an endorsement of individualistic freedom or quite on the contrary an act that goes well beyond the limits of the self? Is the release of the inmates an act of individualistic vigilantism? Through this act, Mattos stops being apolitical: he no longer seems to agree with his previous claim that "the best policeman would maybe be an automaton who knew the law well and obeyed it blindly" (207). Being the best cop is now divorced with obeying the law, and it can only be possible by breaking it. After all, if the Brazilian state incarcerates arbitrarily and massively, obeying its laws would not be something that "the best policeman" should do.

Mattos becomes political because he goes beyond his individualistic self: he does something for others, without even thinking about the consequences that the infraction could have for his career or even for his own freedom. His colleague Pádua warns him that releasing prisoners is futile and no one would care, especially amidst the chaos brought by Vargas's suicide. The things that Mattos has fantasized the most, namely, inverting the rule of the state, i.e.,: imprisoning at gunpoint his own corrupt and abusive colleagues to liberate the prisoners, has for Pádua an effect that will affect no one. It will not only be a useless event but a depersonalized one, with no authorship to be remembered. For Mattos, instead, his act will actually have an effect on someone: himself. It is only thanks to this crucial moment that Mattos manages to surmount his own symbolic paralysis and muteness. In his own way, this is how he acts and speaks. There is here an interesting paradox: acting more individualistically than ever, (engaging in an act that endorses individualistic freedom, as it matters to him only), he merges his self with the inmates: at once, he breaks the law (becomes corrupt) and intervenes in the collective (becomes political), as if Fonseca would be saying that the two were inextricably linked.

Mattos, the good cop, is the promise of a benevolent state. He never takes bribes and usually starts his shift on time, and when he does not it is because he gets delayed trying to assist citizens. Benevolence is encapsulated in the immunity against corruption and politics. Mattos's "neutrality" fulfils the fantasy of Contractualism, a European political tradition that becomes problematic in front of Latin American Personalism. After all, the fiction of a benevolent liberal state relies among other things in the balanced neutrality of its three powers. Contractualism justifies the existence and the authority of the liberal state in this balanced benevolence, that would be preferable both to an absence of order and to the concentration of power in one individual. Mattos's neutrality and benevolence are shattered when he contravenes the law, because he does not only release innocent prisoners, but also criminals.

Mattos's rupture with the fictions of neutrality and benevolence inverts the very nature of a practice that, as I discussed in Chapter 2, Agamben argues is at the core of the state: arbitrariness. If the prisoners were once condemned regardless of them being guilty or not; Mattos does the opposite following the same arbitrary criteria: he releases them in an extra-juridical way, beyond their actual responsibility in previous crimes. At the beginning of the novel, when he checks on the crowded inmates, Mattos admits to them: "None of you should be here. But there's nothing I can do" (22). Till here Mattos remains ambivalent. Why does he think these prisoners should not be there? He does not say if it is because of over-incarceration or because they may not be guilty at all. When he finally releases them, when he realizes that there is something he can do, there is a disambiguation: he does not choose to transfer them to a different facility to balance the overpopulation of the jails of Rio de Janeiro: instead, he frees all the prisoners for good, making a silent statement that stresses the state's arbitrariness.

Since neither Rosalvo nor the prisoners cannot comprehend this arbitrariness in which they are immersed, they endure symbolic unintelligibility, muteness and paralysis before Mattos: "I don't understand, sir,' said Rosalvo [. . .] The prisoners didn't understand the inspector's order and remained motionless inside the lockup" (272). While he orders them to evacuate the cells, the selectively silent Mattos transfers his symbolic muteness to the inmates: "One by one, in silence, the prisoners began leaving" (272). Symbolic disabilities, in *Agosto* too, affect both state officers and their victims.

Mattos does not give any verbal explanation to anyone on why he does this. Again, his muteness speaks for itself. As soon as he orders the uncomprehending prisoners to leave the *xadrez*, his ulcer recurs. Significantly, the smell of the inmates' sickness, an external echo of his own disease, is what strengthens his call. When he enters the cell, the prisoners' "repugnant smell of poverty, dirt, and disease strengthened even further the inspector's resolve" (272). Here Mattos's "sickness" is re-signified as a social product of the state's carelessness towards its subalterns. By smelling the others' disease, his ulcer (his individual drive against the post-dictatorial state) stops being a personal medical condition to become a collective problem.

His crucial decision is a performative statement that reveals not what he thinks but more literally (and affectively) what he had in his guts (his ulcerated stomach): the irreconcilable tensions between his individual drive and the over-incarceration practices of the Brazilian state. In these tensions, Mattos resists the personification of the state like Tagle/Wieder but goes a step further by simultaneously problematizing the figure of the individualistic detective as well.

## FORCE AND AGENCY

Over the course of the novel, the narrator constantly interrupts Mattos's dialogues with his colleagues, superior or suspects, to bring back the ulcer's *leitmotif*. Despite constantly taking pills and drinking milk to alleviate his pain, Mattos never heals. These iterations punctuate the plot, regulating its pace, constantly bringing back the return of the repressed pain. In one of the first frustrating dialogues between Mattos and Rosalvo, not even after his dairy intake, the ulcer's ache recedes. Despite being able to sense the milk much later, the remedy proves to be not enough facing his frustrations, as "the acidity had yet to pass completely" (54). Mattos's pain is a symptom that remains impossible to soothe until the moment of his death. It recurs even at the end of the novel, after he has solved his main tension against the state—the jail evacuation.

Vargas's suicide only worsens Mattos's sickness. Having released the prisoners, he wanders the tumultuous streets of Rio de Janeiro, crowded with people who cannot make sense of the traumatic event. While he walks, he witnesses "the crowd of people forming immense lines near the Catete Palace" to mourn Vargas's corpse (274). Mattos seeks some more milk to find relief, but amid the chaos there are no bars opened. As a result, his "stomach ached fiercely" (274). The impossibility to consume the remedy in the midst of confusion mirrors Mattos's internal impossibility to heal.

A symptom that cannot be soothed is a response to a wound that does not heal. This is precisely how Esposito defines "force." The Italian philosopher, drawing from Simone Weil's reading of the *Iliad*, concludes that state force "is not the wound destined to cicatrize into the 'regularity' of politics, but its in-eliminable foundation" (2017, 78). In the same way that Mattos's tensions against the state, encapsulated in his incurable ulcer, cannot be extirpated from his body; state force resides at the core of the political. Esposito understands force "not as measurement but as a universal constant of, and invariable in, human nature" (78). Similarly, the fact that Mattos's immunity end up being overcome by corruption and politics seems to suggest that not only force but also systematic crime, i.e., corruption, is inseparable from the political. As Esposito himself says elsewhere, order (a given arrangement of society, e.g.,: dictatorships, democracies, etc.) is not supposed to suppress conflict, because "conflict *is* order" (2011, 50; Esposito's italics). Order, then, should not be expected to neutralize force or corruption because they always return as a repressed symptom, like Mattos's ulcer.

As Gareth Williams claims, following Esposito, force is the "most intimate wound of the political, situated at the very heart of [. . .] the political itself" (2016, 6). Mattos's incurable ulcer aches more intensely when the similarly "incurable" force and corruption of the Brazilian state presents itself unabashedly hindering his agency (or Vargas's), almost as if it were the only silent response that he can offer. And perhaps, this is what Fonseca is trying to illustrate with Mattos's ulcerous madness: in an opposite albeit similar way to the portrayals of the Argentine absent and mute state, the representation of an all-pervasive Brazilian state sheds a light to the fictional silhouette of Contractualism, too. Whereas Argentine detective stories would stress the hollowness of the state to emphasize its manufactured foundations, Fonseca conveys a similar sense of this fictional dimension of the state, without relinquishing its overwhelming presence that colonizes the most private corners of its people: its intimacy. In the end, Mattos's inability to embody that "automaton who knew the law well and obeyed it blindly" (207) points to the impossibility of a benevolent state as a whole. If force constitutes the core of the political, then, a social contract based not on force but on tacit consent between the asymmetrical parties that constitute the state (mainly its leaders, its three powers, and its people) becomes implausible.

From the beginning of the story, the narrator delves into Mattos's immunity to corruption and his inability to subject himself to the state's force. His honesty is depicted negatively and explicitly attributed to madness by his colleagues. Unlike Pádua or Rosalvo, Mattos does not fit in the systematic criminal nature of the state. In one of the final scenes, Mattos discovers that Pádua killed "o Turco Velho," the Old Turk, one of Mattos's prisoners. He then accuses him and tells him he refuses to be his accomplice. To which Pádua replies that he is not being one, because there is nothing he can really do to stop him: "I know you're a good cop, but not even Sherlock Holmes could prove I killed that guy [. . .] You need to stop suffering over nonsense. That's why you have the ulcer" (230–231). Pádua sees Mattos's ulcer and madness as a common symptom of this unsolved tension: he believes that Mattos suffers because he wants to, because he deliberately chooses not to play the game. In here as in elsewhere, Pádua insists on reminding Mattos that it is his individualistic desire for autonomy, in the face of the state's force and corrupt nature, that will lead to his downfall.

During one of their first encounters, Mattos has just rehearsed in small doses what he will end up doing on a grand scale: he has released some innocent homeless people that Pádua had locked up. After Pádua admonishes him, Mattos proudly explains that he "cut the red tape and called headquarters" to do it (50). When he unilaterally surmounts the hindrances of the state apparatus, Mattos puts himself above the other policemen in the same way as private detectives once did from outside of the state. But the traditional heroism that this unilateral behavior once had no longer works. That is why Pádua does not applaud him (like Watson would Holmes), but scolds him instead for having done something illegal: "You put yourself at risk for a bunch of scumbags. You expecting some kind of medal [. . .]? One of these days [. . .] they'll open up an internal investigation and kick your ass out" (50). Even though Pádua and Rosalvo constantly commit illegal acts, they do so by following their self-interest insofar as they would not risk their own immunity. The reason why they regard Mattos as a madman is that he is honest when he must be corrupt and gets involved with illegality when he should be protecting himself from the state's rule. The novel's dénouement confirms Pádua's views, since it is Mattos's autonomous agency, amidst the hindering criminal state, that will break his immunity to politics and corruption and subsequently to death. In other words, it is Mattos's urge to unilaterally wield force within the state what will make him fail in the end.

Mattos admires Delegate Hermes Machado, the policeman who imprisons one of the hitmen that tried to kill Lacerda. At one point, Hermes tells him the reason why he joined the police in the first place is because of vanity, which he defines as "man's great motivator": thanks to the police, he has the power to "make arrests, something that no judge, no Supreme Court justice, no president of the Republic can do" (103). Mattos admires in Hermes precisely what he thinks he lacks himself and could possess: omnipotence. Of course, Hermes's omnipotence is nothing but a mirage, a traditional attribute of mythical individualism—a delusion of grandeur. Whereas for the classic private eye, vanity meant the ability to hold the monopoly of truth, here vanity entails what was supposed to be the most impersonal attribute of the state: the monopoly of force.

Being able to wield power within and above the state, in *Agosto,* includes the most important expression of a presidential republic: the personalist leader. Mattos must therefore be read as a literary re-elaboration, a problematic *Doppelgänger* of Getúlio Vargas. Because, paradoxically, neither of them can truly wield power. Whereas Mattos wants to be seen as a good police, the legacy of Vargas is closely linked to that of a good policymaker. Both know how to "police" well, following Foucault's notion of the polysemantic French word *police*, meaning simultaneously "policy," "politics," and the "police institution" (1988a, 153). Often called by his working-class constituency "the father of the poor," Vargas was seen as a benevolent leader, who granted them unprecedented rights to education and health care. During his first administration, in 1932, he granted unrestricted suffrage to women. Nevertheless, due to the anti-democratic pressure that the military and the opposition subjects him to, the Vargas portrayed in the novel can no longer govern.

Equally, Mattos cannot truly "govern" the small jail of Rio de Janeiro as he pleases. Both share a common impotence that is diametrically opposed to the masculine fantasy of omnipotence and sovereignty. Mattos cannot impose his will until the end of the novel. In the meantime, he has to content himself with toying with it only in small doses. When he tries but fails to speak with Senator Vitor Freitas, the politician's secretary tells the policeman that he feels threatened by his draconian tone, and that he should not forget that the dictatorial rule is over, so "a minor-level policeman" like him can no longer intimidate "a federal senator protected by constitutional immunities without suffering the grave consequences of that criminal and arbitrary act" (105). Mattos hangs up, takes an antacid, and moves on to keep working on his case. Again, what he lacks belongs to someone else: Freitas's constitutional immunity, which amounts, once more, to the mirage of omnipotence.

But, why does Fonseca insist on Mattos's toying with the limits of his own agency? What is at stake is the issue of what policemen (who are used to having a free hand to act as they please during dictatorial regimes) are and are not allowed to do in post-dictatorial democracies. To put it differently, Fonseca partakes in the common Southern Cone poetics of failure because he questions who really wields power within the state apparatus. Though Fonseca's ostensible theme is the 1950s post-dictatorship, in which Vargas was a legitimate democratic leader, having relinquished authoritarianism, at the same time he is elliptically writing during and about the new late 1980s post-dictatorial context. Thus, he asks how much the brand-new post-dictatorial Brazilian democracy is truly democratic. *Agosto*, after all, is not only a detective story but also a historical novel that, as such, responds to a typical convention of the genre: problematizing the past to speak about the present.

Therefore, when Fonseca addresses the boundaries of Mattos's agency to wield force, he is writing not only about the 1950s but also about the fresh memory of a recently finished dictatorship and conflictive transition to democracy. The post-dictatorial period in the region presupposed the replacement of the military by democratically elected politicians to lead the state. Especially during the late 1980s, these transnational transitions were promoted as exemplary cases of contractualism's triumph: liberal democracies, local and foreign Fukuyamans would insist, were here to stay, as an irreversible and inalterable order, immune to interruptions.

However, this contractualist fantasies were already present in the speech of Latin American dictators much earlier. The Uruguayan journalist Eduardo Galeano, for instance, says that "in 1965, Roberto Campos, economic tzar of Castelo Branco dictatorship, announced that 'the era of charismatic leaders surrounded by a romantic aura is giving place to a technocracy'" (212). This very same dictatorial motto, ironically, is recaptured in post-dictatorial democratic times. With post-dictatorship, the clearer visible face of constituted power, which once was personified by dictators and authoritarian personalist leaders, has become all-too blurred into civilians that openly compete for and dispute power relying on their constituency.

Reading Fonseca, then, leads to two fundamental questions: Can the state (whose force is inextricable from its very core) function benevolently? And where did constituted power go? In this new order that promises not to allow dictatorial or democratic personalism, underneath which face will constituted power be hidden? *Agosto* does not answer these issues, but it sheds light on the anxieties and tensions that post-dictatorship produces in individuals in the figure of its main detective.

## MADNESS AND KNOWLEDGE

When Mattos releases the prisoners, Rosalvo thinks "the guy has really gone crazy" (271). When Pádua finds out, he defines Mattos with the very same word (272). Both policemen understand Mattos's autonomy as a product not of a political decision but of lack of rationality. Mattos's eccentricity shows clearly when he is contrasted with his foils. Brazilian writer Boris

Schnaiderman describes Mattos as an "intelligent, cultured and sensitive policeman" (2). These are the traits that distinguish him from his fellows. It is in this sense that madness can be read in terms of class. Closer to Dupin, Holmes, Lönnrot or Renzi; Mattos belongs to a higher status than most of his colleagues.

In his essay on *Madness and Civilization*, Foucault defines madness as a complex concept, a notion that changes throughout history. One of the elements that is crucial in its multiple definitions is the close relation that madness holds with exclusion. Since the Renaissance, madmen have often been physically separated from European society in places that were once reserved for lepers. Even if Mattos wants to exclude himself from the state's corrupt network, even though he thinks highly of himself when compared to his working-class colleagues, he cannot be truly excluded, because, as Foucault reminds us, any kind of exclusion produces at the same time another parallel form of community of the excluded (1988b, 7). Mattos, a "functional madman," displays a sophisticated individualism that permeates the representation of the state, which once was a space circumscribed to sheer brutal force. He aims to be detached from society, listening to opera and expressing unconventional ideas for a common officer. These traits outline the ambivalent figure of this individualistic detective, who nonetheless chooses to work for the state.

Due to his madness, Mattos suffers symbolic illiteracy: he reads too much and that prevents him from seeing the world the way he should. As one of his lovers, Salete, points out, excessive reading leads to madness, as she remembers how someone told her, "a man who frequented her house went crazy from so much reading" (66). Like Lönnrot, Renzi or the *Estrella distante*'s anonymous narrator, the fact that Mattos reads too much leads to his inability to read at all. Pádua stresses Mattos's symbolic paralysis in similar terms: "you're not capable of using those shitty guns"(273). Fonseca's detective reproduces here a tradition that harks back to Dupin: because of his upper-class background, which conditioned him to be well-read, Mattos is unable to interact with the Real and its realm of life and death (encapsulated here in the ability of using guns), making him, too, a prisoner of the symbolic order.

Culture, language, books, in short, symbols, instead of clarifying how to read reality, end up stupefying Mattos. Again, the eloquent etymologies behind the detective's surname inform his personality. *Mattus,* in Late Latin, means "stupid": somebody who is in awe for whatever he has learnt (as a "student") and thus becomes paralyzed, incapable of thinking clearly. Reading, for Mattos, does not necessarily amount to understanding what he reads. The abundance of signifiers fails to produce meaning that could reconcile Mattos with the world and its mechanisms.

Mattos's tension against the state, like Tagle/Wieder's, is an inheritance of a European myth not only of individualism but also of madness and symbolic illiteracy par excellence: Don Quixote. Both share what Foucault considers to be "the most important [. . .] form" of madness, namely, by "[Romanesque] identification," whose "features were fixed once and for all by Cervantes" (1998b, 28).[2] Mad because he has read too much, Mattos reproduces the very kind of madness that is Don Quixote's: a "punishment of knowledge" (Foucault 1988b, 26). Both heroes partake in the classic tradition of madness as punitive consequence of an excess of literacy. But madness is not only a consequence of knowledge, "madness fascinates because it is knowledge" itself (Foucault 1988b, 21). After all, madness produces meaning. It matters little if that meaning remains unintelligible for some. The ability to hold knowledge and meaning, (i.e., the monopoly of truth), is one of the main attributes of mythical individualism in Anglo-American sleuths. "The madman often tells the truth" the proverb goes; or, as Foucault claims, since the late Medieval theatre "the Madman [. . .] stands center stage as the guardian of the truth" (1988b, 14). Nevertheless, like Don Quixote, madness will not bring success to Mattos in the same way that holding the monopoly of truth once did to Anglo-American detectives. Instead, his madness leads to his failure.

Schnaiderman notes the influence of Cervantes in the shaping of Mattos: he describes the detective as "a bit Quixotic in his rallies and attempts to humanize the treatment of inmates" (2). Schnaiderman is surely thinking of the passage in Cervantes's novel in which Don Quixote famously releases a chain of galley slaves. Mattos is mad for the same reasons as the Spanish knight, who is perceived by the freed prisoners as somebody who "was not quite right in his head as he had committed such a vagary as to set them free" (Cervantes 311). In these terms, one of Cervantes's Spanish guards expresses his astonishment at the situation: "He wants us to let the king's prisoners go, as if we had any authority to release them, or he to order us to do so!" (309). With both Mattos and Don Quixote, what is perceived as madness is their individualism unleashed against the world, their common delusion of believing that they can wield force in front of the state. When he is first confronted with the galleys, Don Quixote gets puzzled. Sancho, who does not suffer from symbolic illiteracy and is thus well versed in practical things, explains: "That is a chain of galley slaves, on the way to the galleys by force of the king's orders" (297), to which Don Quixote responds with his well-known naiveté: "Is it possible that the king uses force against anyone?" (297). Both Mattos and Don Quixote express themselves as if their authority were higher than it actually is. Don Quixote acts as though he were more powerful than the Spanish King; Mattos acts as though he were mightier than the Brazilian President.

This is what defines their common madness: an individualistic delusion of grandeur, that prevents them from functioning in the world. It excludes them from the world, in Foucauldian terms, by including them in the imaginary community of the heroic madmen. The crumbling of the hitherto stable *ego*'s agency and *mundus*'s force produces a new *mundus* in which not only one *ego* but many egos are diluted. Whereas the knight errant releases the galley slaves because he believes he must succor these "unfortunates who against their will were being carried where they had no wish to go" (219), the reasons behind Mattos's investment in the prisoners' freedom remain a mystery. At the same time, in releasing the inmates, Mattos becomes, like Don Quixote, a myth of individualism.

Like Cervantes's myth, Mattos acts not only because of too much reading but also as a result of grief: whereas Don Quixote grieves the lost world of chivalric romance, Mattos mourns Vargas. The president's suicide letter famously reads: "I take my first step on the road to eternity. I leave life to enter history." But what is "entering history" reduced to once Vargas is dead? A suicide letter, which for any other individual would mean the ultimate trace of intimacy, becomes a narration of the Brazilian state, a story that shapes the ways readers should understand history. Examining the role this letter has in Fonseca's novel can shed more light on the crumbling so far examined: *ego contra mundum*, individualistic agency against state force, madness and knowledge.

## THE BRAZILIAN STATE: MUNDUS CONTRA MUNDUM

### Historiography and Mythology

Vargas's suicide letter ends paradoxically with a sentence that indicates not closure but inception: "Entering history," which only seems to be possible after exiting it. The man's death paves the way for the birth of myth. After all, Fonseca reminds us how other politicians considered Vargas an ageless man (31), i.e.,: eternal. This is precisely how French theorist Roland Barthes defines "myth," as something that "deprives the object of which it speaks of all History. [. . .] In it, history evaporates" (152). Hence, as English historian James Dunkerley notes, "history," in Vargas's letter, points not so much to the past as to the future, not "the general history of the past but the particular history of the great" (30). The letter aims to shape Brazil's future in a very distinct way: "The only future [Vargas] provides for is one under his shadow" (30).

In the novel, the leader's shadow affects, first and foremost, Mattos. Through the affective encounter between the politician's corpse and the detective's sick body, Fonseca somehow amalgamates their figures. The coupling of Vargas/Mattos becomes only prominent when the inspector sneaks into the presidential palace, looking for the president's corpse, while "his stomach ached [. . .] He needed to see Getúlio's body" (Fonseca 268). Here, again, the connection between Mattos's ulcer and the internecine conflicts of Brazilian history are explicit. It is almost as if some part of Mattos has died with the leader, re-signifying what he meant only a few days earlier when he told one of his girlfriends that the president was part of his life (256).

The investigator yearns for contact with the president's corpse before its burial, but their encounter is filled with negative affect, which in turn produces symbolic disabilities. Hastening to leave the ground floor of the Catete palace, which is filled with a multitude that endures symbolic unintelligibility, while "moving to and fro, yelling incomprehensible orders" (269), Mattos finally reaches Vargas's bedroom. Except that he is symbolically blinded, seeing the body but missing the face, as he glimpses precariously between the bedroom's ajar door and the restless multitude. The impossibility of seeing a face amounts to a cancellation of what the French philosopher Emmanuel Levinas calls a "face-to-face" ethics. Without the encounter between Vargas/Mattos's faces, there is a rupture of "the conjuncture of the same and the other" (80), there is no "direct and full face welcome of the other by me" (80). Something gets broken in Mattos in this instant of symbolic blindness, since it is immediately thereafter that he releases the prisoners, almost as if it were its direct consequence.

Mattos's rebellion amounts to a kind of symbolic (mythical) suicide that echoes Vargas's real (historical) suicide. Unlike his leader, Mattos does not kill himself. Nonetheless, his act of releasing the inmates is similar to what Dunkerley defines as "political suicide," i.e.,: "the self-destruction of a political career, policy or party rather than a life" (1). Indeed, his self-destructive drive is not gratuitous. In his last words to Mattos, Pádua asks him whether he knew that August 24th is Saint Bartholomew's Day. The reference to this figure of Christian hagiography alludes to martyrdom, which is often a key component not only of religious history but also of political suicides. "For the faithful," says Dunkerley, "political suicide constitutes a final terrestrial act of vindication of both person and cause" (13). So, it is for the secular Mattos but also for Vargas. It is in this sense that St. Bartholomew finds an echo now in Rosalvo's words, as he concludes that thanks to his suicide, the president would now turn into another saint (Fonseca 271).

Through his death, Vargas becomes a secularized version of a central component of Christianity, that Dunkerley attributes to Salvador Allende only but I believe that also applies to the Brazilian leader. Martyrs project "an image of resurrection" (Dunkerley 19–20), the eternal continuity of the Messiah, the personalist leader, the all-pervasive father who never abandons his orphans despite his absence. Watt concludes that myths "persist in our memories, and in some sense even become a part of us; they are [. . .] larger than life" (233). According to Esposito, "personhood [. . .] is that which, in the body, is more than body" (2012, 11). In the figure of a personalist leader, this "corporeal surplus" is even more pronounced, since the person of the leader survives the death of the body through mythification. Thus, Vargas will not be perceived by his survivors as another statesman, another irrelevant and forgotten proper name that only can be captured by a history textbook. He will be perceived instead as a myth who, like martyrs, will have to be venerated (with all the corresponding rituals) and remembered. The issue is by whom?

## MULTITUDE AND PEOPLE

Beyond his death, what is the actual component that sanctifies Vargas? The answer can be found in Rosalvo's rant, as he blames the military for not having let the aged president die alone, falling into disgrace by his own merits. Instead, they "backed him up against the wall, without giving him a chance" (Fonseca 271). Whereas before the people were already starting to demystify Vargas, the suicide restored his historical stature. This is why, in *Agosto* the Brazilian state is a suicidal state, a state whose members go against each other, which in Rosalvo's words appears in the military going against the very institution it believes it upholds, creating a sort of *mundus contra mundum.*

Paradoxically, this suicidal state produces a new mythical *ego* in the figure of Vargas, a problematic personalist leader that the state eventually attempts to destroy but only ends up magnifying. In turn, this new myth returns the favor by reassuring the state's continuity. In a way, the myth of the Father of the Poor, Fonseca is telling us, can be read as what Roland Barthes calls "a myth of Order" (150). Vargas's letter states his aim of "being always with you" (qtd. in Dunkerley 30). But who exactly is this "you," the recipient of the leader's company? Precisely, the agent that makes Vargas holy: "the people," who will put their leader's picture on the wall again. Right before the suicide, the narrator reminds us that the reputation of the president's administration had been declining and that August "hit its lowest level of popular approval" (Fonseca 246). The President's suicide renews his crumbling contract with his people, including the previously apolitical Mattos. Individualism gets diluted in them but at the same time gets enhanced in the individual figure of Vargas, the statesman.

In his treatise on *The Social Contract*, Jean-Jacques Rousseau already contemplates the "mortality" of the state: "The body politic, as well as the human body, begins to die as soon as it is born" ("The Death of the Body Politic"). What is interesting about this analogy is the inherently self-destructiveness of both bodies. Rousseau does not see the state's death as a consequence of warfare with other states for instance. Instead, the state "carries in itself the causes of its destruction" ("The Death of the Body Politic"). In Fonseca's novel, Rousseau's analogy becomes more literal since the death of the statesman seems to entail the downfall of the state he embodies. In Latin American presidentialist democracies, when personalist leaders such as Vargas die the stability of the state seems to be at stake. Something similar happened more recently when Néstor Kirchner (2010) or Hugo Chávez (2013) did. For Rousseau, states often return to life because of legislative power: the legislature, that for the Swiss philosopher fulfills the function of the heart, guarantees the preservation of the state. Fonseca suggests the continuity of the Brazilian state after 1954 in quite different terms, namely, in direct relation not with impersonal institutions but with the executive branch, the personalist mark that the presidentialist leader leaves in his people.

Paolo Virno distinguishes two competing concepts that are fundamental to read *Agosto*. On the one hand, the Spinozian notion of "multitude" points to "a *plurality which persists as such* in the public scene, in collective action, in the handling of communal affairs, without converging into a One" (2004, 21). On the other hand, the Hobbesian concept of "the people" which "is somewhat that is *one*, having *one will*, and to whom one action may attributed" (Hobbes, qtd. in Virno 2004, 22; Virno's italics). The contrast between the multitude's heterogeneous multiplicity and the people's homogeneous unity is not the only difference between the two. Virno says that, according to Hobbes, the people follow a specular logic, constituting a transparent mirror of the state, becoming its "reverberation," its "reflection" (22). The multitude, instead, "shuns political unity, resists authority," but more importantly it "does not enter into lasting agreements, never attains the *status* of juridical person because it never transfers its own natural rights to the sovereign" (23). To sum up, "the multitude is anti-state, but precisely for this reason, anti-people" (23). Both cannot coexist at the same time and space: "if there are people, there is no multitude; if there is a multitude, there are no people" (23). What is interesting about this distinction is the inability of the multitude to "enter into lasting agreements" (23). Unlike the people, the multitude cannot sign contracts.

When Vargas commits suicide, he renews a contract with his constituency, but in doing so transforms the multitude of bodies that accompanies his coffin into what Hobbes defines as "the people." In turn, his people preserve and justify the existence of the state. The change of category is not a mere semantic distinction, in that it is charged with a fundamental political difference. If it is impossible to contract (to tame) the multitude, the personalist leader's suicide could be read as a renewal of the bond that unites him with his people, as well as a conservative reconstitution of the state. Ultimately, after the riots following Vargas's suicide are contained, everything goes on as usual in Rio de Janeiro. Fonseca encapsulates this restitution of order in the novel's final paragraph, which ends with the weather forecast for August 26th 1954, an image of routine and continuity par excellence. *Agosto* seems to suggest that Vargas's suicide, despite being perceived as leaving chaos behind actually reestablishes unity, reinstating boundaries that otherwise would have been breached. That is what Rosalvo means when he moans about the aborted withdrawing of Vargas's picture from the wall by the people.

After releasing the prisoners, Mattos joins the multitude flooding the president's funeral. While they carry Vargas's coffin, they cry out loud the very name of their leader (a proper noun considered to be sacred) to compensate for his absence. Following Gramsci, Marx, and Derrida, Indian philosopher Gayatri Spivak engages with the notion of the subaltern in direct relation with proper nouns. According to her, the reason why subalterns cannot speak is that they do not own a name; they can only be named through their representative: "the absence of the non-familiar artificial collective proper name is supplied by the only proper name 'historical tradition' can offer—the patronymic itself—the Name of the Father" (73).

Like subalterns, the multitude, an anonymous and orphan entity that cannot be constituted or defined by a person, (in other terms, an agent that cannot be personified), does not own a "collective proper name." But unlike subalterns (or the people), the multitude's impossibility to have a name assigned remains impervious even in front of a leader. Once a collective group can be named, i.e.,: defined, it is no longer a multitude. After all, a prerequisite for signing a contract is having a signature, i.e.,: a proper name. The transformation from the multitude to the people can only happen with this assignation of a proper noun. This is why in Hobbesian terms, the contract between the state and the people is symmetrical and specular: because the people can only exist as long as it is named by its paternalistic and personalist statesman, the sovereign, the masculine embodiment of the state. In the same way that Marx showed the extent to which "a man *named* Napoleon would restore" the French people's "glory" (Spivak's italics 73); Fonseca uses these "patriarchal metaphorics" (Spivak 73) to show how "historical tradition" operates in the mythification of the Brazilian "father of the poor." By "entering history," Vargas, like Louis Bonaparte, restores the mirage of "glory." His proper name becomes a signifier that gives meaning not only to his own legacy but also to the Brazilian people and, therefore, to the preservation of the Brazilian state beyond his death.

Even when the military tries to disperse the multitude, Mattos stays with them. As Virno points out, "in the absence of the state, there is no people" (2004, 22): when the coffin is taken away to be buried, the personalist leader's presence fades away, turning the people temporarily into the multitude again, which in turn endures sheer symbolic muteness: "A sudden, eerie silence fell over the crowd" (Fonseca 275). The fact that the multitude cannot speak may be read as a twofold crisis of representation, that is simultaneously political and literary. Contrasted with the people, the multitude now seems nothing but a group of bodies left alone in their orphanhood. The absence of the representation of a leader mirrors their literary silence. But this silence vanishes (along with the multitude itself), when they shout his name. The elegiac apostrophe produces a renewal of the contract between the personalist leader and its constituency beyond death.

"I leave to the ire of my enemies the legacy of my death [. . .] the answer from the people will come later . . . " (270), reads the note said to be found on the president's deathbed. The note echoes another personalist leader's last words, which are often misattributed to Eva Perón (because it is the epitaph on her tomb) but belong in fact to Túpac Katari, the indigenous Aymara leader: "I die but will return tomorrow as thousand thousands" (Robin & Jaffe, 199). The fabricated message enhances Vargas's myth and gives meaning to martyrdom. This is, after all, what "entering history" means: I may have died but my mythical stature will prevail in my people, who survive me and will act in my name; I, the incarnation of the state, may temporarily be absent, but the continuity of the state remains assured in them. This renewal of the contract has a twofold effect: it reinforces the crumbling state and it suppresses the possibility of a boundless multitude, rioting in the streets, destabilizing social order.

We must only observe how this *multidão* (the original Portuguese uses this word, whereas the English translation often features the more neutral word "crowd") behaves early on in the novel, when it faces the uncharismatic opposition leader, Lacerda. Having survived the attack on his life, he publicly addresses them at the headquarters of his political party, failing to contain their anger. "The shouts from the [multitude] drowned out his words" (Fonseca 148; translation modified), says the narrator. The multitude's boundless voice eclipses the politician's, even when the latter is amplified by a loudspeaker. Vargas's nemesis ends up suffering symbolic muteness, his "inaudible words" (148) being replaced by the national anthem, a paradigmatic instance of the nation-state. The contrast with the funeral scene is evident: there is a disconnect between the leader and the multitude, whose "wrath did not subside" (148), resulting in riots and police repression. Unlike Vargas, Lacerda fails to be in tune with the multitude. The different outcomes of the two scenes show what is often absent in history textbooks, which often reduce their narration of the past to the enumeration of proper names and sheer chronology: that personalist leaders and dates like August 1954 only enter history as long as they are symbolically fed by the multitude.

As Zizek reminds us, following Lacan, "symptoms are by definition never 'innocent'" ("From Jouce-the-Symptom"). Mattos knows what he is doing when he releases the prisoners. Like Don Quixote, Mattos knows he is not insane. He is just using his symptoms (his ulcer, his "madness") to unleash his individualistic drive. Similarly, when Vargas writes that he "enters history" by dying, that is not a pointless act but a self-inscription in the national mythology that the people will recapture. As Waldemer concludes in his reading of *Agosto*, "the violent demise of an important public figure such as Getúlio Vargas is precisely the sort of phenomenon that historiography has tended to privilege" (38). According to him, the novel reminds us that when, "Vargas chose his dramatic exit, he displayed a sound understanding of how history and historiography operate" (38), namely, by producing myths. Dunkerley notes that Vargas's political suicide "was motivated by the loss of power" (27). By using their symptoms, Mattos and Vargas reinstate lost power to project their *ego* above the state. But whereas Mattos's individualism aims to destroy the state; Vargas's strengthens it.

The problematic *Doppelgänger* relationship that connects Mattos with Vargas suggests that the personalist ex-dictator and president, has not only entered history, but also national mythology. Whereas historiography aspires to deal with facts in a scientific way, in order to reveal "truth"; mythology understands myths as sheer language, as narratives that once claimed to seek "truth" but became not facts but artifacts. Vargas's death exceeds the notion of "fact": his suicide turns his life (and legacy) into a monument that overflows rational knowledge. His letter claims that his death cannot be reduced to a date; it is not just data; it is also an encounter between the leader and the people that produces affect.

Furthermore, it is an encounter that does not have to be final, because myths can always be revisited. Myths happen to operate effectively not only in literature but also in certain accounts of history that privilege personalities and their proper nouns over more complex multitudinous process. For instance, what happens to historiographic accounts that take Vargas's letter itself as a document? The authenticity of this letter, Dunkerley reminds us, has been often disputed. Does Vargas's letter belong to the realm of fiction, literature, myth? To what extent can it be considered a document, an aseptic fact? Can *Agosto* itself be considered a document that speaks about Brazil in the 1950s? With this historical novel, Fonseca puts at center stage the thin line that separates what is fake from what is real, history from literature.

In Virno's terms, on the other hand, positivist accounts mimic the renewal of the state's contract: they eliminate the complex and dynamic notion of multitude, turning them into the static Hobbesian notion of the people. "Static" not only in the sense that it is not proactive, but also in the sense that it cannot be understood without the state. Historiography, especially positivist approaches, by definition, aims to reconstruct history in an aseptic way, like the automaton that Mattos first thinks policemen should be. Often neglecting the intellectual paradigm shift produced by the linguistic turn, historiographic accounts, still in the twenty-first century, claim their right to truth, or at least, they posit a closer perspective from which historians can observe history, more privileged, for instance, than novelists. In a nutshell, historiography aspires to act like a mirror, a symbol that according to Foucault epitomizes madness: "a mirror which, without reflecting anything real, will secretly offer the man who observes himself in it the dream of his own presumption" (1988b, 27). Fonseca seems to agree with Foucault in that, like madness, historiography "deals not so much with truth and the world, as with man and whatever truth about himself he is able to perceive" (27).

To put it differently, historiography, despite its scientific aspirations, is not so different to mythology. One definition of myth, according to Watt, is that they aim to respond "factual or rational questions" (228). They are an interpretation of *mundus*. Both history and myth, ultimately, are narratives that use language to give these hermeneutical accounts of the world. They also share their relationship with time: "one of most important functions of myth is that it anchors the present in the past" (Cohen, qtd. in Watt 233). So is the aim of historical novels, but also of any historiographical account. Through the distorted reflection of Mattos on Vargas, Fonseca erases the boundaries that historiography sets to distinguish itself from mythology. In *Myth and Meaning*, Lévi-Strauss wonders: "When we try to do scientific history, do we really do something scientific, or do we too remain astride our own mythology in what we are trying to make as pure history?" (1978, 18). Fonseca's *Agosto* seems to ask the very same question. But, whereas for the French anthropologist, "history has replaced mythology and fulfils the same function" (18), Fonseca seems to be closer to Barthes, for whom there is no real substantial difference between mythology and historiography. This is perhaps Fonseca's comment on historiographic narrations: he believes that historiographic accounts are, like Barthes's myths, basically made of "language" (9). In his semiologic analysis, Barthes claims that "the very principle of myth" is to "transform history into nature" (128). Similarly, historiography renders invisible the ties that it maintains with the ambiguous nature of language.

For Waldemer, the meaning of failure lies precisely in this tension between mythology and historiography. According to him, Mattos's "ultimate failure," combined with "the novel's anticlimactic conclusion" (37) is related to a statement that Fonseca wants to make about history: Mattos fails, so Waldemer claims, because his "history of the crime is consigned to oblivion, not because his interpretations of events is insignificant or incorrect, but simply because it will never enter the official record" (37). Mattos fails, despite having solved the case, because, unlike Vargas, he does not manage to enter history. "Here *Agosto* reminds the reader that historically marked phenomena, prior to 'becoming history,' are themselves potentially evanescent, escaping oblivion only because they are recorded and accorded privileged meaning" (37). At this point, the *Doppelgänger* finds a chasm, where Vargas and Mattos can no longer be amalgamated.

Indeed, there is here as Waldemer points out a "critique of official history's presumed authority" (33). Understanding documents as reliable evidence, historiography often deliberately forgets that in order to access facts it must use language. And words can lead to mirages, distorted mirrors, symbolic illiteracies that often display temptations, such as reproducing personalism through personifications, neglecting the role of the boundless and anonymous multitude. As Barthes puts it, "myth does not deny things, on the contrary, its function is to talk about them; simply, it purifies them, it makes them innocent, it gives them a natural and eternal justification" (143).

It is no coincidence that one of the epigraphs that introduces *Agosto* is from Carlo Ginzburg, a historian who fought against this positivist conception of history, which, like myths, naturalizes events and sanitizes personalities. Fonseca seems to say that historiography, not only literature, ends up obscuring history, because both share the same aesthetic charms, which is closely linked to what Barthes calls the "relation of deformation" that links myth and meaning (121). A kindred relation maintains histography with the true history it purports to portray: it manipulates its object of study through distortion, for instance, by amplifying the figure of a politician over the role of the agent that put him in that place: the multitude.

If "entering history" expresses the extent to which the state prolongs its presence through time; a close reading of the depiction of the Brazilian state in *Agosto* exhibits the way it also colonizes its subjects in space.

## PRIVACY AND COMMUNITY

The Brazilian state appears in Fonseca's *Agosto* visibly spatialized. The plot unfolds in Rio de Janeiro, then the country's capital. The constant presence of the city and its urban spaces cites the all-pervasiveness of the state. Wherever the city is represented, the state reaches that space too. What is interesting about this novel is that state power features mainly not in public but private spaces. This physicality of power, often represented in the façade of public monumental buildings like the Catete Palace itself, is here funneled to that space where whatever is public is supposed to be cancelled out: intimacy. Throughout the novel, the all-pervasiveness of Brazilian state power reaches the utmost intimate corners of the city: brothels filled with politicians coming from the congress that is located on the other side of the street; a small jail; the bedrooms of the president and the inspector, etc.

*Agosto* evidences what French philosopher Louis Althusser claims in his definition of the modern liberal state: namely, that it "is neither public nor private" (244), but permeates both poles indistinctly. Mattos, one of the incarnations of the state in the novel, sways between these two poles, not knowing "what his world" is, feeling "like a stranger in his nebulous world and in the world of others, too" (Fonseca 257). In short, he is alienated both from *ego* and *mundus*. Similarly, the spatial representations of the Brazilian state show the extent to which its power violates the porous boundaries between public and private, neutralizing their distinction, offering a variation: *Agosto* features not only the traditional rivalry of an *ego* against the state, but also the state against itself, a sort of *mundus contra mundum*.

It is in this sense that *Agosto is a critique not only of positivist historiography but, once more, of* contractualist theory. After all, it was Hobbes who famously defined the "state of nature" as a war of all against all, a *bellum omnium contra omnes*. Yet the Rio de Janeiro depicted in this novel is not a lawless territory. By contrast, its *mundus contra mundum* points to a conflictive albeit thoroughly organized social order. This distinguishes *Agosto* from its counterparts: not only subjects but also the capital city incarnates the post-dictatorial state, a liberal democracy that fails to accomplish what social contracts aspire to: namely, consensus not only between the leader(s) and their people but also between leaders themselves. The overwhelming presence of the city shows the structural criminality of the state that paradoxically can ricochet against itself. Ultimately, it is one of the most intimate members of the president's staff, his own bodyguard Gregório Fortunato, who ends up destabilizing Vargas's government and causing his downfall. A downfall that in the long term would have lasting consequences since a decade later, after the coup against Goulart, it would end up delegitimizing any attempt of progressivism in Brazilian politics for almost forty years.

Fortunato is introduced as a "voluminous body" filling a "small elevator" leading to the third floor of the presidential palace, where Vargas's "modest bedroom" (Fonseca 2) is located. The defeat of Vargas's government is somehow announced in this slippage between content and container captured here by the Black Angel's large body in a space he barely fits. Fortunato is characterized by his inability to fit in interior spaces, not only in his workplace but also, according to his wife, "he was becoming a visitor in his own home" (31). Everything about the bodyguard is bigger than it should be, even his own pictographic representation: after he is incriminated, a newspaper features a "large photo" (85) of him, almost as if it would overflow the front page. Like the crooked cops Pádua and Rosalvo, Fortunato is a rogue element of the state, a state that cannot contain itself just as it fails to contain the multitude without transforming it into a people.

Therefore, Fonseca does something new: he does not dismember the state; he enlarges it. Instead of portraying its selective absence, he pictures its overwhelming presence. Perhaps for this reason Fonseca introduces *Agosto* not only through an epigraph from Carlo Ginzburg but also by the famous definition of history from James Joyce's hero Stephen Daedalus in *Ulysses*: like history, the state's presence, too, seems a nightmare from which every character in the novel tries (but fails) to awake. In turn, Joyce's citation echoes Marx's opening of his essay on Louis Bonaparte: "the tradition of all past generations weighs like an Alp upon the brains of the living" (1852, 1).[3] It is in this regard that Fonseca's *Agosto* could not be timelier: the Brazilian state, a state whose nightmarish past does not allow emancipation, a state that cannot help but to destroy itself repeatedly.

Beyond this singularity, Fonseca does share a significant element with his counterparts: his use of literary distortions, which I have been naming "symbolic disabilities." Fortunato, like the Brazilian state, has an elephantiasic body whose limbs are symbolically swollen, unable to be seized inside the scarce spaces that the Catete Palace has to offer. Be it its "small elevator" or the presidential "modest bedroom," the fact that the bodyguard cannot be easily accommodated in these spaces points beyond a mere anecdotal description of his body's features. Equally, the adjectives are there not as an innocent evocation of a character that most of the novel's readers would recall from their own youth. Whereas Vargas plans to enter history, the state's officers cannot enter nor even easily remain within the official space they have been assigned because the state is unable to contain itself.

Vargas's suicide takes place in the very same "modest bedroom" that Fortunato guards at the beginning of the novel. The bedroom is located at Catete Palace, then the president's residential mansion. During the dictatorship, in 1970, the building was turned into the "Museu da República" that still today features Vargas's blood-stained pajamas, a metonymy of intimacy, as one of its most prominent elements. Dying in his bedroom is the fate that Vargas shares with Mattos (who gets killed that same day), as well as with Paulo Gomes Aguiar, the victim in the case that Mattos is investigating and that triggers the whole plot, twenty-four days earlier. Bedrooms hold physical boundaries that aspire to produce intimacy. In *Agosto* they are constantly violated. There is no room for privacy in the novel, as is shown when Alice "violates" Mattos's personal space, redecorating his house, and entangling him with her husband, who is the criminal that the Inspector is (unknowingly) after. When Alice moves into his apartment, she interrupts the typical domestic *vacuum* in which myths of modern individualism are embedded, destroying the detective's isolation and detachment from *mundus*.

Another example can be found when Mattos goes back home only to be assassinated in his own bedroom by the murderer of the case he is investigating: Chicão, "a powerfully built and angry-looking" Afro-Brazilian man who looks like Fortunato (Fonseca 170). In another clear case of a problematic *Doppelgänger* between individuals and state officers, it is no coincidence that Chicão's name features the masculine suffix-*ão*, an augmentative of "Chico," a pseudonym of the proper name Francisco. This augmentative is a morphological articulation of the enlargement of the ever-present state. Chicão, a distorted reflection of the state (as Mattos mistakes him for Fortunato), enters Mattos's house without even having to force the door.

Perhaps the most eloquent example of the state's intrusive presence in its people's intimacy comes when Mattos himself enters Vargas's bedroom, without even having to show his credentials, protected by the chaos surrounding the Catete Palace: "The reception area was deserted." There "was only the bronze statue of the Indian Ubirajara grimacing in rage" (268). Here the confused multitude overshadow the traditional physicality of the state—encapsulated in the bronze statue. The deserted reception enables a state officer to invade the president's room without even having to confirm his identity. An identity that, thanks to Mattos's political suicide of releasing the prisoners, is about to crumble and becomes here, as a prophecy, depersonalized, invisible. Mattos accesses the core of the government without even having to prove how he belongs to the state. In the crime scene, one of the forensics recognizes him, and does not wonder about his presence at the scene. Again, there is no coincidence here: Mattos's presence in the intimate space is perceived as natural because the all-pervasiveness of the Brazilian post-dictatorial state (here incarnated in the inspector) has become all-too naturalized in daily life to the extent that nobody questions it.

The constant permeation, the unrestricted circulation of state agents, shows the extent to which citizens try to maintain a separation from each other by seeking refuge in intimacy, but they fail. Mattos tries to keep his immunity to corruption, thinking highly of himself, believing that he is removed from the world. Nevertheless, he is actually connected with everyone as much as anyone else. This is why he ends up joining the multitude in the end and why he gets to access Vargas's room so freely. Similarly, Vargas tries but fails to maintain his separation from the state's rogue elements or the pressure of the military that wants to oust him. In *Agosto*, *mundus* cannot help but go against *mundum* from within, without clearly demarcating a separate entity.

## FINAL THOUGHTS: COMMUNITY AND CORRUPTION

Beyond this excess of spatialization, Fonseca portrays the Brazilian state as an entity whose parties are inextricable from each other. August of 1954 in Brazil can be definitely read through Walter Benjamin's notion of "a moment of danger" (2003, 391), a delicate historical instant in which the Brazilian state experienced a systematic crumbling, a disintegration of its constituent elements (both its representatives and its people). For Benjamin, the "danger" behind this instant was the appropriation of the past by constituted power, the instrumentation of history as "the tool of the ruling classes" (391). Fonseca rewrites the past not by trying to reconstruct thoroughly the ways things happened. Instead, he snatches the past from historians narrating his own biographic and historical memory of Vargas's suicide, and re-appropriating this moment that, as Benjamin feared, was used as a tool by constituted power.

What is interesting is that Fonseca does so by putting center stage a political phenomenon that could never have been praised by contractualist theorists or positivist historians: corruption. Since, in *Agosto,* it is corruption that is the only binding agent that keeps everything and everyone together, the sole element that agglutinates the crumbling state and produces community. Addressing corruption is one of the many genre conventions that features in detective stories, especially since the origins of hard-boiled fiction. But there is something different about *Agosto*. In the other books here discussed, corruption was perceived as a malignant element that is inseparable from a criminal state against which private detectives would fight. Here, by contrast, corruption, first resisted but later embraced by the public detective, generates not only negative but also positive affective encounters. Corruption brings not only self-destruction at the hands of rogue elements of the state like Fortunato; it also brings connection. It is only after Mattos relinquishes his immunity to corruption, it is only when he, too, becomes corrupt (like Fortunato, Pádua or Rosalvo), that he is able to release prisoners who otherwise would be unfairly imprisoned. Conversely, it is only when he lets himself mix with others that are somehow stained by corruption (like Alice or Vargas and his constituency), in other words, only when he becomes the multitude, that he reconciles with himself.

Fonseca rewrites the *Gemeinschaft-Gesellschaft* dichotomy proposed by the German sociologist Ferdinand Tönnies. Whereas *Gemeinschaft* describes rural societies, organized with ties that are personal, motivated and mutually indispensable; the *Gesselschaft* involves urban societies, organized with ties that are impersonal, arbitrary and responding individualism. Tönnies distinguishes communities from societies in that the former are defined by intimacy: a *Gemeinschaft* is first and foremost "all intimate, private, and exclusive living together" (33).

In the Rio de Janeiro of the 1950s portrayed in *Agosto*, the Brazilian state appears as a criminal network that ultimately does not truly differ from a community. A state that has the keys to all the bedroom doors in which "intimate and private" life happens. A state that entangles all its members, making them dependent on each other, paradoxically, because they follow their own individualistic self-interest. During the past few decades, in many transitions to democratic regimes in Latin America, corruption has been closely linked to individualistic self-interest. Corruption defined the systematic illicit gain of rogue elements of the state (as in Collor de Melo's administration in Brazil [1990–1992] or in Ménem's administration in Argentina [1990–1999], among many others). More recently, corruption was cynically used as an electoral weapon by constituted power to impeach, imprison or delegitimize progressive democratic leaders (Dilma Rousseff in 2013, Lula da Silva in 2018, Cristina Fernández de Kirchner since 2015 to today). In *Agosto*, instead, corruption is tied not solely to self-interest but to what seems to be its opposite: community. There is a democratization of corruption in the novel that breaks with its monopoly at the hands of constituted power in the same way that the fictionalization of the past democratizes history and releases it from the conservative temptations of historiography.

In this twofold democratization, as well as in all the other singularities that seem to distinguish the Brazilian state, there is a claim of the implausibility of the contractualist theory in which not only Southern Cone constitutional republics were built but also their very models. In Latin America, along with "every politician is corrupt," there is often a commonplace that claims that the state is permanently absent. As a result of this absence, this commonplace insists, the state fails to protect the people from themselves. Fonseca, by contrast, shows the opposite. This opposition of absence and presence can be seen in many ways. An absent state does not speak, for instance, as it can be glimpsed in the common symbolic muteness of the Argentine and Chilean state in Piglia and Bolaño. But this opposition can also be read in the relationship that the authors establish with history: whereas in *Plata quemada* el Gaucho Dorda and his partners "escape history" and in *Estrella distante* Tagle/Wieder becomes a Deleuzian line of flight with his elusive aircraft; here Mattos/Vargas do not escape but rather willingly want to enter history.

Nonetheless, the antithesis proves irrelevant because in *Agosto*, the state is tangible in every corner of private life. Despite that, it fails to contain itself and serve its population in the very same way as absent states. Therefore, despite these differences, the authors that I have examined deal with a common problem. By re-elaborating the Argentine, Chilean and Brazilian post-dictatorial experiences and their conflicts with Contractualism, they all reveal what remains concealed in the literary representation of Anglo-American states read in the first chapter: the manufactured dimension of the foundational contract that the apologists of the state claim exists but which, like Vargas's suicidal letter, proves to be sheer mythology.

In the next and last chapter, I will explore the contemporary rewriting of tensions between individualism and state when they are in direct contact with the Mexican-American border. I will examine not only Latin American but also Anglo-American detectives again, now through the lens of a Southern Cone writer such as the Chilean Roberto Bolaño himself. I will show how notions that I have examined, such as symbolic muteness, blindness, illiteracy and unintelligibility, personification, personalism and depersonalization, community and multitude, go a step further in an exacerbation of the poetics of failure.

## Chapter 5

# Coda

## *The Mexican-American Border Seen from Chilean Eyes*

PROJECTING SOUTHERN CONE DICTATORSHIPS
TO NORTH AMERICAN DEMOCRACIES

### From Chile to the Mexican-American Border

"Living in this desert [. . .] is like living at sea. The border between Sonora and Arizona is a chain of [. . .] enchanted islands. The cities and towns are boats. The desert is an endless sea. This is a good place for fish [. . .] not men" (Bolaño 2008, 440–441).[1] This is how Lalo Cura, one of the many state detectives that crowd Roberto Bolaño's *2666*, describes the Mexican-American borderland. Far from Buenos Aires, Montevideo, Concepción, or Rio de Janeiro, Bolaño's novel takes place in Santa Teresa, a fictional town surrounded by the desert. Unrelated to the many homonymous real towns located throughout Mexico or in the south of the United States, Santa Teresa is a token toponomy drawn from Catholic hagiography, that displays at least two layers. On the one hand, it is a tribute to North American hard-boiled tradition: in the 1940s, Canadian author Ross Macdonald named Santa Teresa his fictionalized version of Santa Barbara, California, where his private sleuth Lew Archer operated, following Marlowe's model. On the other hand, Bolaño chooses to set his plot in a vague and fictional town to prevent immediate identification with the city that he is actually talking about: Ciudad Juárez.

At first sight, then, this novel takes place in a desert space unfit for human life, a territory completely alien and diametrically opposed to the mentioned South American urban settings. Nevertheless, deserts, traditionally linked to extreme aridity, are reimagined here in terms of their opposite: the fluid sea. Lalo Cura's aquatic image looks like the antithesis of a desert, the very element that they lack by definition: the water found only in oasis. A desert that is actually an anti-desert, then, Santa Teresa's fluidity points to many elements that would reappear throughout the book. The most obvious is that which porous borders share with big urban spaces: cash flow. In *Plata quemada, Estrella distante,* and *Agosto,* money, (especially dirty money), is an agglutinating element that organizes the social fabric. Equally, imagining the desert as an endless sea resonates with the many aquatic spaces from which the female victims of the crimes portrayed in this book emerge. These spaces follow the logic of what Rita Segato calls "pedagogies of cruelty": the women, reduced to a multitude of dead bodies, appear in streams, oil deposits, even containers filled by nitric acid.

As Brett Levinson and Gareth Williams have noted in their reading of *2666,* the naturalistic brutality of these crimes cannot be separated from one of Bolaño's obsessive *leitmotifs*: the link between political violence in Latin America and Nazism that is already announced in one of his early works, the encyclopedia of fictional far-right-wing writers, *La literatura nazi en América* (1996). A link that would reappear throughout his work, from *Estrella distante* to *2666.* Yet unlike Argentina, Brazil, and especially Chile, neither Mexico nor the United States have experienced fascist dictatorships. Thus, this last chapter will not deal with a series of imports from North to South nor with the circulation of the genre from South to South. Instead, this final case study involves a projection from South to North: a juxtaposition of Southern Cone dictatorships put side by side with the contours of American territory and the crisis of representation produced by feminicidal violence. This desert should be read through a lens that is rooted not only in Mexico or the United States, but in recent Chilean history. A fluid desert has to do more with the German post-war diaspora and its links with the Southern Cone. A desert that is closer to Paul Schäfer's *Colonia Dignidad* and the specters of Erich Priebke, Josef Mengele and Adolf Eichmann wandering in the Patagonia, than to Sonora or Chihuahua.

## AN OBSOLETE RIVALRY

Chapter 1 explored a stable rivalry in which the *ego,* the classic private sleuth, triumphs over a hindering but tamable *mundus,* the image of the Anglo-American state. Chapter 2 noted the ways in which that rivalry was inverted, as a truly monstrous *mundus,* the Argentine state, always defeats a maimed *ego,* divested of all agency. Chapter 3 examined how *Estrella distante* shows how the rivalry starts to crumble and the boundaries between each of its poles get blurrier. Chapter 4 gave an account of an all-pervasive self-destructive *mundus*, the Brazilian state, in which there was no room for individualism, a state that featured a constant violation of intimacy.[2] All these literary re-elaborations of recent history share a transnational, transcultural, and multilingual poetics of failure. In Buenos Aires or in Montevideo, in Concepción, or in Rio de Janeiro, detectives ultimately fail, in one way or another, at the hands of a post-dictatorial state.

The Mexican-American border, a confine where states start and at the same time end, seems alien to this common Southern Cone historical conjuncture. And yet there is in *2666* an exacerbation of the poetics of failure, that has now fully colonized not just individualism but also any possible narrative that could work (even unwillingly) as an apology for the state. In Bolaño's *Estrella distante,* after Pinochet's neoliberal redefinition of the state's contours, the Chilean state's spectrum re-emerges in democratic times more solid than ever to engage in state terrorism to protect its own immunity. Similarly, in Fonseca's description of Brazil in 1954 the state appears to be crumbling but finally survives the death of Vargas, its most important statesman. By contrast, in Santa Teresa individuals and the state are no longer disintegrating; they have already collapsed. In the desert, it is no longer plausible to speak about either individualism or the state.

In a post-NAFTA world, Watt's notion of *ego contra mundum* arrives at its exhaustion, a point of no return. By portraying the asymmetric and selective effects of the distribution of neoliberal depersonalization, Bolaño shows how the narratives that once nurtured these opposing categories are no longer eloquent to explain the world. Even if Bruno Bosteels still reads in the Mexican Paco Taibo's work, "the conflict between the mental superiority of the lonely detective and the essential corruption of the official ruling apparatuses" which "bring us back [. . .] to the old liberal, or anarchist libertarian, dilemma of the individual against the state" (267), in Santa Teresa there is no such dilemma. This asymmetric but stable rivalry, that was first subverted, became gradually blurrier, and started to crumble, no longer exists here and is now completely obsolete to narrate the political and the historical through the lens of detective stories.

## FAILURE AND DEPERSONALIZATION

In the fluid desert of Santa Teresa, what persists beyond this obsolete rivalry is a deepening of a poetics of failure, where "failure" maintains its twofold dimension, both political and aesthetic. What Argentine literary critic Ezequiel De Rosso notes when he describes *Estrella distante* as a "systematic disappointment of the expectations of a reader who is specialized in the genre" (135) is even more evident here. This novel's deliberate refusal to meet the horizon of expectations of the detective genre is related to the refusal of closure. Bolaño's *Estrella distante* at least left room to imagine some sort of closure through the elided execution of Tagle/Wieder. *Estrella distante* and *Agosto* feature *Doppelgängers,* fragmented subjects and occasional depictions of the multitude that sometimes becomes the people. "The Part about Crimes," by contrast, portrays a multiplicity that is even more radical than mere duality or disjointed identities. Despite their problematic personality, the individualistic couplings Tagle/Wieder and Mattos/Vargas could still choose either to melt into or to abandon the multitude as they pleased.

Santa Teresa is a different world altogether. Only seven years separate Bolaño's first detective story from his last one, yet there is a major shift in his literary project. Almost as though he had realized that the narrative strategies, he used to portray the traumas of the Chilean dictatorship, were no longer valid to narrate Latin America, Bolaño uses a different approach to portray the effects of crime in the Mexican-American border. I am not solely alluding to a mere change of setting, but to the degree that depersonalization vanquishes any temptation of personification, the impossibility of creating a solid image of a state. To put it in Benveniste's words that belong to linguistics but can still be understood in political terms, it is as though Bolaño had understood that the "'we' is not a quantified or multiplied 'I'; it is an 'I' expanded beyond the strict limits of the person, enlarged and at the same time amorphous" (1996, 195). In short, the multitude is not made of singularized individual iterations; it is instead a formless expansion of the *ego*.

For this reason, the multitude no longer appears as an optional space to sojourn as a tourist, as Wieder does playfully through his heteronyms or Mattos does when he joins Vargas's followers. Now the multitude is everywhere. Whereas in *Agosto* there was no room to escape the state's presence, in "The Part about Crimes" there is no refuge against the overwhelming power of the multitude. This can be seen in the profusion of characters that crowd the book: detectives, criminals, and a succession of barely distinguishable female victims.

In this novel there is no single detective but all too many, and none of them are heroic, or even anti-heroic. On the one hand, there are the Mexican policemen: Pedro Negrete, chief of Santa Teresa police; his assistant, Epifanio Galindo; Lalo Cura (a play on words that evokes madness), a former drug-dealing thug who is recruited to become a junior patrol officer; Juan de Dios Martínez; and many others. On the other hand, there are the Chicano sheriff of the fictional Huntsville, Harry Magaña, and the ex-FBI agent Albert Kessler. Going further than Fonseca's portrayal of the indistinction between public officers and private sleuth as well as public space and intimacy, Bolaño materializes an even more porous boundary between these poles in his fictional Mexican-American border.

Whereas Magaña and Kessler, for instance, may be public officers in the United States, once on Mexican territory, out of their American jurisdiction, they are no different from a private sleuth and, to a certain extent, vigilantes intruding on another state's sovereignty. This correlation between nationalities and the public and private sector (most Mexicans detectives work for the state; while Americans act as private sleuths) is no coincidence. Mexican officers cite the stiff and slow bureaucracy inherited by and inherent in Hispanic culture, and the American characters allude in part to hard-boiled tradition and more broadly the efficiency and pragmatic characteristics that in Latin America are usually linked to American multinational corporations, institutions, and even military interventions. It is not a coincidence that Bolaño chooses to name the fictional equivalent to El Paso (the American city that neighbors Ciudad Juárez) "Huntsville," a city of hunters.

*2666* is structured in five long chapters. Each, as many critics have noted, pays tribute to different popular genres, which Bolaño adapts and transforms to his own eclectic writing. I will focus on the fourth one, "The Part about the Crimes," which engages with the detective story tradition. The book's longest, this plotless, formless, and complex chapter aims to represent the hundreds of feminicides that have haunted Ciudad Juárez for the past decades.

Starting in 1993, along with the beginning of the implementation of the NAFTA treaty, the reader learns about maquila working-class women heading to work and being murdered in ever more brutal ways. The reader also witnesses a group of local policemen that all too belatedly and slowly take on the task of solving these crimes, inevitably failing every time. The unmanageable multiplicity of the crimes is mirrored in the equally numerous detectives, whose failure grows in proportion to the reader's expectation of closure. The unsatisfied expectations drawn from the failure of local state officers, for instance, increases when policemen from the capital or abroad equally fail to grasp the feminicides, let alone solve them.

This rhetoric of frustrated repetition and accumulation points to socio-economic and historic causes. When American detectives get involved, the reader expects (along with Santa Teresa's characters) that feminicides will finally be stopped. A great deal of 1990s neoliberal policies, such as the NAFTA treaty itself or the Washington Consensus, were informed by such expectations: if we, Latin Americans, cannot solve our conflicts by ourselves, if we are the problem, then opening our borders to foreign investment and multinational corporations, and welcoming institutions located in and regulated by the North (the IMF, the World Bank, the American government, etc.), must surely be the solution. These and other ways in which history informs literature are the main element that this chapter shares with the rest of this book.

## MEXICAN STATE DETECTIVES AND AMERICAN PRIVATE SLEUTHS: IMPOTENT MINDS

### From Knowledge to Depersonalization

Despite its formless and expectation-defying plot, "The Part about the Crimes" does not entirely break with the Latin American detective story tradition. It connects with it in many ways, the most evident of which is the relationship between failed individualism and knowledge. This continuity reappears in the configuration of some of the many detectives that feature in the novel. For instance, the Santa Teresa press defines ex-FBI agent Albert Kessler's legitimacy as an investigator in direct relation to "a tacit acknowledgment": the failure of the Mexican police (2008, 453). Ironically nicknamed an updated version of Holmes, Kessler, the promise both of successful individualism and the benevolence of the neighbor state, holds the monopoly of knowledge: he gives international lectures on crime and works as a consultant for films in which "the good guys always win" (723). However, his theoretical contemplations amount to little when faced with the task before him. For all his erudition, Kessler is yet another spectator of a world that experiences an unintelligible collapse. Ultimately, his knowledge leads to the very same failure that Mexican policemen experience. Kessler is no different than Lönnrot, Renzi, or Mattos, in that he may know a great deal about criminals but cannot really stop them.

Equally, the young Lalo Cura is defined by knowledge, being the only state policeman who reads outdated treatises such as Söderman and O'Donnell's *Modern Criminal Investigation* (1941). Whereas in *Agosto*, madness was in constant tension with rational knowledge; what is "mad" on the Mexican-American border is the very possibility of investigating crime. The books that Lalo reads cause the more experienced Epifanio to admonish him: "Don't you know, you snot-nose bastard, that there is no such thing as modern criminal investigation?" (2008, 414). This echoes what Renzi hears from old Luna in "La loca y el relato del crimen": "What are you going to do with all these papers now? A dissertation?" [. . .] Calm down, kid. Or did you think that we care about semantics in this newspaper?" (2000, 101). Here, too, Bolaño shows a shift in his literary project: whereas in *Estrella distante* knowing how to read snuff movies was still essential for the anonymous author to find Tagle/Wieder, in "The Part about the Crimes," knowledge is a useless delusion, a distracting chess match that succumbs to a *mundus* where only force prevails. Here Bolaño is closer to Piglia and Fonseca as at the same time he goes beyond both them and his own previous work.

A second continuity in Bolaño's novel is the traditional equation of crime and state. This equation appears in Pedro Negrete's encounter with Pedro Rengifo, respectively, the chief of police and one of Santa Teresa's most powerful drug dealers. They treat each other as friends because they are namesakes: both Pedros mirror each other, rendering again the boundaries between law and crime, state officers and drug dealers, indistinguishable. In fact, structural connivance between state and crime pervades the text and points to an unalterable criminal *status quo*. When one of the criminals is thought to have fled Santa Teresa, the American police issues an order to arrest them, but at the same time they do not interrogate any of the "coyotes." The systematic criminal activities practiced both by private and public sector, on the border, they become transnational as it affects agents of society who are involved with both territories: the "coyotes" who help migrants to navigate their clandestine journeys north.

What is original in this novel is to be found less in the rewriting of the tensions between knowledge and failure or the equation of crime and state, than in the more tangible presence of a notion already announced in *Estrella distante* that here takes center stage: depersonalization. To begin with, this can be traced in the way the narrative fleshes out its many investigators and criminals only in a perfunctory way, not focusing on any one in particular. The state officer to whom the novel pays most attention is Juan de Dios Martínez, who as Deckard observes is "one of the more morally invested detectives" (365). Like Fonseca's Mattos, Juan de Dios is the promise of the benevolent state: he is immune to corruption and he sees himself as solely focused in the Quixotic task of undoing wrongs. But whereas Fonseca pays a great deal of attention to Mattos's personality, neither Juan de Dios nor any of his colleagues (Lalo Cura, Epifanio Galindo, etc.) are real protagonists standing out from the other policemen.

"Containing the stories of a teeming number of people," David Kurnick notes, "the novel refuses the orienting perspectivalism of character. The heroic detective simply disappears [. . .]: his witnessing, investigative, emotive, and *collating* functions all migrate to the level of the book's form" (117). The multitude of detectives is but one of the many shapes that the novel takes to express depersonalization: after all, a bunch of useless detectives amounts to no detective at all. As Kurnick claims, "*2666* demands that we take an interpretive distance from the category of the individual. The novel is indeed 'character driven' [. . .], but only in the sense that character here drives beyond itself: Bolaño's individuals relentlessly direct our attention to the structures in which they are enclosed" (118). In other words, when the Chilean author constructs characters, he does so not so much to construct mythic figures as to emphasize the impersonal web of networks in which they are immersed. If Bolaño resorts to personification, he does it to accentuate not individualism but depersonalization.

Kurnick notes that "The Part about the Crimes" lacks a "crusading detective" (116). *Estrella distante* featured detectives that, however reluctant or fragmentary, still constitute a "crusade." Romero and the anonymous narrator's journey through the Chilean diaspora in Europe to find and punish Tagle/Wieder can clearly be read as a path that seeks redemptive closure. So can Renzi's story about the madwoman or Mattos's battle to release the prisoners from the jail. In "The Part about the Crimes," by contrast, crusades are not plausible, because depersonalized subjects are empty and divested of purpose.

Beyond this conspicuous absence, depersonalization appears at a linguistic level. Specifically, with the constant use of the Spanish third person pronoun, *se*, which lacks a clear English equivalent, the closest option being the gender-neutral, and indefinite pronoun "one." Bolaño's pronominal *leitmotif*, thus, often gets lost in Natasha Swimmer's translation, which prefers to use the passive voice or a vague first-person plural pronoun. Spanish linguists Ignacio Bosque and Javier Gutiérrez distinguish two slightly different variations of this pronoun. On the one hand, there are syntactical constructions made with the impersonal pronoun *se* which "lacks an explicit subject" (416). In their treatise on Spanish syntax, they provide a very relevant example of this linguistic oddity: "the sentence *Se vio al criminal salir corriendo* expresses the fact that somebody has seen him, but it does not allude to any specific witness" (416). Therefore, "sentences with *se impersonal* include an implied subject" (416). It is not so much that *se* denies the existence of subjects, rather that *se* makes personhood blurry, keeps it vague, often because it remains unknown even to the speaker. Two of the most important characteristics of the impersonal *se* reside in that "it is circumscribed to an unspecific or indeterminate interpretation" (416) and that "it is circumscribed to people" (416).

On the other hand, we have the passive reflexive *se*, which according to Bosque and Gutiérrez is used in the "typical official language of the government" (419). Whereas recovering the implied subject with the passive reflexive *se* is possible, with the impersonal *se* it is not. They give the example of the sentence "*se firmaron los tratados de paz*," in which the implied subject is substituted by the passive reflexive pronoun *se*, i.e.,: peace treatises were signed (by the ambassadors), for instance (419). The main distinction between these two variations of *se* can be seen in a morphological issue: number. Because the number of agents remains unknown in impersonal sentences, they can only be conveyed in the singular. Passive reflexives can take the plural form because *se* introduces a verb that is in agreement with the objective complement.

Bolaño toys with the blurry boundary that distinguishes the variations of these pronouns. The subject behind one of the novel's *leitmotifs*, *se cerró el caso*, following the criteria established by Bosque and Gutiérrez, is not only implied, it is deliberately ambiguous. At first glance the suggestion is that the case was closed by the police, but the novel's sentences resist personification in specific syntagmata such as "Pedro Negrete," "Lalo Cura" or even the impersonal institution of the fictive Santa Teresa Police as a whole. The agent responsible for closing the case remains unknown. The subjective complement repeatedly remains vacant, implying a multiplicity of potential culprits: drug dealers, the government, corporations, all can wield their force to close a case. At the same time, because the agent remains unknown, there is collective absolution: no one is held responsible. Bolaño's use of the impersonal pronoun is not unpremeditated. It is a morphological articulation of political depersonalization.

After the first feminicide, Negrete asks his staff: "Do we know who she is? [¿*Se sabe quién es*?]," to which "they all said no" (Bolaño 2008, 278). By using *se*, Negrete conceals and reinforces the shield that protects the accountability of individual policemen: all agree to say that nobody knew anything. Even more problematic is that the narrator, too, replicates Negretes's use of impersonality, as if reproducing the official language mentioned by Bosque and Gutiérrez. Of yet another of the unsolved crimes, the narrator says that "the ballistic analysis, which was never made public, was later lost for good [*no se dio a conocer jamás . . . se perdió*]" (280). The impersonal pronoun indicates that nobody in particular has lost the analysis, while at the same time exempting anyone of doing so. Here as elsewhere, *se* systematically denies the possibility of closure at a syntactical level by avoiding the mandate of having to ascribe action to a subject.

This use of the impersonal pronoun is the material way in which depersonalization works as Bolaño's response to individualism, turning it into an "entirely residual" (Kurnick 117) element that no longer holds any mythical dimension. When sentences consistently lack a subject or an agent, actions become orphans: things just happen, events merely take place without anybody to execute them or be accounted for, much like impersonal meteorological phenomena. As Bosque and Gutiérrez note, Spanish verbs are even more charged with impersonality than English ones. *Nieva* or *llueve* are self-sufficient, they do not even require a pronominal subject to express meteorological phenomena, unlike English ("it snows") or even French ("*il neige*") (353). In the same way that we say "it rains" in the impersonal third person (both in English and Spanish), in Santa Teresa women's murders just happen daily, as natural and normal as a rain shower. Women get killed and the language used to describe these killings gives the impression that they are killed "by no one" and that their murders remain unsolved "by no one." Bolaño seems to suggest that the normalization of feminicides (i.e., the process by which they become part of nature) is rooted first and foremost in the depersonalization brought by language.

Esposito deals precisely with the political implications of this impersonal dimension that can be found in language. In his close reading of Benveniste's study of personal pronouns, Esposito focuses in "Benveniste's insistence on the difference of the third person, in both its pronominal and verbal forms, from the first and second person" (2012, 14–15). Unlike *I* or *You*, the third person is the only one that "can be defined as a 'non-person'" (15). Specifically, in Spanish, this is particularly valid not only for the personal pronouns *él/ella* but even more so for the impersonal pronoun *se*, which is a morpheme semantically charged with impersonality. Furthermore, the use of *se* excludes the involvement of whomever pronounces it, connoting "anyone but me." It is used mainly to express lack of agency: nobody does anything to provoke or close cases, cases get closed.

The third person, Esposito claims, is unrelated to the first or the second person, it is rather its negation: "it refers to something, or even to someone, but to a someone who is not recognizable as *this* specific person, either because it does not refer to anyone at all or because it can be extended to everyone" (107). Bolaño's use of *se* dwells between these two poles, "at the point of intersection between no one and anyone" (107). As Benveniste puts it, because the third person "does not imply any person, it can take any subject whatsoever or no subject, and this subject, expressed or not, is never posited as a person" (qtd. in Esposito 107). This definition can be clearly traced in how Bolaño builds characters bereft of their personhood: anyone can commit feminicides and as a result no one is perceived to do.

But what are the implications of depersonalization? It is here when I want to come back to a figure of speech that belongs both to literature and to the system of justice: personification. Diametrically opposed to the impersonal, personification was used since Poe, Doyle and Christie to personify ideas through characters. Whereas the criminal mastermind, like Poe's D—in "The Purloined Letter" or Doyle's Moriarty, embodied evil; their private eyes incarnated the mythical attributes of individualism (personal wit, individual knowledge, etc.), that would restore justice and legality. The very question that defines this early period of the genre relies on personification: the whodunit logic that structures the narrative. The "who" of the question presupposes an individualized subject.

Even if hard-boiled fiction authors like Dashiell Hammett and Raymond Chandler are not so concerned about the enigma of the murderer's identity, they still typically delve into the individual personality of the detective, a unique anti-hero, thus reproducing, albeit in a different way, the mythical attributes of individualism. In fact, Kurnick underlines that in hard-boiled fiction there is already a gesture of depersonalizing crime. He understands "hard-boiled fiction's torque on classic detection as a depersonalization—substituting a systemic criminality (the collusion of state and industry) for an individual mastermind (i.e., Moriarty)—" (117). Unlike Piglia or Fonseca, the Chilean author resists such exploration of the detectives' personality. This is why according to Kurnick "Bolaño takes the process a step further by vaporizing the detective himself" (117). A refusal to resort to personification is here at stake.

Depersonalization is present also in the portrayal of criminals. In the same way that there are no heroic investigators, so there are no well-defined state villains: there is no Tagle/Wieder, no evil dictatorial South American policemen. Beyond their traditional barriers, private detectives and state policemen share a symbolic impotence: they all are bereft of any possibility of wielding force. By depersonalizing individuals and the state, Bolaño does not divest merely individuals of agency, but also the last corners of human condition itself. If there is a villain in the story, it is dissolved in the market, an impersonal social agent that resists personification, because it follows a depersonalized pattern—its most evident metaphor being its invisible hand.

If Poe created a genre that made things (ideas and concepts such as individualism) into persons (characters), Bolaño, a century and a half later, depicts persons as things that serve the market. Through depersonalization, personification becomes commodification. The impotence of wielding force that equally afflicts the characters of "The Part about the Crimes" is insistently portrayed in terms of a series of misunderstandings. In this sense, too, the reader is no longer in Renzi's or Mattos's realm of the mere futility of knowledge, but in that of its impossibility.

## FROM DEPERSONALIZATION TO UNINTELLIGIBILITY

Unintelligibility reappears throughout "The Part about the Crimes," in various guises. To begin with, the anonymous narrator's detailed tone discloses how the meticulous narration of singular crimes "obfuscates more than it reveals" the "illegible unique humanity of each women murdered in Juárez," since "the repetitive prosody [. . .] does not bring into evidence the singularity of the individual lives lost" (Jelly-Schapiro 85), just as it hardly helps the reader to understand feminicides as a structural problem. There is a rupture, between signifiers and their traditionally ascribed meanings, that permeates not only the narrator's voice but the way it depicts its characters. All too often entangled in situations that they cannot grasp even partially, criminals, law officers, bystanders and victims are all affected by symbolic unintelligibility. The narrator's description of one of the murderers as a "clean-looking man, from which it was deduced that he had showered at [his victim] Rebeca's house" (Bolaño 2008, 325) provides precise but irrelevant facts that do not help render things understandable.

Similarly, when one of the murderers confesses unabashedly that he has killed his own mother, his statement as to why he drove a piece of wood into her vagina remains incoherent: "he had done it to teach her [. . .] to take him seriously," he declares to the police, to quickly "lapse into incoherence" (309). In the original, what falls into symbolic unintelligibility is not even the subject but language itself: *sus palabras se volvieron incoherentes*. As if it had agency of its own, this impersonal and incomprehensible language can definitely be identified with one of the many structures that Kurnick sees as enclosing individuals. Words replace people and speak through them in an indecipherable way.

Along with unintelligibility, characters endure symbolic muteness. None of them speak; they are instead spoken by a language that rules them. All the lost agency and voice of depersonalized individuals is condensed here in a language that controls them. Another murderer, a husband who kills his wife, is unable to confess clearly to the police. He mentions his parents but "it wasn't clear whether he meant his own parents or Adela's, who had witnessed the murder" (408). Again, Bolaño breaks with the detective tradition by dissolving yet another fundamental convention of the genre: the criminal's confession, in which evil starts to deploy its rationale. In "The Part about the Crimes," just when we feel we are about to make some sense of it all, meaning escapes. Whereas words were once understood as signifiers to which investigators would rely on to solve cases or understand the motivations behind them, they have become here all too blurry.

Symbolic unintelligibility, like depersonalization, is an all-pervasive force. It permeates the aggressors but also their victims, even their mourning, like the family that grieves for their daughter with "words that meant nothing or whose ultimate meaning only they could understand" (318). Similarly, the mother of another victim mourns her disappeared husband, picturing him in Arizona or California, and "these thoughts paralyzed her (in them everyone, including her husband, spoke a different, incomprehensible, language)" (316). The wife never hears from her husband again after he leaves home to cross the border. In addition to causing symbolic unintelligibility, his disappearance also provokes symbolic paralysis. Almost as if the absence of subjects would provoke the absence of meaning. It seems that unintelligibility is actually caused by depersonalization.

For this reason, it is important not to read this "incomprehensible language" in a simplistic way: Santa Teresa, a border town immersed in bilingual interference, gives the reader the initial impression that unintelligibility is linked to a twofold language barrier. On the one hand, between the local dialect and the standard Mexican Spanish from Ciudad de México; on the other, between Mexican Spanish and American English. As for the first boundary, the narrator claims that the homeless of the clandestine garbage dump El Chile (where bodies are often found) speak an inscrutable slang (466).

Non-fiction narratives like the Mexican author Sergio González Rodríguez's *Huesos en el desierto* (2002) had already addressed these feminicides and contributed to a great deal of "The Part about the Crimes." Originating in a series of articles that were published in the Mexican newspaper *Reforma* during the late 1990s, *Huesos en el desierto* is part essay and part literary journalism as it blends reporting, editorializing, and self-reflection to document the way in which masculine misogyny operates in the Juárez feminicides. Bolaño, who had not been to Juárez, builds on his work to take the representation of feminicides to a fictional setting and turns González into a character of *2666*, a Chilango investigator who also endures unintelligibility. González fails to follow the inscrutable Norteño jargon of the local policemen. But their dialect is incomprehensible even to themselves: "They said: *engarróteseme ahí*, or *metateado*, or *peladeaje*, or *combiliado* [. . .] as if they were uttering the names of gods or steps in a ceremony that even they didn't understand but everyone had to obey" (297).

Later in the novel, not even the local Juan de Dios Martínez can escape this curse. After watching midnight Mexican and American TV shows filled with "channels with crippled madmen who [. . .] uttered unintelligible greetings, in Spanish or English or Spanglish, every last fucking word unintelligible" (420), he suffers from symbolic impotence ("he simply *couldn't* turn off the light" [420]) and insomnia. Both the "foreign" journalist and the local policemen are trapped in the same impossibility of knowledge, communication or understanding.

As for the second boundary, the intrusion of the English language on the Mexican-American border seems to explain the all-pervasiveness of unintelligibility. The murder of Lucy Anne Sander, an American tourist in Santa Teresa, triggers US interference into the feminicide cases, embodied in the American Sheriff Harry Magaña, who is introduced in a sarcastic tone that underlines his hybrid condition of Chicano. Like González, Magaña is alienated from the policemen's jargon and their local (lack of) *modus operandi*. He does not understand puns, *albures*, the masculine practice of word play in Mexican Spanish that entails often misogynist sexual double entendre. Although Magaña seems Mexican to others, his accented Spanish and his poor vocabulary define him as a "gringo" (326). He himself later admits that even after weeks trying to solve the case of Lucy Anne, south of the border, his Spanish worsens instead of improving (347).

But whatever it is that alienates the Chilango Sergio González, the local Juan de Dios and the Chicano Harry Magaña, whatever excludes them from the state police, it is also what at the same time includes them. There is no clear distinction between the internal and the external boundaries of Santa Teresa. In the end, all the characters share the same symbolic disability: none of them can understand the feminicides through language. It matters little whether González cannot follow Norteño or whether Magaña becomes paradoxically less fluent in Spanish, because their local counterparts are circumscribed to the same impossibility of knowledge as they are. This is an impossibility that goes beyond specific tongues: Magaña dreams of his American hometown. In the dream, he hears someone crying out loud: "We have to get the girls at the bead factory!" (352). It is a voice pointing at the *maquiladoras*. The reader does not know whose voice this is, but its depersonalized force is eclipsed again by an unintelligible language: "he photocopied documents that seemed to be written in a language not of this world" (352).

Another key character, Florita Almada, has visions in which the murderers "speak [. . .] a mixed-up Spanish" (450). But this linguistic mixture does not amount to any terrestrial language either: they do not speak Spanish, nor English, it is partially a "made-up language," that Florita somewhat understands partially. She identifies the signifiers, but misses their meaning, as "some words are incomprehensible to me" (450). Magaña's nightmares as well as Florita's visions, affected both by depersonalization and unintelligibility, are obscured by this otherworldly language that is not even Spanglish. Something similar happens to Erica, when she asks the police in English if they know who killed her friend Lucy Anne. The police's answer is filled with symbolic unintelligibility to the extent that they looked at her "uncomprehendingly" even after a nurse translates the question to Spanish (322). Whatever is lost in all these cases does not lie in specific language barriers between Spanish and English, or Norteño and Chilango, since not even translations can make these conundrums intelligible.

In short, it is not so much a problem of tongues (*lenguas*) but of language (*lenguaje*) itself. This is precisely how Benveniste understands the universality of pronouns, as "both a problem of languages in general and a problem of individual languages" (1978, 217). According to him, if "all languages possess pronouns" (217) it is because pronouns point to "a problem of language in general" (217). For this reason, Bolaño consistently uses the impersonal third-person pronoun, a linguistic universal that goes beyond its realization in Spanish. The constant use of *se*, in this sense, mirrors the unintelligibility of this otherworldly language in which characters speak, hear, dream or hallucinate.

An early sign of how unintelligibility resides in language more than its specific cultural realizations takes place when one of the first victims is found by a janitor of a nearby school. Here, unintelligibility materializes itself even beyond words. Shocked after seeing the victim's impaled corpse, the janitor goes back to the school where he finds the cook. She addresses him with "a gesture as if to ask how it had gone" to which he responds with "another gesture, impossible to decipher" (Bolaño 2008, 294). In Santa Teresa, even gestures fail to convey meaning. What otherwise might have been an efficient signifier in nonverbal communication, here is not enough. This nonverbal unintelligibility shows the extent to which language, beyond its particular realizations in specific tongues, is insufficient to apprehend brutality.

It is in terms of unintelligibility that Rita Segato opens her interpretation of the Juárez feminicides. For her, "the only viable hypothesis for the enigmatic crimes that [. . .] presented themselves as unintelligible" is that they "seem to partake in a big communicative machine whose messages become intelligible only for those who [. . .] study thoroughly the code" (2008, 80). According to Segato, the problem is that Mexican society has failed to understand these crimes in a semiotic way, missing the "expressive dimension" of violence, and as "any detective knows: [. . .] any act of violence, as any speech act, has a signature" (93). Segato ascribes meaning to acts that seem to be beyond rational explanation. For instance, she argues that "in the language of feminicides, the female body also means territory" (93) and rapes are an "allegorical act par excellence of the Schmidtian definition of sovereignty: legislative control over a territory and over the body of the other as [its] annex" (84). To sum up, Segato believes that feminicides are a complex tongue, a cryptic code that nonetheless is still readable (91). If only they could be decoded properly; if only we knew how to read them, the feminicides could be understood, i.e., "solved," and systematic violence against women could be stopped.

Santa Teresa offers a gloomier prognosis: in "The Part about the Crimes," unintelligibility wins out, because Segato's signifiers of violence resist the temptation of meaning. It is not just that Bolaño leaves the reader without closure. He also systematically avoids offering clear patterns that could enable interpretation. Whereas it is true that most murdered women work in the maquilas, others do not: Isabel Urrea, one of the first victims, for instance, is a middle-class journalist. Some women are mothers, and some are pregnant, but others are not. The narrator's reminds the reader ironically that not even the places in which bodies are found follow a clear pattern: despite "some voices that were timidly beginning to be raised," the police found one of the victims' corpse at home, "not in a vacant lot, or a dump, or the yellow scrub of the desert" (2008, 309). Bolaño leaves his readers, too, without signifiers. Whereas detective fiction traditionally invites the reader to become another detective, to identify patterns or to be suspicious of certain characters, here none of this is possible.

The irony reappears when the police takes the reiterated amputation of breasts as serious evidence that they are after a serial killer. Similar to the ones they would see in one of those "gringo movies" (370), they conclude too quickly. But in fact, these are nothing but deceptions that point somewhere else: there is no language to understand and no code to decipher. What in classic Anglo-American detective stories, or even in their Southern Cone reformulations, was unintelligible only to simple-minded state policemen or to confused detectives, is here unintelligible to society as a whole.

In his *Introduction à la littérature fantastique,* the Bulgarian critic Tzvetan Todorov examines a literary genre, the fantastic, that is closely linked to early detective stories, especially in the figure of Poe who set the foundations of both. Todorov observes that classic realistic stories that feature the irruption of a disturbing supernatural element (Hoffmann, Nerval, Maupassant) often depict a world characterized by he calls "pan-signification," a world in which "relations exist on all levels, among all elements of the world" (1975, 112). This is a "highly significant" world, in which "everything is charged with meaning. Even more: beyond the primary, obvious meaning, one can always discover a deeper meaning (a super-interpretation).

[. . .] Every object, every being means something" (112–113). What Todorov states about these supernatural stories, can also be said about traditional detective fiction. In Poe, in Conan Doyle, in Christie, even in the Southern Cone detective tradition, the world still has legibility, and everything is legible in the world. Every little thing is as a potential clue. Yet in Santa Teresa, this omnipresence of signifiers and its full potentiality of meanings are now obsolete.

Bolaño thus depicts state officers and private detectives who suffer from this structural symbolic unintelligibility that causes them to fail to solve the feminicides. What they miss is not so much how to read messages, but the fact that such messages are no longer readable; not that individual signatures are hidden beneath complex communicative acts, but that individual agency is not enough to apprehend the nature of these crimes. In a nutshell, they fail because depersonalization is not legible. As Williams says in his reading of the novel, "in the desert we are left without legibility" (2016, 17): breaking with the detective story tradition, there are no longer symbols for readers to read or detectives to detect. Everything remains within the realm of the unintelligible. And whatever cannot be understood becomes invisible.

## FROM UNINTELLIGIBILITY TO BLINDNESS

Because events that are beyond interpretation become all too natural, they escape visibility. Unintelligibility, linked to linguistic disruptions, provokes blindness, too. The same symbolic blindness that once affected the state (in the Anglo-American tradition) and individualistic heroes (in their Southern-Cone replication), now permeates both sides of the opposition as yet another form of depersonalization. Witness cannot see the crimes as "there wasn't enough public lighting" (Bolaño 2008, 295) says the narrator, constantly commenting (again ironically) on how hard it is for the inhabitants of Santa Teresa to see, due to the precarious conditions in which they live.

However, it is equally hard for them to be seen: the witnesses who find the first corpse, for example, agree that "we've never seen her before. She isn't from around here" (278), and later a teenager girl "one day left school and was never seen again" (317). The poetics of failure takes center stage when even facial composure becomes impossible, as the police fail to reconstruct a "convincing sketch" of one of the murderers (420). Invisibility is often stressed as one of the attributes that haunts most characters, especially but not limited to the victims. For example, the cars in which they are typically kidnapped often have tinted windows that hinder any possible witness's vision. In the same way that the narrator gives the impression that there is a hidden language that no character can fully grasp; there seem to be things that cannot be seen by most of them either.

Nonetheless, the inability both of rendering things visible and of becoming visible is not plainly literal, but also symbolic. In the same way that (inter) linguistic barriers are insufficient to surmount language unintelligibility, the lack of proper streetlights is hardly enough to explain this constant impairment of sight. On the one hand, women's invisibility, in Santa Teresa, points to the almost ghostly aspect of their bodies, which reflects their lack of social ties within the city: "No one claimed or acknowledged the body. As if the girl had come to Santa Teresa alone and lived there invisibly until the murderer [. . .] took notice of her" only, this time, to enhance her invisibility by killing her (368). There are multiple iterations of this description along with the *leitmotiv* that often accompanies reports of the discovery of a corpse: the lack of passport to identify the person behind the body. Whereas documents are often understood as a metonymy of legality, their constant absence cites the profound lawlessness in which these women are immersed on a daily basis. After all, documentation that presupposes social visibility and guarantees a minimum degree of rights. Their lack is but another way in which Bolaño highlights how everyone (in Mexico, Central America, the United States and beyond) is symbolically blind towards these depersonalized victims.

The destruction of their faces, perhaps the most significant part of the female body in Western poetry (Petrarchism, Neoplatonism, Spanish Golden Age, etc.), as they are mutilated or dissolved by nitric acid is yet another trait of depersonalization. After all, the main element that a piece of identification requires is the bearer's face. The destruction of faces mirrors its material correlation, namely the absence of documents: divested of their faces, the distinctive human feature that could compensate for their lack of legal identity, that could distinguish them as unique persons, they become depersonalized entities, prevented from seeing (literally) or being seen (symbolically). Whereas in the Rio de Janeiro of Fonseca's *Agosto* there is an ephemeral suspension of Levinas's ethics of the "face-to-face" when Mattos cannot see the face of Vargas's corpse, in Santa Teresa this suspension has become the norm. Without faces, the female victims can no longer partake in the "the conjuncture of the same and the other" located in "the direct and full-face welcome of the other by me" (80). In this mutilation, they lose personhood.

Symbolic blindness does not only affect the victims. As with unintelligibility, every character is subject to it, even the murderers. The Cifuentes siblings, both suspects of having committed feminicides, seem like imperceptible ghosts. They, too, have no photograph to prove their existence and witnesses describe them in "vague, when not contradictory" terms (2008, 389). Miguel, one of the main suspects in the murder of Lucy Ann Sander, "vanished into the bushes" (319) right before she disappears, as well. The one character who seems to be immune to symbolic blindness is Florita Almada. A Tiresias/Cassandra-like prophet and psychic who speaks up for the safety of women on Mexican TV, Florita alone publicly denounces the brutality that takes place in Santa Teresa. She expresses her accusations in terms of visions, continually using the verb "to see." The narrator stresses that "she had been granted the gift of sight. She saw things no one else saw" (336) and tells us that she could offer "a meaningful explanation for everything that happened to her" (336). Amidst a desert of unintelligibility and invisibility, Florita can interpret, i.e.,: she can see beyond, much more than the myriad of detectives.

Paradoxically, Florita is partially blind: "She became a seer" but "seer meant someone who sees, and sometimes she didn't see anything" (336). The paradox resides, of course, in the fact that, like Tiresias, she is said to be the only one that can truly see, despite her own physical sight impairment. Significantly, she remarks on the policemen's symbolic blindness, encapsulated in their "dark glasses [. . .] Why do they cover their eyes, I ask?" (361). These sunglasses are reminiscent of and mirrored in the tinted windows of the assassins' cars: they obscure what goes on behind them, making it impossible for the reader (infected with both unintelligibility and symbolic blindness too) to understand and see. Both the sunglasses and the tinted windows elicit the expectation of "a hidden truth" that remains invisible or rather inexistent. In one of her last appearances, Florita finishes her speech with a shift. She stops using the verb "seeing" to now switch to "talking." By repeating that she is talking about Santa Teresa (362), she makes clear the one symbolic disability that she is not immune to: deaf-muteness. Like Cassandra, her prophecies, visions and warnings are systematically ignored.

But what about Bolaño? What is his symbolic blindness? Despite the triumph of unintelligibility, there is in the book an insistence on narrating the feminicides through fiction or fictionalized versions of the real. Santa Teresa is, after all, not in fact Ciudad Juárez. The 111 cases of feminicides of the book are not strictly speaking a paraphrase of the historical ones. I read this insistence as an underlying presumption: the belief that literature can still hold some constituent power against constituted power. As Deckard notes, "given the proliferation of documentary and journalistic books about the feminicides, including the reporter Sergio González's [. . .] the novel might be said to justify its own necessity by demonstrating this failure" (360). Written testimony or audiovisual documentaries are rooted in an attempt to portray facts accurately. In a very similar way to Piglia and Fonseca, Bolaño seems to be saying that facts are not enough.

Over the past few decades, as Spanish-American critic Alberto Moreiras recalls, "high literature has suffered a drastic loss of cultural capital [and] is no longer effective [. . .] in the fight against late-capitalist globalization" (192–194). Bolaño's literary project seeks to regain this effectiveness for fiction. *2666* contends that facts are not as convincing as their poetic re-elaboration. Fiction, not testimony, not trans-medial discourses, not journalism, ought to be more effective to narrate the desert, to engage with history and politics. "The Part about the Crimes" can thus be read as an attempt to report feminicides by recovering literary mythification when everything else, audiovisuals, journalistic articles, academic thought, forensic evidence, has failed.

If depersonalization leaves no room for mythical literary heroes, which myths does Bolaño side with? Certainly not Florita Almada's Tiresias or Cassandra. Because, unlike her, the narrator deliberately does not give voice to the victims. Whereas in Southern Cone detective stories it was the state and the private investigators who suffered from symbolic muteness, in Santa Teresa this same silence systematically affects the victims as well. Schapiro talks about the "muteness of the individual victim" (86), in that the (soon to be) murdered women barely speak in the novel. The reader does not hear from them except through the statistical data conveyed by the narrator. The reader learns their age, their weight, their height; sometimes, even their full names. But the narrator never explores their thoughts about a situation that affects them first and foremost. Bolaño chooses not to make them speak, keeping them in a symbolic muteness that has to be a calculated narrative strategy, a literary project that contests not only documentary discourses, but also literature itself, even beyond the tradition of the detective genre.

After all, a great deal of the Latin American left during most of the twentieth century followed Marx's imperative taken from his description of the nineteenth-century proletariat: "they can not [sic] represent one another, they must themselves be represented" (1852, 84). Through poetry or novels, writers such as Neruda, Guillén, Vallejo, García Márquez, Arguedas, among many others, understood literature as a commitment with the different expressions of Latin American subalternity, and that engagement had necessarily to be funneled through a ventriloquism of the voice of the oppressed. Thus, in his poem "Heights of Macchu Picchu," Neruda claims "I come to speak through your dead mouth" (96) and demands to "speak through my words and my blood" (97). Neruda's poetic voice, thus, personifies the voice of the oppressed.

By contrast, Bolaño refuses to let these women speak through him, voluntarily imposing a veil (a symbolic blindness) on himself. Unlike Neruda and a great deal of the Boom and the Post-Boom generations, he does not engage with what Moreiras defined as "a prosopopoeia of the dead," i.e.,: a "foundational trope that will bring posthumous, metonymic life to those who already have died" (200). In this gesture, too, the Chilean novelist breaks up with the tradition of personifying ("prosopopoeia" is the technical term for personification) ideas in characters. He holds onto literature without turning to the traditional literary strategies of seeing everything through fiction and relinquishing the inherited entitlement of representing what cannot be represented by itself. He positions himself at an equidistant place in the Latin American tradition, far from the Boom and the subsequent generation of writers who engaged in *testimonio*.

Bolaño situates himself against his forerunners' stress on literary aesthetics, because unlike them he prefers not to pretend to decipher nor to embody that space that remains ever unintelligible: the voice of the dead. In the same way that in *Agosto*, when Fonseca represents the heterogeneous and unintelligible multitude as bodies who in front of a personalist leader are turned into the homogeneous and readable notion of people; the "prosopopoeia of the dead," when seizing the subaltern's voiceless voice, makes it readable and erases it simultaneously. Bolaño chooses not to pursue this strategy.

The myth that remains for Bolaño to side with, thus, is no other than Sisyphus. Bolaño rolls the immense boulder of narrating these feminicides. He clearly seems to know that he is failing but assumes his stoical task as necessary. Much like the Santa Teresa's amorphous group of fatigued policemen, "soldiers trapped in a time warp who march over and over again to the same defeat" (2008, 416). Bolaño writes from this defeated Latin-American left that no longer believes in what they consider to be outdated strategies of engaging with politics. Whereas Kurnick observes the absence of an individualistic hero, Williams suggests that the actual hero is repetition, "the true master" (2006, 9) of the novel. And Sisyphus (that Marx equated with the limitless "labor of accumulating" [1987, 185]) is nothing but sheer repetition.

As Trelles Paz argues, Bolaño's detectives are "demoted heroes" that "present themselves as invulnerable [. . .] because, even when they imagine the failure of their quests and battles, they still undertake them" (360). Florita tries to show what has been hidden. Bolaño, alternatively, shows what has already been shown repeatedly and *ad nauseam* by journalists such as González and others, even by himself over the course of hundreds of pages. Like his detectives, he does not relinquish the (pre-announced) failed attempt. Except that he does so by defying his ineffective forerunners' narrative choices. He proposes a new way of narrating from a (defeated) post-dictatorial left: rather than humanizing victims, he articulates their own (and his own) symbolic muteness and blindness in order to make "audible the gendered structures of reification" (Shapiro 86). Otherwise, what if any is the need of narrating yet again these crimes other than, as Deckard says, to spot a discursive failure? If Florita can "see" the feminicides through visions (without seeing them), Bolaño, without having witnessed these feminicides, invites the reader to experience the magnitude of their brutality through literary discourse, by imagining beyond facts and personifications, challenging both literary tradition and the presumptions of the Latin American left, as well as surpassing the need to appropriate voices that after all are impossible to seize.

## THE MEXICAN-AMERICAN BORDER: AN INFERTILE BODY

### Money and Depersonalization

Money plays a pivotal role in "The Part about the Crimes," as it does in the tradition of detective stories it is built on. But Bolaño confers on it an original element: instead of merely triggering crime and its investigation, here money (and especially the market that enables its accumulation) replaces the state as the main structural framework that is inherent to crime. Unlike the state, which has officers, money depersonalizes crime, liquifying its main agents: detectives, policemen, criminals, but most importantly, the victims. Money is behind the elegiac if often monotonous catalogue of the murdered women. Filled with names and surnames, this catalogue elaborates on the victims' origin and the socio-economic function that their bodies once performed in life. Thus, the 111 fictional women, an accumulation of corpses through the pages, is reminiscent of the capital they would produce and enable to be accumulated while working for multinational companies.

Whereas financial accumulation entails the transformation of socially necessary labor into money that in turn generates capital, the novel's piled-up corpses imply the transformation of female necessary labor into their own commodification and their subsequent death. Unlike the former, the latter is the product of economics and the aftermath of social surplus. It is in this regard that Shapiro describes this list in terms of accounting as a "ledger of murders" (85): the catalogue of victims is a book of economic transactions, which enhances the notion of female corpses as yet another negative asset on a foreign corporation's ledger.

Capital accumulation, along with the thorough description of women's mortal remains, is depicted in "The Part about the Crimes" as an irrational heap. Reading Benjamin Franklin's autobiography, Weber comments on "the earning of more and more money [. . .] so purely as an end in itself, that from the point of view of the happiness of, or utility to, the single individual, it appears entirely transcendental and absolutely irrational" (1992, 18). Whereas accumulating capital is often understood as a useful means for human happiness, Weber claims that making money is closer to an irrational command divested from any purpose. Wealth accumulation, thus, enables and actually encourages its willful perpetuation and exponential growth.

Likewise, Santa Teresa is the site of the assassination of women without any political aim. In the same way that the multitude of characters that crowd the novel are subjected to language, they are also subjected to money. As Deckard notes, "the accumulation of characters' stories, like the accumulation of bodies, seems without purpose, ultimately realistic in its very meaninglessness" (364). The purpose of these killings does not respond to any issues that could be explained in utilitarian terms. They lack the rhetoric of immunity used by the Southern Cone dictatorial states: no criminal justifies the feminicides as a means of extirpation of a foreign agent from the body of the nation, like Tagle/Wieder does when he compares communism with leprosy, a disease that must be eradicated. Enumerating corpses, like accumulating capital, is purely "an end in itself" (Weber 1992, 18). This lack of purpose is mirrored in the absence of systematicity: as Brett Levinson points out, "each [murder] functions as one more atrocity in a disconnected but repeating series" (182). At first glance, they look like isolated events. It is worth spelling out, though, that this absence of connection is only superficial and paradoxical. What is at stake in these iterations is not so much related to the repetition of disjointed events but to the common thread that unites most of its victims: their gender. Almost without exception, all are women who are killed between their teens and their thirties years of age, i.e.,: with a few exceptions, most of them are within a reproductive period.

Just as their executioners do not acknowledge that their depersonalized murders follow any particular political agenda (they kill their victims neither because of their relationship with any political party nor because they are activists of a subversive cause), there is no single intellectual author behind the crimes. There is no "great Latin American dictator" orchestrating a systematic genocide that is supposed to decimate some ideology, nor is there a conventional serial killer murdering for private motives. In Santa Teresa, evil, too, resists personification: it is not incarnated in a character but disembodied and scattered through the population. Feminicides are perpetrated in a spontaneous and erratic fashion, that is closer to the dynamics of wealth accumulation than to genocides perpetrated by military dictatorships. As Natasha Wimmer puts it, "capitalism, the World Bank and the international drug trade replaced caudillos, death squads, and political persecution as the new faces of evil" (qtd. in Deckard 1). Unlike either the Anglo-American canon of detective fiction, its Southern Cone replications, or even more broadly the above-mentioned Latin American *littérature engagée* (Asturias, García Márquez, Cortázar, among many others) that would partake in the dictator novel, in "The Part about the Crimes" the criminal mastermind is not incarnated in just one social agent.

Zizek claims that the great lesson to learn from Carl Schmitt is that "the enemy is by definition always [. . .] invisible, it looks like one of us, it cannot be directly recognized [. . .] The big problem and task of the political struggle is that of providing/constructing the recognizable IMAGE of the enemy" (2002, 110). The boom generation constructed this recognizable image by personifying the state in the singular figure of the dictator. Bolaño, according to Williams, still believes in the Schmittian opposition of "the inherited trenches and fortifications of the friend/enemy divide" (2009, 139). But unlike his forerunners, he re-constructs the enemy by disembodying (depersonalizing) its image.

Williams claims that *Estrella distante* partakes in "an eternal return of the same with only nominal difference" (139). But in *2666*, there is a difference that goes beyond the nominal: the use of the third person, "because it does not refer to anyone at all or because it can be extended to everyone" (Esposito 2012, 107). Anyone and everyone kill: thieves, policemen, drug dealers, businessmen, workers, husbands. None of them has much in common with each other. The only true thing that they have in common is that they are not women. In the Mexican-American border imagined by Bolaño, there is room only for the purest arbitrariness and depersonalization: the fact that anyone kills, as I say above, creates a mirage of absolution, in which nobody does.

However much these feminicides are bereft of clear political purpose, though, they do not necessarily lack a cause. Despite this absence of connection, murderers do not kill women for no reason. They do it because they are women, the only social agent that escapes the logic of "everyone kills." As Kurnick claims, "these crimes submit to no overarching logic and have in common only an evident structural misogyny" (130). The victims, although equally depersonalized, still have a common gender identity, while the blurriness of the perpetrators' personality finds its limit in the structure that affects all of them: masculine domination.

Santa Teresa's subjects are not important as individuals *per se*; they are reduced to the functions they perform in society. Far from being free as promised by neoliberal *doxa*, everyone is subjected to language, money and also to gender. According to Bourdieu, "sexual harassment does not always aim at the sexual possession that seems to be its exclusive goal: in some cases, it may aim at sheer possession, the pure affirmation of domination" (1999, 21). Something similar could be claimed about the way Bolaño depicts these killings preceded by anal, vaginal and oral rape as well as by the amputation of breasts and nipples: beyond any utilitarian purpose, the feminicides are rather an end in themselves, in the same way that financial accumulation can be. This does not free them from having a distinct cause: the reinforcement of masculine domination in the face of the feminine body.

## FROM WASTE TO INFERTILITY

In "The Part about the Crimes," male characters treat women as a disposable excess, even though they are indispensable. Or precisely because they are. Like Piglia in Plata quemada, Bolaño inscribes money, popularly valued for its utilitarian dimension, as the other side of a same token: ashes, waste. In his reading of the novel, John Kraniauskas invokes the notion of the homme jetable (44), literally, the man who can be dumped, i.e.,: derelict human beings, whose condition was produced by economic inequality inherent to capital accumulation. Kraniauskas attributes the concept to Étienne Balibar, but in fact it is Bertrand Ogilvie who coined the term. In the mid 1990s, drawing from the Latin American idiom población chatarra (the people who live among rubbish dumps and whose socio-economical condition blurs the boundaries between their bodies and the place where they roam), Ogilvie takes the idea of disposable human beings to describe "these masses of population that do not access the national and international circuits of production and exchange" (128). Likewise, Balibar understands them from the perspective of structural unemployment brought by "the destruction of traditional activities [which . . . ] leads to a situation [. . .] in which millions of human beings are superfluous" (12). Balibar goes on to say that nobody needs them and precisely for this they are at the same time "excluded from labor

[. . .] and kept within the boundaries of the market" (12). Waste, in Ogilvie/Balibar's definition, works then as a metonymy: humans, reduced to a labor that can now be discarded, become residual themselves.

As Ludmer reminds us in the beginning of El cuerpo del delito, Marx had already equated a "superfluous population" with the criminals that were removed from "the labor market" (1963, 388), in his analysis of wealth creation, a century before Ogilvie/Balibar. According to Marx, even criminals and the unemployed, at first sight the most superfluous sectors of the population, are indispensable for capital, because they accomplish extremely productive aims: they lower wages and create institutions without which capital could not function. Marx mentions "the whole of the police and of criminal justice, constables, judges, hangmen, juries" (388). An updated version of Marx's list could include police reporters and the more recent industries related to forensics and criminology or even entertainment, in the shape of detective fiction books, films, TV shows or videogames. While crime takes a part of the superfluous population off the labor market and thus reduces competition among the laborers—up to a certain point preventing wages from falling below the minimum—the struggle against crime absorbs another part of this population. Thus, the criminal comes in as one of those natural "counterweights" that bring about a correct balance and open up a whole perspective of "useful" occupations (388).

This twofold nature, both indispensable and excessive at the same time, is the peculiar element of the feminine victims depicted by Bolaño, who not only are integrated in the labor market, but actually constitute the heart of its productive growth in Santa Teresa. In a nutshell, they embody an aporia: they are superfluous (their bodies constantly discarded) and yet also absolutely essential for the economic circuit in which they are immersed, since the economy of the town operates to a great extent because of their labor. Like Juárez, the mythical urban space created by Bolaño both attracts women (with the lowest rates of female unemployment and the highest rates of feminicides in all of Mexico) and repels them (by discarding their bodies as garbage).

The women described in this elegiac "ledger of murders," therefore, are not solely residual; they also perform a highly productive function. They are an excess created by the same financial capital to which they are simultaneously indispensable, not only in terms of production but in terms of reproduction, since there cannot be society without women's labor and fertility. If they are "disposable," as Shapiro notes, they are also "replaceable" (86). While each individual woman can be substituted by another, women as a whole cannot.

Both waste and productive drive, these female characters should be read not only in the light of Ogilvie's *homme jetable* but in terms of another similar and contemporary albeit more pertinent notion: Agamben's *homo sacer*. In his reading of this "figure of archaic Roman law" (1998, 47), the Italian philosopher discusses its "inclusive exclusion" (7). Again, this twofold dimension is embodied in each of the female characters that appear in Bolaño's fictional list: they are sacred bodies because of their indispensable attributes for capital accumulation (as a docile and inexpensive workforce) while at the same time they also are sacrificed bodies because of their condition of excess.

The narrator's forensic tone that never fully engages affectively with the victims records the extent to which the logic of masculine domination considers the feminine body to be the excess of a society without which it could not function. Cast aside by the selective and unequal distribution of capital that has affected generations of Mexican and Central American workers, these female victims, transformed into the waste of society, work in the maquilas of Santa Teresa in subhuman conditions. Their existence is no different from the "bare life" of the *homo sacer*, which Agamben defines as "a life that may be killed by anyone—an object of a violence that exceeds the sphere both of law and of sacrifice" (1998, 57).

Whereas the Oxford English Dictionary defines "sacrifice" in terms of slaughter as offering and the DRAE defines *sacrificio* in terms of "killing for a cause," Bolaño's list of women does not fit in neither of these definitions. Rather these victims are located, like Agamben's *homo sacer*, in "a zone of indistinction between sacrifice and homicide" (55). As seen in the figure of the third person, anyone—thieves, policemen, drug dealers, businessmen, workers, husbands—can "kill with impunity" (47) and "this violence [. . .] is classifiable neither as sacrifice nor as homicide" (54). Both within and beyond the law, women are immersed in Santa Teresa's market and exposed to the vulnerability it generates. Their dismembered bodies are a foil for the sovereign masculine body of the state, which lawfully decides who is liable to be killed "without committing homicide and without celebrating a sacrifice" (55). This *impune occidi*, the sovereign's ability to kill the *homo sacer*, ratifies the reading that the feminicides depicted by Bolaño should be understood not as a means (a sacrifice for a bigger cause) but as an end in themselves, in line with Weber's interpretation of capital accumulation and Bourdieu's views on masculine domination. If these feminicides have an aim, it is the self-reinforcement of the dominant order (regardless of its origin, whether class, gender or sovereignty). If Bolaño portrays them is to emphasize the extent to which we lack freedom in times of free trade agreements and are instead ambushed and trapped in its economic and political structures.

In these terms, without meaning or motivation, the narrator portrays the maquiladoras' shed as spaces built "without rhyme or reason" (2008, 396). Bolaño maps this blurred boundary in a "zone of indistinction" between what is productive and what is expelled from production, between Mexican and Central American female labor and insatiable North American capital, between abstract depersonalization and concrete bodies, between the dominated female corpses and the masculine territory in which they are found. Furthermore, this anomic threshold of neoliberal democratic states is more than just some mere decorative scenery to impress the reader; it is above all a metonymy of the corpses themselves. Bodies are found in ditches, ruins, waste-grounds, cliffs, deserts, vacant lots, highways, streets, alleys, hills, cars ready to be sent to the scrapyard, dumpsters, warehouses, industrial parks, streams, oil deposits: the spaces in which the female corpses emerge are hostile territories that have their climax in a container filled with nitric acid.

As Schmitz and Verdú Schumann note, "the mediating role of the body" is a cornerstone of classic detective fiction, because "the body functions as a key witness" of the crimes that sleuths investigate (15). And this turns out to be even more evident if we pay attention to Barrientos Tecún comparative study on the portrayals of the body in Southern Cone and Mexican detective novels: "the body works as a fundamental element because [. . .] violence, ultimately, is exerted against the body" (78). More specifically, he notes how "corporeality has left very deep traces in Latin American literature, to the extent that it is not far-fetched to claim that the body became its great main character" (77). As Barrientos Tecún observes, "corporeality becomes, thus, the sign that encapsulates the tragic recent history" (84). It is in this sense, too, that Bolaño (through his Chilean lens) inscribes "The Part about the Crimes" in the detective fiction tradition, building bridges with his Southern Cone literary counterparts: along with the body of the *desaparecidos* in Chilean, Argentine or Brazilian novels, this posthumous text puts center stage the mutilated female body as the main character of the genre.

Beyond the detective stories tradition, the conjunction of the female body (with its fertility) and death, ever more sinister and crueler, recalls another literary tradition: Bolaño's prose is informed by Spanish Golden Age poetry, which placed the ephemeral degradation of the female body in contrast to their youth. The tercets of Spanish poet Luis de Góngora's sonnet, "While trying to compete with your hair," evoke this well-known trope. Here, the lyric masculine voice sings to his female addressee, inviting her to enjoy herself before it is too late: "enjoy neck, hair, lip, brow, / before, what in your golden age / was gold, lily, carnation, shiny glass / turn into not only silver or drooping violet, / but also you and it together / into earth, smoke, dust, shadow, nothing." Bolaño, who, as Kraniauskas points out, was above all "a poet who only began to write novels towards the end of his life in [as] a means of making money" (37), rewrites Góngora's *tierra* and *polvo* through its most dreadful by-products: these spaces in which bodies emerge impersonally.

As with Ogilvie's *población chatarra*, the corpses and these residual spaces are merged and mixed up: they are the ruins that allude to any commodity that is first coveted and swiftly excreted by a voracious market, abandoned under the open sky of the border. Female corpses, like the waste in which they are camouflaged, are concealed from the public sphere. Bodies are "thrown" on dumps in order to be hidden and invisible. These macabre spaces are not only the physical site of the crimes, Bolaño seems to say, but also, like language and money, they are somehow their culprits. Since the dark streets themselves render these women invisible, swallowing them up "like black holes, and the laughter, that came from who knows where, was the only sign [. . .] that kept residents and strangers from getting lost" (2008, 497). These somber spaces are thus metonymies of the bodies decomposing next to and along with the garbage. All these spaces converge in Santa Teresa, a huge garbage dump, which should be read as an update of the Latin American boom, if closer to the hellish realism of Rulfo's Comala than to the magical Macondo of García Márquez.

Sergio Villalobos-Rouminot underlines this hellish dimension of Santa Teresa (193–205). By contrast, Kurnick questions this "image of hell" because "there is nothing metaphysical about the violence on the US-Mexico border depicted in *2666*" (132). Kurnick is right when he claims that this is not a religious hell, but it is still a literary hell. It may not be a religious space for punishment (quite on the contrary, nobody gets what they deserve) but a space only functional to the accumulation of capital, waste, habit and crime, all embodied in women's corpses. It is no coincidence that the first victim mentioned is named Esperanza. Like in Fonseca, onomastics announces and informs the nature of the text: Esperanza is an allusion to Hesiod's *Works and Days*, for which Elpis, the ancient Greek embodiment of Hope, is the last human attribute that remains immune to the catastrophe unleashed by the opening of Pandora's box. Hesiod's text is the source of the Spanish proverb *la esperanza es lo último que se pierde*, that roughly translates in English as "hope is the last thing to die." Esperanza, of course, also cites the famous verse of Dante's *Inferno*: "Abandon hope all ye who enter here," a literary hell that amounts to a city, a *città dolente*, much like Santa Teresa. The fact that the reader is warned to abandon all hope in Santa Teresa from the start should not be neglected as it has been in most of the readings of the novel: the horizon of expectations, Bolaño warns the reader, are now different from the genre's models. Once more, depersonalization absorbs personification, which does not work any longer: hope, like individualism or the modern state, can no longer be funneled through a literary character because reified humans have no personality at all.

Literary tradition also informs this "secular hell" in the sense that it evokes the antithesis of the traditional space of fecundity named in the Latin trope *locus amœnus:* the *locus eremus*, the infertile wasteland that engulfs women during their reproductive years. It is no coincidence that Bolaño locates the origins of this 1980s neoliberal accumulation, linking it to an infertile but still commodifiable plot of land, that landowners sold to the then brand-new maquiladoras (2008, 432). These spaces, which are infertile and infantilizing, suggest a displacement: they evoke the place (spatial and non-spatial) that society has already prescribed to female bodies even when they are (re)productive. The thin border between space and bodies entails a sinister logic.

Society finds women's bodies in the same place that it had initially put them while still in life: in that of waste.

## NEOLIBERALISM AND IMMUNITY

The female corpses are separated by these infertile spaces through an ostensibly porous boundary. This boundary, then, must be read as a breeding ground for what Esposito calls "contagion," those infectious forces that aim to overcome the resisting counterforce of immunity. If Segato is right when she reads the female body as an allegory of territories to be conquered, then the thin threshold that separates both biological and political bodies must be understood as a common element, through which waste flows seemingly without any restrictions.

This is what is at stake when the novel describes corpses decomposing in contact with the contaminated water of a stream. In an even more somber tone, when one of the last women is found all that remains of her body is her skeleton, her flesh having been absorbed by the ground a long time before. Corpses are infected by and merged with the space in which they emerge. After all, the "contagion" of infectious phenomena such as depersonalization, and its by-products (unintelligibility and symbolic blindness as well as the complex relationship between money and waste), circulates among and affects the different bodies of society involved in the feminicides: victims, victimizers, witnesses, accomplices. As Esposito claims, the risk of contagion "has to do with trespassing or violating borders" (2011, 2). If contagion is so all-pervasive, it could give the impression that there is no border, no real distinction between bodies (women's and the state's, the biological and the political).

"The Part about the Crimes," of course, is more complex than that. Along with the list of female victims, Bolaño offers a series of fictitious American multinational companies, conveniently settled in this all too porous border, for whom the female victims work. These evoke the historical maquiladoras, factories that have been present on the Mexican-American border since the 1960s, but that multiplied exponentially after the signing of NAFTA in 1994. A disembodied image of the market, these maquiladoras can be read following what Esposito names the "immunitary paradigm." When everything else trespasses thresholds, the maquiladoras inherit the Anglo-American private's sleuth exemption that gives them the entitlement to not be trespassed. Whereas Dupin or the Continental Op were immune in front of society, the only ones who "owe nothing to anyone" (2011, 5), here it is a depersonalized market that owns this privilege.

The meaning of *immunitas*, according to Esposito, is diametrically opposed to its dialectical antonym: *communitas*. Whereas the first means that which lacks the *munus* (the Latin prefix *im* meaning "without"); the second one means that which bears it (*cum,* its contrary, means "with"). "Those who are immune," he says, are exempted to engage with the *munus*, (which in Latin means "a task, obligation, duty" [5]). To put it differently, the immune ones are "exempted [. . .] from [. . .] paying tributes or performing services for others" (5), they are absolved "from the obligation of the *munus*, be it personal, fiscal, or civil" (5). Indeed, these maquiladoras are excused from paying duty to the Mexican state due to neoliberal policies that favor the privilege (the immunity) of the market over the commonality of inhabitants of Santa Teresa.

Moreover, these maquiladoras constitute an illusion of immunity for their employers and employees. They produce the temptation of unrestricted individualistic accumulation for their former, while at the same time they create the mirage of trickle-down economics, a nineteenth-century *laisser-faire* theory, regurgitated by 1980s neoliberalism. This theory forecasts that unrestricted capital accumulation, in the end, should drip into the working class, as a natural consequence of lower taxes and the promotion of business in underdeveloped areas.

This is what is at stake when the narrator says that one of the female victims, a worker in one of the maquiladoras, was expecting a promotion before being murdered by her partner, after quarrelling with him about whether to emigrate to the United States. It is due to that expectation that she prefers to stay rather than to emigrate. She never set foot north of the border and her bosses at Nip-Mex (the fictional maquiladora that employs her) like her. As a result, she "had hopes of a quick promotion and a raise" (Bolaño 2008, 488). She refuses the gloomy prospect of geographical mobility (becoming an illegal alien in America) for the equally flickering promise of social mobility (being promoted in an American company in Mexico in a future that never quite materializes). These two somber options amount actually to no option at all. The lack of choice is precisely what gets her killed: as Nip-Mex, the multinational company that promises a better future for its workers, ends up enabling their workers' destruction, through the precarious conditions that makes them consider fleeing the country or staying to wait for a better future that is constantly postponed.

Whereas in the other novels examined in this book, the narratives that once endorsed individualism and justified the existence of the modern state are gradually crumbling, in *2666* they have already collapsed. The portrayal of trickle-down economics as sheer deceit, as pure fantasy, is only one instance of this downfall. "The Part about the Crimes" outlines the shadows projected by a boundless market that has engulfed the state and the individuals. After several decades of neoliberal policies in Latin America (accentuated in the

1990s with NAFTA and the Washington Consensus) that naturalized the otherwise problematic link between individual agency and social mobility, Bolaño offers a paradox: the triumph of the market, rather than empowering individuals as its slogans promise, actually paralyzes and devours them. Capital accumulation, as well as its promising carrot and stick, works to a great extent thanks to the immunity held by the American company, which become wealthier and more powerful due to their exemption from paying their fiscal *munus*. And they do so at the expense of both the Mexican state, which loses valuable tax income to strengthen its public institutions, and its individuals who, far from sharing the freedom circumscribed to the market, are subjected to the rigid structuring structures of gender, class, and political sovereignty examined above.

On Bolaño's Mexican-American border, the market is not solely summarized in the maquiladoras, but also in the drug trade. As Kraniauskas notes, what links the two is "the importance of laundering" (42). What they have in common is a sort of oligopoly of immunity: they are the only social agents entitled to avoid what is required from the rest of the community, since neither maquiladoras nor cartels must pay taxes, owe explanations to civil society, or be punished when committing illegal acts. Holding the privilege of immunity unilaterally is what reinforces their power.

Esposito's *immunitas*, nonetheless, is a productive and ambivalent concept: it is helpful for reading not only the market but also the Mexican state. According to Kraniauskas, Santa Teresa is "neither the USA nor Mexico" (43), the two states that allow and welcome this indulgence towards the transnational market. By contrast, it is a "narco-territory" that "is simultaneously global whilst, parasitic, crossing and containing some of each [country]" (43). It is in this vein that one of the novel's countless Mexican characters tells Magaña that ultimately Northern Mexico and Southwestern United States are all the same (Bolaño 2008, 527). Despite the blurriness of the border that separates these territories, there is still a seamlessness, a series of elements that enable a reading of the Mexican state and its subjugation to the immunitary paradigm.

There is an example early in the chapter: an anonymous senior member of the maquiladora Multizone-West, "a subsidiary of a multinational that manufactured TVs [. . .] hoped the body would be removed as soon as possible" (282). After bribing the police, he alludes to the issue of taking responsibility. The senior member asks the police whether they will "take care of everything," while he bribes them (282). Immunity, linked to the impersonal third-person, exhibits its reactive counterforce against community: nobody murders, nobody solves the crimes, nobody takes responsibility, to ultimately create the mirage that nobody dies, even as feminicides continue to accrue. "Taking care of everything" means to accept illicit money and remain silently complicit; it implicitly entails perpetuating the immunity of the market, which in turn subjugates the state and individuals.

Another instance of this subjugation can be found when a nurse and witnesses argue about who will respond for one of the first victims, as no one really knows her. As a result, nobody pays for her ambulance and she dies in the streets, while the argument takes place. Individuals and the state alike become paralyzed and are incapable of acting on time due to indifference, precarity and financial constraint. Several pages later, Efraín Bustelo, a low-level state policeman, investigates one of the suspects, who works for another fictional maquiladora, File-Sis. He asks the company for a list of workers, but the corporate response consists solely of maintaining its immunity at all costs, as they claim not to have any employees registered on their payroll while they, too, bribe him. The records are gone, if they ever existed, and corporations will do anything to endorse that void. Equally, when Magaña's body is disappeared after he is murdered, the American consul demands the state of Sonora to locate his whereabouts. Pedro Negrete, chief of the state police, uses the transient dimension of the border as well as Magaña's clandestine situation to reassure the state immunity.

But the main element that distinguishes the way immunity works is that while they are successful in protecting the market, they now fail to do the same with the state. This distribution of immunity has effects that are at the same time selective and asymmetric. Like depersonalization, it benefits constituted power at the detriment of constituent power, putting the state officers somewhere in the middle. This in-between location points to the dominant-dominated position of the state in relation to the market, to use Bourdieu's terms. After a few years of consecutive feminicides, Klaus Haas, a German store owner, is saddled with responsibility for the crimes. But, as Kurnick points out, of course this "revelation is wholly anticlimactic," because the reader knows very well that "while Haas is obviously a violent man, he is just as obviously not 'the' author of the hundreds of killings, if of any" (130). In fact, Haas is but the most prominent of the constant scapegoats that the police find to cover its own failure, since the beginning of the chapter.

Equally, once the first suspected murderer is quickly absolved, his innocent colleague is incriminated in his place by the police, because the appearance of justice (the fiction of order) is more important (and less costly) than investigating criminals. In Santa Teresa, the state does speak: it says, "here is the criminal." Even when it knows it is not. Whereas Anglo-American detective stories depicted an incompetent state that did not know, and Southern Cone ones perceived a criminal state that did not want to know, the state on the Mexican-American border is portrayed as more concerned to make its citizens think that it knows, because, like the market, it needs to produce mirages to sustain itself within the margins of constituted power. The state's need to make its citizens believe in its all-pervasiveness itself reveals its own frailty.

Nevertheless, these mirages of the state do not fully work either. In the same way as we do not believe in the individual and its narratives, Bolaño seems to posit that we no longer believe in state narratives. This is what distinguishes Santa Teresa's scapegoats from, for instance, the ones that feature in Piglia or Fonseca: while in Argentina and Brazil scapegoats expose the close ties between state and criminality; in the Mexican-American border, scapegoats work as a failed *deus ex machina*: they are introduced to suddenly solve an insoluble conflict. Like Magaña and Kessler, scapegoats appear in the plot as an ephemeral restoration of meaning, which show signs of a possible happy ending, only to immediately frustrate it. They are thus more related to a failed attempt to strengthen the immunity of the state than to merely underline its criminal nature.

In Piglia there is a state that still succeeds in its production of scapegoats: in "La loca y el relato del crimen," the innocent Antúnez goes to jail in place of Almada, the real murderer. Similarly, in Fonseca's *Agosto* scapegoats are there to remind the reader of the systematic over-incarceration of Brazilian prisons. But in "The Part about the Crimes," state scapegoating fails, because after Haas is imprisoned, the feminicides just keep on growing. Even if Piglia or Fonseca were far from offering a veiled apology of the state as their Anglo-American models would do, they still believed in the efficacy of its crumbling voice. Bolaño goes even further, showing that state's narratives, in the same way as that of its coeval individualism, fail to withstand close examination.

This is what is being conveyed when the narrator mentions partial resolutions of isolated cases and how they boost, albeit ephemerally, the police's reputation and the overwhelming sense of failure. But as new feminicides accrue, state detectives' success is short-lived. These iterations work as yet another example of how the police is no longer immune, because its smoke screens cannot compete with its more unmanageable structural failure. Gradually, the narrator stops engaging with the state's voice, which communicates, but "vaguely," unabashedly subjected to shunning public responsibility, excusing itself in implausible coincidences, in the impersonal third-person as well as in the border's seamlessness. Far from enduring the symbolic muteness circumscribed to its female victims, the Mexican state speaks. But its language is weak, and (as its policemen) impotent.

## FINAL THOUGHTS: DEPERSONALIZATION AND MULTITUDE

Neoliberal depersonalization and its by-products (unintelligibility, blindness and immunity) affect all social agents, but they do so in an asymmetric and selective way. On the one side, there are the victimizers and their accomplices. For them, depersonalization is actually something positive. The novel pictures murderers, along the state and the market, as amorphous ghostly entities. They all hide themselves beneath a diffuse web of agents, who are either anonymous (nameless fugitive men, multinational companies, cartels) or whose names cannot function as the subject of a sentence, unable to compete against the all-pervasive impersonal third person.

Whereas the market appears in the form of illegal (narcos) or legal (maquilas) business (i.e., not clearly personified in any prominent character), the state also resists personification, shrouding itself in the sundry mass of failing policemen that amount to no successful detective. These different forms of depersonalization all point to self-protection. They can be read as counterforces that aim to immunize the market and the state, to wash them away from any public liability regarding the feminicides. Both the market and the state are more concerned about maintaining their immunity to social disapproval than about restoring social order. In other words, they are more engaged in protecting and polishing their own image, in ensuring that they face neither costs nor damages. Whereas the market denies the identities of its employees; the state refuses to be held responsible for the flawed protection of its citizens. In doing so, both secure power in their invisible hands. On the other side, there are the victims, the female workers, whose depersonalization, far from benefiting them in any way, turns them into bare life. All the freedom and agency that they lack belongs exclusively to their victimizers.

In a nutshell, the asymmetry that affects victimizers and victims is none other than the one that structures the problematic hierarchy between constituent and constituted power. In "The Part about the Crimes," beyond all-pervasive depersonalization and its by-products, and although there are no mythical heroes left in the plot, the reader still knows very well who the depersonalized villains are. Obviously, these two types of powers can often be juxtaposed: constituent power can easily become constituted once it has been absorbed by the structure of the state, and inversely even then constituted power can still be productive and creative in the same way as constituent power. Despite this, the asymmetric distribution of depersonalization's effects (positive for some parts of society, detrimental for others) inextricably separates the victimizers from the victims.

Ultimately, the mute and invisible victims amount to a multitude, a heterogeneous group of bodies that can neither be reduced to the Mexican people (most of them, after all, are Central American migrants, i.e., transnational bodies) nor to the traditional working class. By contrast, this multitude is exhibited in the broader notion of constituent power. Bolaño makes the point that not all the victims are workers, but they are all women. In his novel, gender makes obsolete the use of class or the nation-state's people. A depersonalized and faceless multitude, these mutilated victims are equally opposed to personification and to any kind of state representation.

If Santa Teresa's depersonalization benefits constituted power, is the opposite possible or even conceivable? Is there room for a depersonalized justice that could be functional to constituent power instead? At first sight, Bolaño seems to say there is not. His multitude is divested of its agency and affective constituent power, enduring symbolic muteness, blindness and unintelligibility. It remains ever unable to relish the privilege of exemption that is circumscribed to constituted power. But, perhaps, the destruction of personification and individualism has the potential to subvert the oppressive dimensions of the market and the state, whose laws pretend to be impersonal, but are all too often racialized and gendered.

Thinking beyond but also from Bolaño's *2666*, more recent grassroots feminist movements in Latin America such as *Ni Una Menos* could constitute an example of a political agent that aspires to such impersonal emancipation. *Ni Una Menos* seeks collective justice against gender-based violence in radically unprecedented ways: unlike many other political movements, it eschews a personalized figure that could work as their leader. Thus far, it has not been absorbed by personalist politicians who could have championed (and possibly neutralized) their agenda, within the state apparatus. In other words, it is a movement that remains within a realm of depersonalization to favor the oppressed.

Like Santa Teresa's maquila workers, *Ni Una Menos* is a multitude because it does not allow room for individualism, but also because it goes beyond the notion of the people, since it transcends spatial and chronological borders: it exceeds the territorial boundaries of specific states (spanning from Montevideo to Ciudad Juárez) and it confronts successive administrations, belonging to the whole political spectrum (from Cristina Kirchner and Dilma Rousseff to Mauricio Macri and Jair Bolsonaro): a group of bodies that is emancipatory because it does not settle for merely holding accountable specific victimizers, but aims instead to transform our patriarchal society (and its oppressive structuring structures) as a whole, so that feminicides such as those depicted by Bolaño remain audible.

When Esposito analyzes the history of impersonality in the literary tradition, he refers to the "novelist's withdrawal behind the scenes" (2012, 131) that finds its apex first in Flaubert and later in Kafka. Bolaño's withdrawal is even more radical, because through the systematic use of the third impersonal person he withdraws, like Flaubert and Kafka, his own voice but also the character's. Still, his constant use of the impersonal third-person can be read in a different light. Perhaps, it can be understood as a new expression of the path that, according to Esposito, was inaugurated by French novelist Maurice Blanchot in the 1950s: a different way of engaging with the collective, the multitude, through making visible its non-personal dimension. When Charles de Gaulle returns to power in 1958, Blanchot writes against him that "the power of refusal is accomplished neither by us nor in our name, but from a very poor beginning that belongs first of all to those who cannot speak" (qtd. in Esposito 2012, 132). Perhaps, this is the meaning of the impersonal third-person *leitmotif* that punctuates the narration of every crime, *se cerró el caso*, "the case was closed": in the path inaugurated by Blanchot, Bolaño, too, "makes impersonality not only the mode and form of the political act, but also its content" (132). Perhaps, this is the ultimate political implication to this linguistic feature: the inversion of the oppressive impersonality of the law, the market and the state into an impersonal emancipatory form of collective justice.

Even more, there is a deeper reading that goes beyond the skepticism of the book. Feminicides, as Segato defines them, are "crimes without a personalized subject that are performed on an equally depersonalized victim" (2008, 93). Due to their depersonalized characteristics that impede us from apprehending them and that grant the long-term impunity of their authors, Segato identifies feminicides with genocides, crime against women as crimes performed by a sort of "second state," a parallel state that in Mexico takes the shape of the *narcoestado* (97). That is why she stresses the importance of creating "new juridical categories" (93). Detective stories and the system of justice they portray are entrenched in the principles of liberal Contractualism, rely heavily on personhood. They depend on the opposite of depersonalization: personification. From their inception with Poe, detective stories are structured around the subject, either in the figure of the private detective, embodiment of individualism, or the criminal mastermind, often also been personified in a single individual. In short, the personification of the individualistic subject is fundamental to the construction of the detective genre. Bolaño's narrative strategy of liquifying individuals, and focusing on the multitude as a whole, can thus be read in a different, less dreary light. If "the multitude produces the common and the common enables the multitude to produce further" (Beasley-Murray 260), Bolaño' reformulation of the detective story, exposing the asymmetric distribution of immunity, can also be read as a radical recovery and re-signification of something that has all too often been bastardized in almost three decades of post-Communism and the growing naturalization of the immunitary paradigm: the idea of community.

*Chapter 6*

# Final Thoughts
## *From Failure to Community*

### FAILURE

Why think about the state today? In 1999, British Scholar Susan Strange coined the neologism "Westfailure" as part of a claim that "the system known as Westphalian has been an abject failure" (345). According to Strange, state sovereignty "has failed" (346) because of its inability to "manage and control the financial system" (345). Strange writes right after the late 1990s Asian financial crisis, and although she clarifies that she does "not mean to say that it is collapsing, only that it has failed to satisfy the long-term conditions of sustainability" (346), the role of the state since has become even more problematic. Collapse, according to Strange, is slow: "the signs of decline and ultimate disintegration appear some while before the edifice itself collapses" (346). As these Latin American detective stories imagine the post-dictatorial state, they also expose the signs of its collapse.

After all, as Beasley-Murray suggests, "it is in Latin America that the failure of modernity's social contract is most evident" (285). Even more so than in other regions of the Global South, like Africa or South Asia, where the fantasy of liberal Contractualism was not as tied to the constitution of their states. This failure manifests itself from Concepción, Montevideo, Buenos Aires and Rio de Janeiro to Ciudad Juárez. A recurring theme of these texts is that the narrative of individualism no longer works in a genre where it once did. Whereas individualism persist elsewhere, in Latin America, by contrast, the detective, private or public, always fails, in one way or another, at the hands of the post-dictatorial state. At the same time, even if the state wins out, it still fails to secure at least a mirage of Contractualism at the hands of an order that privileges constituted power only. The way these detective stories imagine the state, following Bourdieu's terminology, is as a dominated dominating force. On the one hand, it dominates the individual and the people; on the other, it is dominated by the market. This also resonates with Strange's Westfailure in terms of the inability of the state to contain the "financial system."

This common understanding of failure also features in non-fictional texts written by the authors I have analyzed. In the last volume of his posthumously published diary, for instance, Piglia writes extensively and explicitly about failure. He sees failure as part of his individual self, "the secret story of my life" (2017, 154). Piglia believes that the very "condition of art" (70) is failure, the "driving force" both of his diaries (154) and his novel *Respiración artificial* (71). This can also be claimed about "La loca y el relato del crimen" as well as *Plata quemada*. Putting failure center stage, then, constitutes a poetics: in Piglia's words, "a sort of negative epic" of "those who have failed" (71). This poetics is not individual, but collective, linked to his generation and their defeat by constituted power.

As Ana María Amar Sánchez claims, defeat is central to understand this use of failure: in Latin America, "where governments are behind the crimes and laws protect murderers, success is always suspicious" (qtd. in Hoyos 64). Whereas for Hoyos, this "culture of defeat" appears in Colombian detective stories as a "trait of national identity," defeat is central and transnational in the poetics of failure of the authors that I have examined. In a diary entry from 1982, Piglia observes that as dictatorship in Argentina ended, so did (in parallel and perhaps surreptitiously) "an age in which a better reality was possible, an era in which he and his friends [. . .] had triumphed because they were still alive and fighting but they had also been defeated, their bodies filled with scars, they were survivors, they were casualties of war" (2017, 159). Similarly, in the last article of his posthumous book *Entre paréntesis*, Bolaño defines his own novel, *Los detectives salvajes*, as the attempt to portray a "generational defeat" (2004b, 327). A similar case can be made about *Estrella distante* and *2666* or even Fonseca's *Agosto*. According to Strange, the fact that the Westphalian state "survives despite its failures only shows the difficulty of finding and building an alternative" (346). The stories that I have examined oscillate between these two poles: the prolongation of the ruin and the implausibility of choice.

In 1991, Gilles Deleuze claimed in an interview for *Le Nouvel Observateur* that "the bloody failure of socialism is on everybody's lips, but no one sees capitalist globalization as a failure, in spite of the bloody inequalities that condition the market and the populations who are excluded from it" (379). Now, almost three decades after the dissolution of the Soviet Union, Deleuze's observation seems more relevant than ever. During the last quarter of the twentieth century, the foundations of global capital were rooted in the unrestricted transnational circulation of commodities (NAFTA and the proliferation of free trade agreements that mimicked it) and even of labor (via Mercosur or the Schengen Area) across the boundaries of porous states. The world order produced by the Great Recession of 2008 has challenged these foundations with a surge of personalist leaders in mainstream politics who aim to restore nationalist, protectionist, and/or racist policies, thus marking a new stage in the ever-changing history of capitalism.

Strange diagnosed already in the late 1990s our present scenario: "immigrants, unemployed, refugees, peasants, and all those who already feel that globalization does nothing for them and are inclined to look to warlords, Mafias or extreme-right fascist politicians for protection" (346). The uneven effects of globalization, i.e.,: of transnational neoliberalism, are what led Strange to claim that the foundations of the Westphalian state, once an indispensable requirement for the existence of global capital, were starting to crumble. This gradual transformation redefines the silhouette of what the state used to be and what it is becoming, even if this collapse leads to a new conservative order, even if all this redefinition takes place for the sake of the survival of capitalism itself.

Written during the 1990s, most of these Latin American stores share Strange and Deleuze's interpretation of failure: they question classic Contractualism as well as the different regional translations of neoliberalism, that during post-dictatorship were deemed unquestionable thanks to the disintegration of the Eastern Bloc and the subsequent installation of what French journalist Jean-François Kahn named *pensée unique*, the single thought that regulated the limits of what was politically possible. Despite its multifaceted aspects, Piglia, Bolaño and Fonseca offer a counter-narrative with a common critique: faced with the triumphant narrative of globalization (whose flaws, as Deleuze noted, went unnoticed by most); they put a poetics of failure at center stage. But this prominence of failure and its oscillation between ruins and lack of choice does not have to be read as a bleak prognosis of the future in a nihilistic and unidimensional way. Beyond this ambivalent oscillation, the poetics of failure offers, instead, a more emancipatory possibility: a different understanding of community.

## COMMUNITY

In *Communitas. The Origin and Destiny of Community* (1998), Esposito offers a re-reading of the concept. He opens with a concern that is reminiscent of Deleuze's words: "Nothing seems more appropriate today than thinking community, nothing more necessary, demanded, and heralded by a situation that joins in a unique epochal knot the failure of all communisms with the misery of new individualisms" (2009, 1). After examining the meanings of community for Heidegger and Bataille, among others, Esposito argues that a return to the idea of community can have an emancipatory dimension that is far from the nostalgic and oppressive way in which the concept currently features in mainstream politics, but also far from the defeated Communist order. Communism is dead, long live the Community!

To imagine the future of community, Esposito, paradoxically, looks to a remote past: he harks back to the Latin etymology of the word. What is common, he concludes, is not what is proper (the territory, the land, the nation), because what is "proper" is private. This distorted notion of the common is more defined by exclusion than by inclusion, because what is private always belongs to a necessarily limited number of owners. Instead, community should be understood as "what belongs to more than one, to many or to everyone, and therefore is that which is 'public'" (2009, 3). What is common, then, is not circumscribed to boundaries of ethnicity, class, religion or gender, it rather belongs to everybody. For Esposito, "community" cannot be confined to the realm of *we* (that is so often appropriated by constituted power), it is rather intertwined with the impersonal third person that operates throughout Bolaño's "The Part about the Crimes": community is anyone and no one.

According to Esposito, then, community is not a property, not an asset that belongs to subjects. "It isn't having, but on the contrary, is a debt, a pledge, a gift that is to be given, and that therefore will establish a lack" (2009, 6). It is in this regard that his understanding of the concept is indebted to Agamben's "coming community," whose members are not "tied by any common property, by any identity" (1993, 5). The common and the proper, far from being synonyms, are then antonyms. Agamben also defines the members of the coming community in terms of lack, as "they are expropriated of all identity" (5). In other words: community cannot be identified with attributes but with depersonalizing lacks.

More importantly, *communitas* is diametrically opposed to *immunitas*. Whereas *immunitas* is that which lacks a *munus*, a duty to others, *communitas* is what includes that duty, *cum munus*. But this duty is not an attribute, it is a lack, a debt towards society: "The *munus* is the obligation that is contracted with respect to the other [. . .] *Munus* [. . .] is giving something that one can *not keep* oneself and over which [. . .] one is not completely master" (Esposito's italics, 2009, 5). In the same way that in "The Part about the Crimes" subjects are surpassed by an unintelligible language, they are transcended by *communitas*. Esposito claims that "community cannot be thought of as a body, as a corporation in which individuals are founded in a larger individual" (2009, 7). To put it differently, community cannot be subject to the state nor to a personalist leader that represents it. Community cannot be reduced either to the people or to civil society.

The poetics of failure resonates with Esposito's radical hermeneutical shift of community's meanings. This sense of community appears in brief albeit fundamental narrative glimpses, such as when, in *Agosto*, Mattos and the multitude in Rio de Janeiro are divested of Vargas's coffin. It reappears in the mourning for the speechless women of Bolaño's "The Part about the Crimes" or the *desaparecidos* under Pinochet that feature in *Estrella distante*. But more broadly, these iterations of community are intertwined with the poetics of failure because the latter posits the dissolution of traditional representations of individualism and the state, the I and the We, and it rethinks both categories as bodies filled not with lacks, that in these detective stories take the shape of symbolic disabilities.

The poetics of failure overcomes the myth of individualistic detectives while it aims to challenge the very possibility of personification itself, in a literary and a political way: respectively, in the pulverization of the private eye and of the sovereign. Once the symbolic disabilities of the state have infected individuals as well, everyone in the community, individualistic heroes and state officers, the private eye and the policemen, are structured by their lacks: blindness, deafness, muteness, impotence, infertility, paralysis, illiteracy, and unintelligibility, and so on. Everyone and anyone are equalized by lacks, thus constituting an acephalous and impersonal community.

The poetics of failure also shares the impersonal dimension of Esposito's *communitas*, as shown in the arc whose path goes from personification to depersonalization, from a solid and stable *ego* to the impersonal third person. From the ruins of a crumbling post-dictatorial state, a potential for a new understanding of community arises. Despite the attempt to personify individualism or the state, detectives and policemen are ultimately engulfed by community. Because, as Esposito puts it, "community isn't an entity nor is it a collective subject, nor a totality of subjects, but rather is the relation that makes them no longer individual subjects because it closes them off from their identity with a line, which traversing them, alters them" (2009 139). This "line" is the *cum*, the "with" in *communitas*.

As a result of this line, there is no room for individualism or for the state as we know it in this understanding of community. Tagle/Wieder, first portrayed as a great individualistic personality, ends up melting into the thin air of the Chilean diaspora in Europe, and ultimately becomes indistinguishable from his victims. Something similar happens to Mattos when he becomes political and corrupt and, subsequently, when he joins the multitude in the streets: his individuality is dissolved to be assimilated by the crowd. The systematic use of the third person, in "The Part about the Crimes," swallows up any Deleuzian "specks of dust" of personhood. This is also a way of reading the presence of the multitude that invades both the individual and the state in these narratives. Even if Esposito does not explicitly mention the multitude, ultimately, it is not that alien to the common: both are "only lack and not possession, property, or appropriation" (2009, 139). If the community cannot be identified with the people, it must then be aligned with the multitude.[1] The poetics of failure, then, pulverizes the incarnation of the traditional masculine sovereign while at the same time offering the emergence of an impersonal multitude, one that aims to be emancipated from class and gender oppressive mechanisms.

## NEITHER INDIVIDUALISM NOR THE STATE

Watt finds that the twentieth century rewriting of the classic myths he studies, specifically Mann's *Doctor Faustus* (1947) and Tournier's *Vendredi* (1967), no longer display "an endorsement of individualism" (274). After examining these detective stories, something similar can be said about the private eye in Latin America. Likewise, Adorno once wrote that Kafka's work exhibits "a skepticism towards the *ego*" (250). As shown in this book, a kindred skepticism hovers over the works of Piglia, Bolaño and Fonseca, who in this regard are inheritors of Kafka. After all, Renzi, Romero and Mattos are far from being heroes, reproductions of a masculine self that in Anglo-American detective fiction has traditionally been represented as a flawless and stable *ego contra mundum*. Not even their anti-heroism is heroic.

By contrast, this Kafkaesque "skepticism towards the *ego*" constitutes a radical critique of individualism at a time when the individual was at the core of neoliberal politics. German-Catalan theorist Robert Caner-Liese claims that Kafka aimed to "unmask this *ego* that presents itself as compact, consistent, univocal and solid" (16). Caner-Liese cites Adorno's description of a self who is gifted with an "identical, instrumental and virile character" (Horkheimer and Adorno 26), and who "believes to be able to amplify his limitless masculine domination" (Caner-Liese 16). Piglia, Bolaño and Fonseca are indebted to this Kafkaesque critique of the self, as all their individuals are utterances of failure. Following an arc, in which the *immunitas* of the masculine embodiment of sovereignty gradually vanishes, from Borges's Lönnrot to the multitudinous detectives of Santa Teresa, this skepticism towards the *ego* leads to an engulfing of individualism by an all-pervasive community.

To articulate this skepticism, all these narratives resort to detective stories as a means of social commentary. But they also share something less evident: in one way or another, they all establish a dialogue between this tradition and at least one other genre. They all combine a dominant genre, detective fiction, with a peripheral one that adjoins them. Piglia's "La loca y el relato del crimen" and *Plata quemada* draw from Walsh's non-fiction novel; Bolaño's *Estrella distante* and *2666* can be read as responses to both the dictator novel and *testimonio*; Fonseca's *Agosto* engages with the historical novel. Despite their differences, what these adjoining genres have in common is that they all rely heavily on factuality. In this tension, between the mirage of data transparency and literary elaboration, between myth and historiography, between imagination and information, the former always overcomes the latter. Yet mythification is not meant, as it once was, to endorse individualism but to destroy it.

On the other hand, most of the narratives examined in this book put at center stage an *alter ego*, which is the very condition of existence of another literary genre: autofiction. A genre that is fundamentally contemporary with the post-dictatorial context in Latin America (and more broadly, with post-modern literature), autofiction toys with factuality to render it irrelevant. Emilio and Renzi, after all, are Piglia's middle and second last name, and as I mention in Chapter 2, Renzi and Piglia follow a parallel life path. The preface to *Estrella distante* states that the story was written in Blanes, where Bolaño spent the last years of his life and where the story's denouement takes place. The anonymous narrator/author claims to have written the story with the help of Arturo B., a pseudonym that alludes to Arturo Belano, a character that reappears constantly in Bolaño's work. Fonseca, like Mattos, was also a policeman who became a commissioner during Vargas's last administration. Nonetheless, these alternative selves are not at the service of glorifying the subject; they partake instead in a common strategy of fragmenting it. A similar case can be made for the *Doppelgängers* (Gaucho/Nene, Tagle/Wieder, Mattos/Vargas) and madmen (the Madwoman, Mattos and Lalo Cura) that also permeate these texts. As Foucault claims, "madness is the *déjà-là* of death" (1988b, 27). This inherent preeminence of death reminds the reader of the limits of individualism, at a time in which its alleged boundless powers (of consumption, of production, etc.) are constantly advertised. *Alter egos*, *Doppelgängers*, and madmen are all different forms of attenuations, fragmentations of individualism, that lead to its ultimate engulfment by community.

Unlike Kafka, who still believed in (and feared) the power of the state, with its oppressive bureaucracy; the poetics of failure espouses a skepticism that is not only aimed towards individualism but also towards the state. This twofold skepticism is what distinguishes Piglia, Bolaño, and Fonseca from their Anglo-American precursors. As Giardinelli observes, "almost all North American detective fiction writers, even the most radical ones, ultimately, have always trusted the deep virtues of the state and its ability to regenerate" (224), despite their apparent disdain towards the state. In *Realidad y ficción en Latinoamérica* (1975), the Chilean Jaime Validivieso notes that this narrative of perfectibility produced in the United States "a society and institutions in which people put their trust in, even when they have flaws, because they think that the germ of improvement will come out from them" (Giardinelli 228).

As we have seen, Poe and his heirs are deeply immersed in the perfectible potential of the state. They may toy with the incompetence of its officers, they might question its efficiency or even its good intentions, but ultimately, they still think the state is necessary. They cannot think outside of nor beyond the apology for classic Westphalian sovereignty. Perfectibility, i.e.,: the pursuit of a "more perfect union" within the boundaries of the state, as established in the Preamble to the American Constitution, is never truly questioned. By contrast, in Latin America, as Giardinelli says, this sense of trust towards the state is much rarer, as rare as the success of "individual efforts and personal audacity" (228). Therefore, the poetics of failure constitutes a truly radical criticism, that arises from the fact that in Latin America the state failed to camouflage its servility towards constituted power and it foundered to secure the mirages of Contractualism.

This book shows how the tensions between individualism and the state are inaugurated, reproduced, and consolidated in Anglo-American detective fiction to be later problematized, subverted, and overcome in Latin America. Ultimately, this book lays the foundations for *how* we should read and study detective fiction henceforth. By focusing on the exceptionality of these reformulations, I hope to have shed light on their truly radical critique of the state and individualism. Against Watt's *ego contra mundum*, Piglia, Bolaño, and Fonseca rewrite this opposition, transforming *ego contra mundum* into *nec ego nec mundus*: neither the individualism nor the state. In their stead, they announce the emergence of a radical and unprecedented community.

# Notes

## CHAPTER 1

1. This sentence is not included in Buttigieg's English translation of Gramsci's *Prison Notebooks*. The original Italian text states: "l'atteggiamento del sentimento pubblico verso l'apparato della giustizia, sempre screditato e quindi fortuna del poliziotto privato o dilettante."

2. Except for Chesterton's Father Brown stories, religious agents are generally absent from early detective stories.

3. Joy N. Humes's translation of Goldmann's essay does not include a series of paragraphs that appear in the French text, amongst which there is this observation that is located in page 183 of the original, which states: "disparition de l'individualisme sur le plan de l'économie (processus que les penseurs marxistes ont enregistré sous la forme [. . .] de passage du capitalisme classique à l'impérialisme) et la transformation homologue du roman caractérisée précisément par la disparition du personnage individuel et du récit biographique" ("Introduction aux premiers écrits de Lukács," in Lukács, Georg, *La théorie du roman*, Gallimard 2005, 183).

## CHAPTER 2

1. Donald A. Yates (1956) and Chilean detective fiction writer Díaz Eterovic (31) remind us that this practice was also common during the first half of the twentieth century in Chile. Writers like Camilo Pérez de Arce and Alfredo Etcheverry published detective stories under the pen names James Endhard and Terry Beech. As Díaz Eterovic notes, "the more English-sounding was the pen name, the better" (31).

2. Chilean and Brazilian national literatures use parody as a mechanism of importing detective fiction in their respective literary fields, too. For a history of Chilean detective fiction and its early uses of parody, see Franken Kurzen, *Crimen y verdad en la novela policial chilena actual*, p. 9. For Brazil's use of parody, see Chapter 4 of this book.

3. See Julio Premat, "Los espejos y la cópula son abominables" and Francisca Noguerol, "Neopolicial latinoamericano: el triunfo del asesino."

4. Spanish has even more aquatic metaphors than English, as in *el hundimiento general de una economía,* or *un escándalo que salpica la imagen de una corporación.*

## CHAPTER 3

1. Vicente Huidobro's verse is used as an epigraph with the authorization granted by the Fundación - Museo Vicente Huidobro, Cartagena, Chile.

2. See p. 66.

3. For the dictatorial uses of language, see Feitlowitz's *A Lexicon of Terror* and Calveiro's *Poder y desaparición.*

## CHAPTER 4

1. Portions of Chapter 4 were originally published as "Entering History through Literature: Personalism and Personification in Agosto's *Fonseca,*" *Chasqui,* vol. 49, issue 2, November 2020, 72–89.

2. The translation was modified because Foucault uses *romanesque* in the original. The original English translation states "romantic," which misses the sense of *romance,* related to the novel more than to Romanticism.

3. Other translations prefer "nightmare," instead of the weight of a Mountain Range to convey Marx's German original "lastet wie ein Alp."

## CHAPTER 5

1. Portions of Chapter 5 are derived from "'A language not of this world': Depersonalization and Unintelligibility in Robert Bolaño's 'The Part about the Crimes,'" an article published in *Journal of Latin American Cultural Studies,* 2021, ©Taylor and Francis, available online at www.tandfonline.com/doi/abs/10.1080/13569325.2020.1798219.

2. A lack of individualism, of course, does not necessarily imply an absence or a rejection of the notion of "individuals." In Fonseca, individuals are still at play. Hence, the exploration of Mattos's personality in detail, following the tradition of North American hard-boiled fiction, or even the mythical figure of Vargas's personalism.

## CHAPTER 6

1. The fact that this multitude is defined by its engulfment of individualism and by its subsequent lack of personality (it doesn't have a "we" that would exclude those

who do not share "our" attributes), does not necessarily mean that these multitude may not allow for individuals. After all, Bolaño still introduces us to characters, however precarious and depersonalized they may be. Whether the Spinozian notion of multitude must be understood as a subject of political struggle or not exceeds the scope of this book as it is an ongoing discussion in political theory.

# Bibliography

*Online Etymology Dictionary,* www.etymonline.com.
*Dizionario Etimologico,* www.etimo.it.
Adorno, Theodor W. "Notes on Kafka." *Prisms. Studies in Contemporary German Thought.* Translated by Samuel and Shierry Weber, Massachusetts Institute of Technology Press, 1983, pp. 243–271.
Agamben, Giorgio. *The Coming Community.* Translated by Michael Hardt, University of Minnesota Press, 1993.
———. *Homo Sacer: Sovereign Power and Bare Life.* Translated by Daniel Heller-Roazen, Stanford University Press, 1998.
———. *State of Exception.* Translated by Kevin Attell, University of Chicago Press, 2005.
Althusser, Louis. "Appendix 2: Ideology and Ideological State Apparatuses." *On the Reproduction of Capital. Ideology and Ideological State Apparatuses.* Translated from the French by Ben Brewster. Verso, 2014, pp. 232–272.
Archbold, John William. "Las masculinidades de los hombres homosexuales en *Plata quemada*, de Ricardo Piglia." *Cuadernos de literatura del Caribe e Hispanoamérica,* 22, 2015, pp. 107–122. doi.org/10.15648/cl.22.2015.7.
Arenas Oyarce, Mauricio. "La articulación del fracas en dos autores latinoamericanos: *Arturo, la Estrella más brillante* de Reinaldo Anenas y *Estrella distante* de Roberto Bolaño. *Acta Literaria,* N° 47, II Sem, 2013, pp. 51–67.
Avelar, Idelber. *The Untimely Present: Post-dictatorial Latin American Fiction and the Task of Mourning,* e-book, Duke University Press, 1999, pp. 107–135.
———. "Alegorías de lo apócrifo: Ricardo Piglia, duelo y traducción." *Ricardo Piglia. Valoración múltiple,* Instituto Caro y Cuervo, 2000, pp. 1–9.
Ayala Gauna, Velmiro. "La pesquisa de Don Frutos." *Cuentos correntinos,* Castellví, 1955, pp. 50–59.
Balibar, Étienne. *Politics and the Other Scene.* Translated by Christine Jones, James Swenson, Chris Turner. Verso, 2002.
Barrientos Tecún, Dante. "La novela policíaca en Centroamérica: un género marginal. El caso de *La muerte en Si menor* (1997) de José Mejía (Guatemala, 1939)." Edited by Néstor Ponce and Raúl Caplan. PONCE, *Lectures du récit policier*

*hispano-américain*, actes du Colloque du Groupe de Recherches Inter-Langues de l'Université d'Angers (GRILUA), 2005, pp. 15–25.

———. "¿Detectives? ¿asesinos? ¿Justicieros? ¿quién es quién? El enigma de la identidad en las novelas de la violencia peruana (*Lituma en los Andes*, *Abril rojo*) y el narcotráfico en México (*Trabajos del reino*)," "Les formes hétérogènes du roman policier. Violence et pouvoir dans le roman latino-américain," *Cahiers d'études romanes*, 31, 2015, pp. 109–120. doi.org/10.4000/etudesromanes.5027.

Barthes, Roland. *Mythologies*. Translated by Annette Lavers, Farrar, Straus and Giroux, 1991.

Beasley-Murray, Jon. *Posthegemony. Political Theory and Latin America,* University of Minnesota Press, 2010.

Belsey, Catherine. *Poststructuralism. A Very Short Introduction*, Oxford United Press, 2002.

Benjamin, Walter. "Critique of Violence." *Reflections. Essays, Aphorisms, Autobiographical Writings.* Translated by Edmund Jephcott, Schocken, 1978, pp. 277–300.

———. "On the Concept of History." *Selected Writings (1938–1940)*. Translated by Edmund Jephcott, Harvard University Press, 2003, pp. 389–411.

Benveniste, Émile. "The Nature of Pronouns." *Problems in General Linguistics*. Translated by Mary Elizabeth Meek, University of Miami Press, 1978, pp. 217–222.

———. "Relationships of Person in the Verb." *The Communication Theory Reader*. Translated by Paul Cobley, Routledge, 1996, pp. 195–204.

Blanco Calderón, Rodrigo. "Piglia y Gombrowicz: sobre el fracaso y otras estrategias de escritura." *El lugar de Piglia: crítica sin ficción.* Edited by Jorge Carrión, Candaya, 2008, pp. 35–43.

Bolaño, Roberto. "El infame Ramírez Hoffman." *La literatura nazi en América*, Seix Barral, 1996.

———. *Distant Star*. Translated by Chris Andrews, The Harvil Press, 2004a.

———. *Entre paréntesis. Ensayos, artículos y discursos (1998–2003)*, Anagrama, 2004b.

———. "The Part about the Crimes." *2666,* Farrar, Straus, Giroux, 2008, pp. 278–498.

Borges, Jorge Luis and Bioy Casares, Adolfo. "The Twelve Figures of the World." *Six Problems for Don Isidro Parodi*. Translated by Norman Thomas, Dutton, 1983, pp. 17–36.

Borges, Jorge Luis, "Death and the Compass." *Labyrinths*. Translated by Donald A. Yates. Edited by James E. Irby and William Gibson, New Directions, 1962, pp. 76–87.

———. "Our Poor Individualism." *Other Inquisitions*. Translated by Ruth L. C. Simms, University of Texas Press, 1964, pp. 33–36.

———. "Sobre el cuento policial." *Borges oral*, Emecé, 1979, pp. 76–80.

Bosque, Ignacio and Gutiérrez Rexach, Javier. *Fundamentos de sintaxis formal*, Akal, 2008.

Bosteels, Bruno. "The Post-Leninist Detective." *Marx and Freud in Latin America: Politics, Psychoanalysis and Religion in Times of Terror,* Verso, 2012, pp. 253–272.

Bourdieu, Pierre. *Outline of a Theory of Practice*. Translated by Richard Nice, Cambridge University Press, 1977
———. *Masculine Domination*. Translated by Richard Nice, Stanford University Press, 1999.
———. *On the State. Lectures at the College de France, 1989–1992*. Translated by David Fernbach, Polity, 2014.
Braham, Persephone. *Crimes against the State, Crimes against Persons*, University of Minnesota Press, 2004.
Brecht, Bertolt. "De la popularidad de la novela policiaca." *El compromiso en literatura y arte*, Península, 1984, pp. 341–346.
Brescia, Pablo. "*Whodunit*: Borges y el policial en las revistas literarias argentinas." *Inti: Revista de literature hispánica*, 77, 2013, pp. 265–275.
Brownson, Charles. *The Figure of the Detective*, MacFarland, 2014.
Bruce, Susan and Wagner, Valeria. "Introduction: A Textbook Case." *Fiction and Economy*, Palgrave Macmillan, 2007, pp. 1–23.
Calabrese, Elisa. "Casos policiales: una genealogía del enigma en la Argentina." *Anales de literatura hispanoamericana*, 2007, pp. 37–47.
Calveiro, Pilar. *Poder y desaparición. Los campos de concentración en Argentina*, Colihue, 1998.
Caner-Liese, Robert. "'Fugacitat Eternitzada.' Temps i perspectiva en els assaigs d'Adorno i Benjamin sobre Kafka." *Comprendre*, vol. 15/I, 2013, pp. 5–27.
Capdevila, Analía. "Una polémica olvidada (Borges contra Caillois sobre el policial)." *Boletín del Grupo de Estudios de Teoría Literaria* 4, 1995, pp. 65–78.
Carini, Sara. "El trabajo, al lector: Nuevas formas de representación del poder en *Trabajos del reino* de Yuri Herrera." *Ogigia* 12, 2012, pp. 45–57.
Catelli, Nora. "El laboratorio Bolaño." *Babelia. El País*, September 13, 2002.
Cervantes, Miguel de. *Don Quixote*, Xist, 2015. Kindle.
Chandler, Tertius and Fox, Gerald. "World's Largest Cities 100 A.D. – 1968," *3000 Years of Urban Growth*. Elsevier, 2013, pp. 303–341.
Chandler, Raymond. *The Long Goodbye*, Random House, 1953.
———. *Farewell, My Lovely*, Paperback, 1988.
———. *The Simple Art of Murder*, Faded Page, 2014.
Christie, Agatha. *The Mysterious Affair at Styles*, e-book, Anna Ruggieri, 2017.
Clayton, Michelle. "Cómo habla la plata." *Ricardo Piglia: una poética sin límites*. Edited by Adriana Rodríguez Pérsico and Jorge Fornet, Universidad of Pittsburgh Press, 2004, pp. 135–144.
Conan Doyle, Arthur. "The Adventure of the Yellow Face," 1893, sherlock-holm.es/stories/pdf/a4/1-sided/yell.pdf.
———. "The Adventure of the Red Circle," 1917, sherlock-holm.es/stories/pdf/a4/1-sided/redc.pdf.
———. *A Study in Scarlet*, Oxford University Press, 1993.
———. "The Norwood Builder." *The Sherlock Holmes Mysteries*, Penguin, 2014, pp. 298–321.
Cselik, Ágnes. "Los conceptos de tiempo y espacio en las obras de Ricardo Piglia: 'La loca y el relato del crimen." *Études Romanes de Brno*. 30, 2009, 2, pp. 121–128.

De Grandis, Rita. "Lo histórico y lo cotidiano en *Operación masacre* de Rodolfo Walsh." *Actas Irvine-92: Actas de XI Congreso de la Asociación Internacional de Hispanistas*. Edited by Juan Villegas, vol. 5. *Lecturas y relecturas de textos españoles, latinoamericanos y US latinos*, pp. 305–313.

De Rosso, Ezequiel. "Una lectura conjetural. Roberto Bolaño y el relato policial." *Roberto Bolaño: la escritura como tauromaquia*. Edited by Celina Manzoni, Corregidor, 2002, pp. 133–143.

Deckard, Sharae. "Peripheral Realism, Millennial Capitalism, and Roberto Bolaño's *2666*." *Modern Language Quarterly*, 2012, pp. 351–372.

Delaney, Juan José. "Sobre los orígenes de la literatura fantástica, policial y de ficción científica en la Argentina." *Historia crítica de la literatura argentina*, Emecé, 2006, pp. 607–634.

Deleuze, Gilles. "We Invented the Ritornello." *Two Regimes of Madness. Texts and Interviews 1975–1995*. Translated by Ames Hodges and Mike Taormina, Columbia University Press, 2007, pp. 377–381.

Derrida, Jacques, "The Purveyor of Truth." *Yale French Studies*. Translated by Willis Domingo, James Hulbert, Moshe Ron and M.-R.L. 52, 1975, pp. 31–113.

———. *Of Grammatology*. Translated by Gayatri Spivak. John Hopkins University Press, 1997.

Díaz Eterovic, Ramón. "Crimen, poder y verdad en la novela criminal chilena." *Diseños de nuevas geografías en la novela y el cine negros de Argentina y Chile*. Edited by Sabine Schmitz, Annegret Thiem, Daniel A. Verdú Schumann, Iberoamericana Vervuet, 2013, 31–44.

Dunkerley, James. "Political Suicide in Latin America." *Political Suicide in Latin America and Other Essays*. Verso, 1992. pp. 1–38.

Engels, Friedrich. *Selected Correspondence, Marx and Engels on Literature and Art, Progress Publishers, 1976*.

Enzensberger, Hans Magnus. Politics and crime. Seabury Press, 1974.

Esposito, Roberto. *Communitas. The Origin and Destiny of Community*. Translated by Timothy Campbell, Stanford University Press, 2009.

———. *Immunitas: Protection and Negation of Life*. Translated by Zakiya Hanafi, Polity, 2011.

———. *The Third Person. Politics of Life and Philosophy of the Impersonal*. Translated by Zakiya Hanafi, Polity, 2012.

———. *The Origin of the Political: Hannah Arendt or Simone Weil?* Translated by Vincenzo Binetti and Gareth Williams, Fordham Press, 2017.

Even-Zohar, Itamar. "The Position of Translated Literature within the Literary Polysystem," *Literature and Translation*. Acco, 1978, pp. 117–127.

Feitlowitz, Marguerite. *A Lexicon of Terror: Argentina and the Legacies of Torture*, Oxford University Press, 1998.

Feinman José Pablo. "Estado policial y novela negra argentina. Los héroes 'difíciles'". Literatura policial en Argentina y en Italia. Edited by Giusseppe Petronio, Jorge Rivera y Luigi Volta. Corregidor, 1991. 143-153.

Fonseca, Rubem. *Crimes of August*. Translated by Clifford E. Landers, University of Massachussets Press, 2014.

Foucault, Michel. "Prison Talk." *Power/Knowledge, Selected Interviews and Other Writings.* Translated by Colin Gordon, Leo Marshall, John Mepham, Kate Soper, Pantheon Books, 1980, pp. 37–54.

———. "The Political Technology of Individuals." *Technologies of the Self: A Seminar with Michel Foucault.* Edited by Luther H. Martin, Huck Gutman & Patrick H. Hutton, University of Massachusetts Press, 1988a, pp. 145–162.

———. "Stultifera Navis." *Madness and Civilization: A History of Insanity in the Age of Reason.* Translated by Richard Howard, Vintage, 1988b, pp. 3–38.

———. "Useless to Revolt?" *Power (The Essential Work of Foucault 1954-1984. Vol, 3),.*Translated by Robert Hurley, The New Press, 2001, pp. 449–453.

———. "10 January 1979." *The Birth of Biopolitics Lectures at the Collège de France, 1978-1979.* Translated by Graham Burchell, Springer, 2008, pp. 75–100.

Franken Kurzen, Clemens. *Crimen y verdad en la novela policial chilena actual.* Universidad de Santiago de Chile, 2003.

Frelick, Nancy, "Introduction." *The Mirror in Medieval and Early Modern Culture.* Brepols, 2016.

Fresán, Rodrigo. "Arquitectura del encierro." *El lugar de Piglia: crítica sin ficción.* Edited by Jorge Carrión, 2008, pp. 304–307.

Galeano, Eduardo. *The Open Veins of Latin America. Five Centuries of Pillage of a Continent.* Translated by Cedric Belfrage, Monthly Review Press, 1995.

Gamerro, Carlos. "Para una reformulación del género policial argentino." *El nacimiento de la literatura argentina y otros ensayos,* Norma, 2006, pp. 79–91.

———. "Disparen sobre el policial negro," *Clarín,* 13, August 2008.

García, Miguel Ángel. *Immigrazione italiana nell'America del Sud (Brasile, Uruguay, Argentina), Federazione italiana lavoratori emigranti e famiglie,* 2003.

Giardinelli, Mempo. *El género negro. Orígenes y evolución de la literatura policial y su influencia en Latinoamérica.* Capital Intelectual, 2013.

Glick, Elisa. "The Dialectics of Dandyism." *Cultural Critique,* 48 (Spring, 2001), pp. 129–163.

Gobbo, Marcelo. "Autobiografía de un estilo." *Piglia. Una poética sin límites,* Instituto Internacional Literatura Iberoamericana, 2004, pp. 41–54.

Goldmann, Lucien. "The Early Writings of Lukács." *TriQuarterly.* Tanslated by Joy N. Humes, Northwestern University Press, 1967, pp. 165–181.

González, Horacio. "The Journalist as the People's Detective." *The Argentina Reader.*Translated by Mark Alan Healey. Edited by Gabriela Nouzeilles, Graciela Montaldo, Robin Kirk and Orin Starn, Duke University Press, 2002, pp. 495–499. doi: 10.1515/9780822384182-070.

Gramsci, Antonio. "Sul romanzo poliziesco." *I Quaderni dei Carceri,* quadernidelcarcere.wordpress.com/2015/05/10/sul-romanzo-poliziesco/.

Grimal, Pierre. *Love in Ancient Rome,* University of Oklahoma Press, 1986.

Halperín Donghi, Tulio. *El revisionismo histórico argentino como visión decadentista de la historia nacional,* Siglo XXI, 2005.

Hammett, Dashiell. *Red Harvest,* Vintage, 1992.

Harvey, David. *A Brief History of Neoliberalism,* Oxford University Press, 2005.

———. *A Companion to Marx's Capital.* Verso, 2010

Horkheimer, Max and Adorno Theodor. "The Concept of Enlightenment." *Dialectic of Enlightenment. Philosophical Fragments.* Translated by Edmund Jephcott, Stanford University Press, 2002, pp. 1–35.
Hoyos, Héctor. "Del detective al fisgón: el policial costumbrista en Colombia," *Lingüística y literatura*, 55, 2009, pp. 52–71.
Hutcheon, Linda. *A Theory of Parody: The Teachings of Twentieth-Century Art Forms*, University of Illinois Press, 2001.
Jakobson, Roman. "La dominante," *Huit questions de poétique*, Seuil, 1977, pp. 77–85.
Jelly-Schapiro, Eli. "'This Is Our Threnody': Roberto Bolaño and the History of the Present," *Critique: Studies in Contemporary Fiction* 56:1, 2015, pp. 77–93.
Jofré, José Luis. "Empresas públicas: de estatales a privadas (1976–2001)" *Revista Confluencia*, 3, number 6, summer 2007, pp. 267–289.
Kracauer, Siegfried. *The Detective Novel.* Blackwell, 2005.
Kraniauskas, John. "A Monument to the Unknown Worker," *Radical Philosophy*, 2016. pp. 37–46.
Kurnick, David. "Comparison, Allegory, and the Address of 'Global' Realism (The Part about Bolaño)," *Boundary.* May 2015, pp. 105–134.
Lacan, Jacques. "Seminar on 'The Purloined Letter,'" translated by Jeffrey Mehlman, 1972, www.lacan.com/purloined.htm.
Lafforgue, Jorge y Rivera, Jorge B. *Asesinos de papel: ensayos sobre narrativa policial.* Colihue, 1996.
Lambert, José. "Production, tradition et importation: une clef pour la description de la littérature et de la littérature en traduction," *Revue Canadienne de Littérature Comparée*, 1980, pp. 246–252.
Lévi-Strauss, Claude. *Tristes Tropiques.* Translated by John Russell, Criterion, 1961.
———. *Myth and Meaning. Cracking the Code of Culture.* Routledge, 1978.
Levinas, Emmanuel. "The Face to Face—An Irreducible Relation." *Totality and Infinity. An Essay on Exteriority.* Translated by Alphonso Lingis, Martinus Nijhoff, 1979, pp. 79–80.
Levinson, Brett. "Case Closed: Madness and Dissociation in *2666*," *Journal of Latin American Cultural Studies* 2009, vol. 18, 2–3, pp. 177–191. doi: 10.1080/13569320903361879.
Link, Daniel et al. *El juego de los cautos.* La Marca Editora, 1992.
Ludmer, Josefina. *El cuerpo del delito. Un manual.* Perfil, 1999.
Lukács, György. *The Theory of The Novel. A Historic-Philosophical Essay on the Forms of Great Epic Literature.* Translated by Anna Bostock. Massachusetts Institute of Technology Press, 2005.
Lynd, Juliet. "The Politics of Performance and the Performance of Narrative in Bolaño's *Distant Star*," *Chasqui: Revista de literatura latinoamericana*, 2011, pp. 180–188.
Mandel, Ernst. *Delightful Murder. A Social History of the Crime Story.* Pluto, 1985.
Manzoni, Celina, et al. *Roberto Bolaño: la escritura como tauromaquia.* Corregidor, 2002.

Marx, Karl. "Apologist Conception of the Productivity of All Professions." *Theories of Surplus Value*. Translated by Emile Burns, Progress Publishers, 1963, pp. 387–388.

———. "Chapter 3: Money, Or the Circulation of Commodities," *Capital. A Critique of Political Economy. Volume 1. The Process of Production of Capital*. Translated by Samuel Moore and Edward Aveling. Edited by Friedrich Engels, 1867, Wordsworth, 1987, pp. 138–194.

———. *The Eighteenth Brumaire of Louis Bonaparte*. Translated by Saul K. Padover, 1852, Cosimo Classics, 2008.

Mattalia, Sonia. "La ficción paranoica: el enigma de las palabras," *Ricardo Piglia. La escritura y el arte nuevo de la sospecha*. Edited by Daniel Mesa Gancedo. Secretariado de Publicaciones. Universidad de Sevilla, 2006, pp. 109–126.

———. *La ley y el crimen. Usos del relato policial en la narrativa argentina (1880–2000)*, Iberoamericana/Vervuert, 2008.

Mintz, Samuel. "Leviathan as Metaphor," *Hobbes Studies* 2, vol. 1, 1989, pp. 3–9.

Moreiras, Alberto. "The Aura of Testimonio," *The Real Thing. Testimonial Discourse and Latin America*, Duke University Press, 1996, pp. 93–224.

Negri, Antonio. "Constituent Power: The Concept of a Crisis." *Insurgencies: Constituent Power and the Modern State*. Translated by Maurizia Boscagli, University of Minnesota Press, 2009, pp. 1–36.

Neruda, Pablo. "Heights of Macchu Picchu." *Translating Neruda: The Way to Macchu Picchu*, translated by John Felstiner, Stanford University Press, 1980, pp. 202–241.

Noguerol, Francisca. "Neopolicial latinoamericano: el triunfo del asesino," *Ciber Letras*, 2006, pp. 1–15.

Nyman, Jopi. *Men Alone: Masculinity, Individualism and Hard-boiled Fiction*, Brill, 1997.

Ogilvie, Bertrand. "Violence et représentation: la production de l'homme-jetable," *Lignes*, 1995, pp. 113–141.

Paiva Padrão, Andréa. "Buenos Aires como espaço literário em Borges: 'La muerte y la brújula,'" *Terra Roxa e Outras Terras: Revista de Estudos Literários*, 12, 2016, pp. 24–33.

Parodi, Cristina. "Borges y la subversión del modelo policial," *Borges: desesperaciones aparentes y consuelos secretos*. Colmex, 1999, pp. 77–97.

Paz Soldán, Edmundo. "Art's Place in Narco Culture: Yuri Herrera's *Kingdom Cons*," *Review: Literature and Arts of the Americas*, 46: 1, May 2013, pp. 26–32.

Pellicer, Rosa. "Ricardo Piglia y el relato del crimen," *La escritura y el arte nuevo de la sospecha*, Universidad de Sevilla, 2009, pp. 89–105.

Picabea, María Luján. "¿Qué define al policial argentino?" *Ñ*, 15, June 2012. www.clarin.com/literatura/policial-argentino-de-santis-martinez-lafforgue-battista_0_rk3zrl73PXg.html.

Piglia, Ricardo. *Cuentos de la serie negra*. Alianza, 1986.

———. "Sobre el género policial," *Crítica y ficción*. Seix Barral, 1986, pp. 67–70.

———. *Prisión perpetua*, Sudamericana, 1988.

———. "La loca y el relato del crimen," *Prisión perpetua*, Lengua de Trapo, 2000, pp. 93–102.

———. "Teoría del complot," *Ramona: revista de artes visuales*, 23, Buenos Aires, 2002, pp. 4–15.

———. *Money to Burn*. Translated by Amanda Hopkins, Granta, 2003.

———. "Escritores norteamericanos," *La Biblioteca. Revista fundada por Paul Groussac.* vol. 15, "El arte de narrar. Variaciones sobre Ricardo Piglia." Primavera, 2015, pp. 124–152.

———. *Los diarios de Emilio Renzi. Los años felices.* Anagrama, 2016.

———. *Los diarios de Emilio Renzi. Un día en la vida.* Anagrama, 2017.

Poe, Edgar Allan. "The Murders of the Rue Morgue," *Selected Tales.* Oxford University Press, 1980a, pp. 105–135.

———. "The Mystery of Marie Rogêt," *Selected Tales.* Oxford University Press, 1980b, pp. 142–185.

———. "The Purloined Letter," *Selected Tales.* Oxford University Press, 1980c, pp. 200–216.

———. *The Raven and The Philosophy of Composition*, e-book, Project Gutenberg, 2017.

Premat, Julio. "Los espejos y la cópula son abominables. Notas sobre *Plata quemada*," *Ricardo Piglia: una poética sin límites.* Edited by Adriana Rodríguez Pérsico and Jorge Fornet, Universidad of Pittsburgh Press, 2004, pp. 123–134.

Quintero, Santiago. "Posdictadura chilena en 'el planeta de los monstruos': una lectura desde Raúl Zurita y *Estrella distante* de Roberto Bolaño." *Des/memorias,* edited by Adriana López-Labourdette, Silvia Spitta and Valeria Wagner, Linkgua, 2016, pp. 156–176.

Rama, Ángel. "Rodolfo Walsh. La narrativa en el conflicto de las culturas." *Ficciones argentinas: Antología de lecturas críticas.* Norma, 2004, pp. 261–302.

Richard, Nelly. *Cultural Residues: Chile in Transition.* Translated by Theodore Quester and Alan West-Durán, University of Minnesota Press, 2004.

Robin, Diana and Jaffe, Ira. *Redirecting the Gaze: Gender, Theory, and Cinema in the Third World.* State University of New York Press, 1999.

Rodríguez Carranza, Luz. "Escorias de la década infame." *Texto y Teoría: Estudios Culturales* 33, 2004, pp. 229–244.

Rodríguez Pérsico, Adriana. "*Plata quemada* o un mito para el policial argentino," *Piglia. Una poética sin límites*, Instituto Internacional Literatura Iberoamericana, 2004, pp. 113–121.

Rousseau, Jean-Jacques. *The Social Contract*, e-book. Translated by Maurice Cranston, The University of Adelaide Library, 2014.

Sarlo, Beatriz. *Borges, un escritor en las orillas.* Ariel, 1995.

Sasturain, Juan. *Manual de perdedores.* Sudamericana, 2011.

Schmitz, Sabine and Verdú Schumann, Daniel A. "Prefacio," *Diseños de nuevas geografías en la novela y el cine negros de Argentina y Chile.* Edited by Sabine Schmitz, Annegret Thiem, Daniel A. Verdú Schumann, Iberoamericana Vervuet, 2013, 9–24.

Schnaiderman, Boris. "*Agosto* e os caminhos da narrativa," *O Estado de São Paulo,* 14/11/1990.

Segato, Rita. "La escritura en el cuerpo de las mujeres asesinadas en Ciudad Juárez: territorio, soberanía y crímenes de segundo estado," *Debate feminista*, 37, 2008, pp. 78–102.

———. *La guerra contra las mujeres*. Traficantes de sueño, 2016, pp. 91–107.

Setton, Roman. *Los orígenes de la narrativa policial en la Argentina. Recepción y transformación de modelos genéricos alemanes, franceses e ingleses*, Iberoamericana / Vervuert, 2014.

———. "Paul Groussac (1848–1929): 'El candado de oro'/'La pesquisa,' dos versiones del inicio del cuento policial en la argentina," *Lingue e Linguaggi*, 2012, pp. 249–262. Doi: 10.1285/i22390359v7p249http://siba-ese.unisalento.it.

Shklovsky, Viktor. "Art as Technique," *Literary Theory. An Anthology*. Edited by Julie Rivkin and Michael Ryan. Wiley Blackwell, 2017, pp. 8–14.

Spitzer, Leo. "Linguistic Perspectivism in the *Don* Quixote," *Linguistics and Literary History; Essays in Stylistics*. Russell & Russell, 1962, pp. 41–86.

Spivak, Gayatri. "Can the Subaltern Speak?" *Colonial Discourse and Postcolonial Theory*, 1994, edited by Patrick Williams and Laura Chrisman, pp. 66–111.

Stavans, Ilan. *Antihéroes. México y su novela policial*. Planeta, 1993.

Strange, Susan. "The Westfailure System," *Review of International Studies*, 25, 1999, pp. 345–354.

Sumalavia, Ricardo. "¿Dónde está la novela policial peruana?," *Quehacer. Revista del Centro de Estudios y Promoción del Desarrollo*, October 2017.

Taibo II, Paco Ignacio. "La (otra) novela policíaca," *Los Cuadernos del Norte*, vol. 8., no. 41, March–April 1987, pp. 36–41.

Taussig, Michael. "Maleficium: State Fetishism," *The Nervous System*, Routledge, 1992, pp. 111–140.

Tavares dos Santos, José Vicente and Niche Teixeira, Alex. "Figurações da Violência: uma apresentação enigmática," *Sociologias*, 15, 2013, pp. 14–25.

Todorov, Tzvetan. "Typologie du Roman policier." *Poétique de la prose*. Seuil. 1971.

———. *The Fantastic: A Structural Approach to a Literary Genre*. Translated by Richard Howard, Cornell University Press, 1975.

Tönnies, Ferdinand. *Community and Society*. Translated by Charles P. Loomis, Dover, 2002.

Trelles Paz, Diego. *Detectives perdidos en la ciudad oscura. Novela policial alternativa en Latinoamérica de Borges a Bolaño*. Copé, 2017.

Valle, Amir. "Marginalidad y ética de la marginalidad en la nueva ciudad narrada por la novela negra latinoamericana," *Anales de Literatura Hispanoamericana*, 36, 2007. pp. 95–101.

Vila-Matas. "Bolaño en la distancia." Review of *Los detectives salvajes*, *Letras Libres*, April 30th, 1999.

Villalobos Rouminot, Sergio. "A Kind of Hell: Roberto Bolaño and The Return of World Literature," *Journal of Latin American Cultural Studies* 18:2–3, 2009, pp. 193–205. doi: 10.1080/13569320903361887.

Viñas, David. "Una hipótesis sobre Borges: de Macedonio a Lugones." *Revista de Crítica Literaria Latinoamericana* 2.4 (1976): 139–142.

Virno, Paolo. "Do you Remember Counterrevolution?" in Hardt and Virno, *Radical Thought in Italy: A Potential Politics*, translated by Maurizia Buscagli, Cesare Casarino, Paula Collili, Ed Emory, Michael Hardt and Michael Turits, University of Minesota Press, 1996, pp. 241–259.

———. *A Grammar of the Multitude: For an Analysis of Contemporary Forms of Life.* Translated by Isabella Bertoletti, James Cascaito and Andrea Casson, Massachusetts Institute of Technology Press, 2004.

Waldemer, Thomas. P. "Rubem Fonseca's Cold Case: The Ephemeral and the Historical in *Agosto*," *Romance Notes*, vol. 47, Number 1, Fall 2006, pp. 33–39.

Walsh, Rodolfo. *Cuentos policiales argentinos*, Emecé, 1953.

———. *Operation Massacre*. Translated by Daniella Gitlin, Seven Stories Press, 2013.

Watt, Ian. *Myths of Modern Individualism*, Cambridge University Press, 1996.

Weber, Max. *The Protestant Ethic and the Spirit of Capitalism*. Translated by Talcott Parsons, Routledge, 1992.

———. "Politics as a Vocation," *Essays in Sociology*. Translated and edited by H. H. Gerth and C. Wright Mills, Routledge, 2005, pp. 77–128.

Williams, Gareth. "Sovereignty and Melancholic Paralysis in Roberto Bolaño," *Journal of Latin American Cultural Studies*, 18, 2–3, 2009, pp. 125–140.

———. "*2666*, or the Novel of Force," unpublished paper, presented at the SFU School for International Studies and Latin American Studies, October 2016.

Wilson, Jason. "The Tragic, Seamy Underbelly of Buenos Aires," *The Independent*, Jan 30rd 2004. www.independent.co.uk/arts-entertainment/books/reviews/money-to-burn-by-ricardo-piglia-trans-amanda-hopkinson-76358.html.

Yates, Donald A. "The Spanish American Detective Story," *The Modern Language Journal*, vol. 40. n. 5. May 1956, pp. 228–232.

———. *El cuento policial latinoamericano: Introducción, antología y biografías*, Ediciones de Andrea, 1964.

Zizek, Slavoj. "From Jouce-the-Symptom," 1997, lacan.com/frameXI2.htm.

———. "From *Homo Sucker* to *Homo Sacer*," *Welcome to the Desert of the Real! Five Essays on September 11 and Related Dates*. Verso, 2002, pp. 83–111.

———. "Mankell, the Artist of the Parallax View," 2005, lacan.com/zizemankell.htm.

# Index

absolution 82, 165–166, 179, 182, 199
Adorno, Theodor 9, 65, 200
affect 37, 131, 134, 141–142, 147, 153,
Africa 50, 195,
African American detective authors 4
Agamben, Giorgio 9; Bolaño 117, 181;
 the coming community 198; the
 *homo sacer* 181, 182; the state of
 exception 61, 117, 133
Alfonsín, Raúl 81
Allende, Salvador 92, 95–99,
 102, 119, 142
Althusser, Louis 9, 150
American Independence 23
Anagrama (Publisher) 93, 95
apocryphal stories 82–83
arbitrariness 75, 153; Bolaño 179;
 Fonseca 132–134; Piglia 76;
 Walsh 61, 84–88
Argentina 2–3, 5, 6, 8, 47–89; detective
 fiction from 6, 8, 9, 45–89; (post)
 dictatorships of 2–3, 5, 9, 45–46, 50,
 57–86, 95–96, 101, 109, 114, 125–
 126, 158, 196, 204; early detective
 fiction of 47–49; economy of 3, 48,
 73, 79, 81–83 political history of 9,
 47–48, 51, 53, 56, 60–65, 73–74,
 78–85, 125–126, 128, 144, 154,
 191; history of detective fiction in
 15, 47–89; immigration in 47–48;
 literature of 47–89
Arlt, Roberto 83
Asia 195
Auschwitz 65
avant-garde poetry 93–94, 101, 108–116
Avelar, Idelber 69, 82, 94,
Ayala Gauna, Velmiro 50–52, 64, 67

Balibar, Étienne 180–181
Balzac 1–2
Barcelona 56, 93, 119
Barrientos Tecún, Dante 183
Barthes, Roland 9, 141–143, 148–149
Bataille, George 198
Bayer, Osvaldo 60
Beasley-Murray, Jon 73, 85–86, 89,
 101, 192, 195
Benjamin, Walter 9, 61, 80, 153; the
 police 36, 40–41
Benveniste, Émile 9, 127, 160, 166, 170
Biopolitics 26, 86, 96
Bioy Casares, Adolfo 47–50, 52–53,
 67, 71, 124
Blanco Calderón, Rodrigo 69
Blanes (Spain) 93, 100, 102, 119, 201
body: affect 37, 142; the body politic
 36, 96, 135 143–144, 178, 182;
 community 198; crime 183;

217

depersonalization 173; detective fiction 183; *desaparecidos* 183; dismemberment 25, 35, 180; emptiness 77–78, 82; the face 142, 173; female corpses 8, 171, 180, 182, 187; feminicides 8, 171, 180, 182, 187; immunity 5, 57, 96, 187; infertility 177, 183; Levinas' face-to-face ethics 142; masculinity 36, 78, 180, 182; mindless 5, 77; monstrosity 25, 37, 77–78, 150–151; obesity 37, 150–151; personalism 142, 143–144; personhood 143, 173; personification 77; shapeless 25; sickness 108, 129–135, 142, 178; soulless 77, 82; the state 20, 22, 35–41, 72–82, 106–121, 129–134; symbolic disabilities 5, 22, 35–41, 62, 72–82, 106–121, 129–134, 150–151; as territories to be conquered 171, 185

Bolaño, Roberto: *2666* 2, 7, 93, 99, 103, 111, 157–193, 196, 200; absolution 165, 179; accumulation 120, 161, 176–187; Anglo-American models 4, 99, 100, 103, 106, 116, 121, 157, 162, 166–167, 172, 185; arbitrariness 179; Argentine literary tradition 92, 112, 114–115, 183, 192, 202; authorship 7, 100, 113–114, 175–176; class 97, 114, 120, 161, 171, 182, 184, 186–187, 191; community 104, 187, 193, 197–202; Chile 93, 158; the Chilean dictatorship 158; the Chilean diaspora 6, 94, 106, 118, 164, 199; Conan Doyle 172; depersonalization 6–8, 101–103, 107, 113, 117, 119, 121, 159–192, 198–199, 204–205; drug-dealing 160, 163, 165, 179, 182, 187, 190, 192; *Entre paréntesis* 4, 105, 196; *Estrella distante* 6–7, 91–121, 125, 128, 154, 158–164, 179, 196, 199–201; Europe 93–95, 99–103, 111, 118, 164, 199; facts 168, 175, 177; feminicides 161, 166–167, 169–192; freedom 182, 187, 190; generational failure 104–105, 113, 196; gender 95–96, 107, 109, 113, 158, 160–161, 167, 165, 169, 171–192, 198–200; González Rodríguez, Sergio 169; individualism 2, 6–9, 91, 94, 97–104, 114, 117, 119–120, 159–160, 162, 164–167, 173, 184, 186, 189, 191–192, 195, 199–202; immunity 95, 103, 111, 120, 159, 163, 174, 178, 184–190, 192–193, 198, 200; immunity to corruption 163; impersonal pronouns 164–166, 168, 170, 187, 189–190, 192, 198–199; impunity 103, 113, 117, 121, 164, 182, 184, 187, 192; knowledge 96, 100, 103, 113, 115, 119, 162–163, 166–167, 169–170; *La literatura nazi en América* 92, 118, 158; *La pista de hielo* 92, 104; literary originality 92, 100–101, 105, 163, 177; *Los detectives salvajes* 93, 104–105, 113, 196; madness 67, 160, 162, 201; the market as a depersonalized agent 167, 185, 190–192; Bourdieu's masculine domination 180, 182, 188, 196, 200; memory 93–94, 116; the Mexican-American border 2, 7, 93, 155, 157–163, 168–169, 177–189; Mexico 92–93, 157–158, 169, 173, 181, 184, 186–187, 192; mirrors 97–98, 163, 174; money 99–101, 106, 158, 177–180, 183, 185, 187; the multitude 6, 8, 115–117, 119, 158, 160, 163, 176, 178, 190–192, 199–200, 204–205; negation 102, 165–166, 173; Neruda 96, 176; parody 91–93, 111; performance art 93, 95, 97, 108–109, 111, 112, 115, 116; personification 6–7, 94–103, 110–111, 116–117, 160, 164–167, 176–179, 184, 191–192, 199; Poe 99, 172; poetry 93–94, 96, 100–102, 106, 108–116, 173, 176, 183; post-dictatorship 3, 9, 45–46,

92, 99, 101–102, 106, 119–121, 158–159, 177, 195, 197, 199, 201; restoration of justice 103–104, 119, 166, 190; ruins 182–183, 196–197, 199; silence 6, 106–111, 117–118, 121, 175; Sisyphus 176; sovereignty 97, 114, 116, 161, 171, 182, 187, 199–200; the state 2–3, 6, 8–9, 91–99, 102–111, 113–121, 157–163, 167–168, 170, 172–179, 182–192, 199–202; structural misogyny 179; symbolic blindness 103, 118, 172–177, 185, 190–191, 199; symbolic impotence 162, 167, 169, 189, 199; symbolic illiteracy 6, 95, 106, 108–109, 111–120, 199; symbolic muteness 6, 7, 103, 106–111, 117–121, 132, 168, 174–175, 177, 189, 191, 199; symbolic paralysis 6, 106, 115, 117–120, 168, 187–188, 199; symbolic unintelligibility 7, 106–108, 111, 115–118, 162, 167–176, 185, 190–191, 198–199; the third person 164–166, 179, 182, 190, 198–199; verbosity 106–107, 121; vigilantism 103, 106, 118–120, 161; visibility 167, 172–174, 179, 183, 190–192; waste 180–185
Bolsonaro, Jair 191
Bonasso, Miguel 64, 68
Borges, Jorge Luis: Bioy Casares 47–50, 52–53, 67, 71, 124; Caillois 15; the *década infame* 53; Hollywood crime cinema 52; immunity 52–58; individualism 5, 48, 50, 52–57, 61, 63; "La muerte y la brújula" 52–67; language 57, 62, 67; literacy 5, 55–57; knowledge 5, 48, 50, 55–57; *Martín Fierro* 52; misreading 54–56; parody 47–56, 67–68; Poe 2, 46, 52–53, 57; punishment 56; restoration of the social order 52, 54, 56; *Seis problemas para don IsidroParodi* 47–50; the state 5, 46, 52, 55–58; Yrigoyen 53, 56

Bosteels, Bruno 159
Bourdieu, Pierre 8; dominated-dominating structures 22, 188, 196; masculine domination 180, 182, 200; *habitus* 85; the state 42; Weber 42
Braham, Persephone 3, 53
Brazil: Argentine detective fiction 123–125; (post)dictatorship of 123–129, 131, 134–135, 137–138, 147, 150–152, 155; early detective fiction in 124; history of 125–127; history of detective fiction in 123–125; over-incarceration in 132–134, 189
Brecht, Bertolt 2
Brescia, Pablo 49–50, 53
*Broadchurch* (2013–2017) 45
Brownson, Charles 32, 34, 69, 72, 81
Buenos Aires 48–49, 51, 53, 56, 58–59, 63, 65, 71, 74–75, 81, 157, 159, 195
Bulwer-Lytton, Edward 115
Burkhardt, Jacob 14, 16

Calabrese, Elisa 56
Calveiro, Pilar 61, 88, 95, 204
Caner-Liese, Robert 200
Capanema, Gustavo 128
Capdevila, Analía 15
Castelo Branco, Humberto de Alencar 125–126, 138
Catelli, Nora 67–68, 99
Catete Palace 135, 142, 149, 151–152
Cervantes's *Don Quijote* 102, 113 madness 140–141, 147; Watt's myths of modern individualism 4, 19–20, 25–27, 63, 140; Chandler, Raymond 3–4, 8, 17, 31, 39, 51, 63; individualism 13–14, 22, 24, 29, 44, 166; the state 17, 22, 29, 38, 46, 82, 88–89; corruption 26, 29, 40, 82; *The Simple Art of Murder* 13; *The Long Goodbye* 63; *Farewell, My Lovely* 44, 82
Chávez, Hugo 144
chess 32, 48, 58, 130, 162
Chicago 14, 76; the Chicago Boys 96

Chile: the Andean Condor 94–95; the Chilean diaspora. *See* Bolaño and the Chilean diaspora. counter-revolution 96, 105, 112, 119; dictatorship of. *See* Pinochet; the *desaparecidos* 6, 97, 109, 183, 199; economy of 120; Argentine literary tradition. *See* Bolaño and literary tradition; history of detective fiction in 91–92, 103–104, 203; neoliberalism in 3, 73, 76, 96, 99, 105, 112–120; (post) dictatorship of. *See* Bolaño and post-dictatorship; the foreign policy of the United States 94, 97

Christie, Agatha 3, 13–18, 22–23, 28, 31, 40, 43, 46, 51, 56, 166, 172

Ciudad Juárez 161, 167, 169, 171, 181, 191, 195; Santa Teresa 157, 175

civilization and barbarism 48–52

class 182, 186, 187, 191, 198, 200; the Argentine middle 82, 85; the Argentine working 82; the Brazilian working 137; the Chilean upper 97, 114, 120; the European bourgeoisie 15–16, 24, 28; *población chatarra* in Latin America 180–183; the European proletariat 16, 24, 28–29, 31, 38, 48, 175–176; resentment 76–77; the upper-class hero 24, 28, 31, 38, 48, 52, 139; parody 48, 52, 68; policemen as working 24, 28–29, 38, 48, 76–77, 139; the precarized detective 68; traditional working 191; the female Mexican working 161, 170–171, 182, 184–191

Cohen, Marcelo 93

Collor de Melo, Fernando 154

Colombia: the dirty war 86; detective fiction in 1, 67, 196

Colonization of the Americas 23

community: civil society 187, 198; the common 192, 198, 200; Communism 193, 197–198; *communitas* 9, 186, 197–199; constituted power 198; depersonalization 191, 199; the *desaparecidos* 199; Esposito's *munus* 198; *immunitas* 198; impersonality 187, 191, 198–199; individualism 23, 28, 187, 197–202; individuals 18, 23, 28, 198–200; the multitude 8, 57, 153, 155, 199–200; the nation 197–198; the people 77, 153, 198, 200; personalism 154, 197–198; poetics of failure 8, 104, 155, 197–202; the state 8, 27, 77, 139, 149–155, 198–202; symbolic disabilities 199; the third person 187, 198–199

Conan Doyle, Arthur 2–3, 5, 13, 15, 26, 46, 89, 166, 172, individualism 2, 19, 24, 32, failure; 12, 22, 31, 39, 41, 43, the state 17, 18, 20, 37, 40–41, *A Study in Scarlet* 12, 28, 30, 34, 38–40; "The Adventure of the Yellow Face" 43; "The Adventure of the Red "Circle" 33, 39; "The Norwood Builder," *See* Conan Doyle and failure

Concepción (Chile) 63, 65, 92–93, 97, 101, 115, 157, 159, 195

connivance between the state and crime 73, 87–88, 163

Contractualism 6, 35–36, 195; apology of 89, 138, 155; critiques of 89, 133, 150, 155; corruption 153; Latin American personalism 133, 154; personhood 192; Rousseau 143–144; the state 202

Contreras, Manuel 96, 113

the Continental Op 13, 17, 21–30, 32, 34–41, 44, 185

constituent power 87; constituted power 188, 190–191; feminism. *See Ni Una Menos*; immunity 188; the multitude 8, 175

constituted power 7, 96, 104–105, 114–116, 153–154, 175, 188–191; the state 87, 89, 104, 128, 138, 195–196, 198, 202

contagion 26, 185

Convertibility plan (Argentina) 82

counter-revolution: individualism 24; neoliberalism 96, 105, 112; revolution 72, 96, 112
corruption: community 27, 153–154; democratization of 154; as an electoral weapon 154; immunity to 26–27, 52, 131, 133, 135–136, 152–153, 159; individualism 26–27, 124, 131, 154 as a monopoly of constituted power 154; Latin American political history 154
Cortázar, Julio 179
crime: the criminal mastermind 6, 22, 34, 54–56, 94, 97, 166–167, 179, 192; the law 34, 61, 66, 69, 103–104, 133, 135, 163, 167, 173, 181, 192, 196; money 30–32, 40, 72, 74, 79–84, 99, 106, 158, 177–178, 180, 183, 187; organized 73, 86; politics 83, 87, 133, 135; punishment 12, 26, 43, 56, 61–62, 66, 71–72, 79, 81, 103, 111, 124, 164, 184, 187, 192; resolution 31, 81, 104; tough criminals 79; true 45
crime fiction. *See* detective fiction
crisis of representation 72, 95, 107, 146, 158
Cuban Revolution 105

Dandyism 31–32; queerness 31–32; the state 31–32; sublimation 31
Dante Alighieri 49, 184
death flights 95, 106, 111; defeat 11, 22, 42, 54–55, 66, 69–70, 72, 74, 84–85, 99, 105, 126, 150, 158, 176–177, 196, 198
delegitimization of unions 82, 150, 154; De Rosso, Ezequiel 97, 103, 105, 107, 113, 159
Deckard, Sharae 163, 175–179
Delaney, Juan José 49
Deleuze, Gilles 196–197
democracy: constituted power 126, 138; Fukuyama's end of history 138; transition to 3, 120, 121, 138

depersonalization: asymmetric 159, 188, 190; Benveniste's personal pronouns 160, 166, 170; Blanchot 192; as collective justice 103, 191; constituent power 188–191; constituted power 188–191; detective fiction 6, 8, 74, 160, 166–167, 172, 175, 177, 179, 188; Esposito 119, 166, 179, 199; Flaubert 192; *Ni Una Menos* 191; immunity 159, 188, 190; individualism 6–8, 74, 101–103, 119, 155, 159, 162, 164–167, 184, 191, 199; Kafka 192, 200; the multitude 6–8, 119, 155, 160, 163, 190–193, 199; the third person 164–166, 170, 179, 182, 190, 199; personhood 7–8, 164, 166, 199; personification 6–7, 101–103, 155, 160, 164–167, 177, 179, 184, 190–191, 199; personality 102, 160, 163, 165–167, 199, 204; selective 188, 190
deregulation 82
Derrida, Jacques 8: the figure of the detective 31, 33, 38, 121; Lévi-Strauss 117; Plato's *pharmakon* 96; phono-centrism 121; Saussure's signifier and meaning 121; writing 117, 121
Descartes, Rene 23
detectives: armchair 39, 50; disintegration of 74, 97, 159; fascination towards 22, 33; immunity 5, 23, 25–27, 35, 41, 52–53, 56–58, 62, 66, 95, 103, 120, 124, 131, 135–136, 138, 153, 159, 163, 174, 188–192, 200; as an intellectual myth 33; legibility 54–56, 71, 95–97, 139, 162, 172; powers of observation of 33–34, 38, 72; as private eyes 5–7, 11–14, 18–22, 25–29, 32–49, 52–58, 61, 63, 67, 69, 71, 73–74, 118, 123, 137, 199–200; the problematic personality of 67, 160; as public eyes 7, 123–124; reluctant 6, 50, 100, 130, 164; state 123–155, 162–177;

as superheroes 25–27; sidekick of 12, 18, 21, 23, 25, 30, 37, 42, 56, 68, 76, 79, 100, 129; toughness of 39, 71, 74, 78; voice of 21, 33, 35, 40, 61–62, 71, 74, 107; wit of 21–22, 25, 33, 36, 40, 44, 59, 69, 100, 166
detective fiction: in Argentina 1–9, 45, 47–93, 104, 114, 128, 135, 183; auto-fiction 67 in Brazil 1–3, 45, 65, 123–155, 183, 203; in Chile 1–3, 6, 45, 65, 82, 91–121, 167, 183, 203; in Colombia 1, 67, 196; in Cuba 1, 3–4, 45; the dictator novel 6, 103, 179, 200; factuality. *See* Bolaño and facts; female authors 8, 14, 68; gender. *See* Bolaño and gender. *See* also Piglia and gender.; globalization 50–51, 112, 175, 196–197; journalism 50–53, 58–60, 67–68, 71, 73, 76, 79, 126–127, 169, 171, 175, 177; Judaism 29, 36, 53–58, 101, 114; memory 64–66, 80, 82, 93; in Mexico 1–3, 7, 63, 93, 157–193; neoliberalism 3, 73, 76, 82, 84, 86, 114, 161, 195–202; non-fiction. *See* Walsh and non-fiction; the historical novel. *See* History and the historical novel; Latin American *neopolicial* 1; literary quality 1–2, 4, 91; *literatura gauchesca* 51, 74, 76, 78, 80, 125, 154; parody. *See* parody; proper nouns. *See* proper nouns; precarity 51, 68, 124, 173, 186, 205; race 4, 19, 45, 116; reception of 3–4, 8, 65; restoration of justice/social order 12, 27, 34–35, 43, 52, 54, 56, 60, 62, 64–65, 68, 71–72, 81, 84, 95, 103–104, 119, 124, 143, 166, 189, 190; the Scotland Yard 12, 15, 17–18, 20, 22, 28, 30, 32–34, 37, 41, 54, 66; in Spain 3; in TV shows 45, 63, 66, 181; in the United Kingdom 11–46; in the United States 11–46; the western 8
dictator novel 6, 103, 179, 200

dictatorship and trauma 61, 64, 66, 79–80, 92, 135, 160
Díaz Eterovic, Ramón 1, 3, 63, 71, 91, 103, 129, 203
DINA (Dirección Inteligencia Nacional) 110
Don Frutos Gómez 50–52, 59, 68, 125
*Doppelgängers*: auto-fiction 201; Bolaño 98–101, 107; community 201; Fonseca 137, 147, 149, 52, 160, 201; madness 201; rectification of history 107; Spanish composite surnames 101
Dunkerley, James 141–147; Allende 142; history 141; martyrdom 146; personalism 141–147; political suicide 142; Vargas 141, 143, 147
Dupin, August 2, 50–51, 53–54, 69, 99; individualism 5, 11–46, 48, 54– 59, 67, 106, 121, 123–124, 139, 185; loneliness 23–24; the state 11–46, 139
drug-dealing. *See* Bolaño and drug-dealing

Eastern Bloc 197
El Paso 161
Engels, Friedrich 1–2
enigma 31, 48, 53, 70, 166, 171
entertainment 63, 66, 181
Enzensberger, Hans Magnus 87–88
Esposito, Roberto 9; Agamben's coming community 198; Benveniste's third person 166; Derrida's *pharmakon* 96; *communitas* 9, 186, 197–199; *compensatio* 103, 109; contagion 26, 185; depersonalization 166, 179, 199; force 57, 103, 135, 185; *immunitas* 5, 9, 26, 57, 103, 186–187, 198; individualism 5, 198–199; the multitude 199–200; the *munus* 26, 186–187, 198; social order 8, 104; surrogacy 110; the third person 9, 166, 179, 187, 192, 198, 199; Europe 3–4, 6, 15–16, 20, 23, 29, 35,

36, 48, 52–53, 93–95, 99, 101–103, 111, 118, 133, 139–140, 164, 199
Even-Zohar, Itamar 49, 64–65
excess: surplus 177–178; unemployment 180–181

failure: community 8, 27, 155, 195–202; communism 112, 197; as crisis of representation 72, 118; displacement of 44, 66; early detective fiction 18, 27, 30, 42–43; force 41–43, 72, 88, 196; generational 105, 196; history 9, 62, 84, 148, 159; individualism 5–6, 8–9, 18, 34–35, 39, 42–46, 52–54, 56, 61–63, 65–66, 71, 80–82, 84, 103–104, 119, 121, 124, 130–131, 136–137, 140, 155, 159, 162–163, 172–173, 189, 195, 197, 199–202; literature 63, 68, 71, 81, 84, 105, 175, 201; myths of individualism 44, 63; mythology 148, 155; neoliberalism or globalization 197; personalism 155; personification 155, 199; poetics of 8–9, 54, 62–65, 72, 82, 104, 124, 137, 155, 159, 173, 196–202; the police 18, 35, 41–42, 45, 87–88, 161–162, 173, 188–189, 199; politics 8, 84; post-dictatorship 9, 45, 57, 62, 69, 81, 83–84, 137, 159, 177, 195, 197, 199; representation 6, 72, 82, 118, 155; sovereignty 68, 195, 200, 202; symbolic disabilities 6, 35, 41, 57, 61, 118, 199; technology 42
fascism 158, 197; communism 110; neoliberalism 114; poetry 111–112
Faulkner, William 116
Faust 4, 19, 27, 46, 200
FBI 45, 66, 160, 162
feminicides 14, 161, 165–192, Bourdieu 180, 182, 188; as crimes of "second state" 192; feminism. *See Ni Una Menos*; genocides 179, 192; Segato 171; unintelligibility 170–172
Feiling, Carlos 68

Feinmann, José Pablo 64, 66–67, 86, 88
Feitlowitz, Marguerite 204
feudalism: abandonment of 23; vestiges of 15–16
Fonseca, Rubem: affect 131, 141–142, 147, 153; arbitrariness 133, 137, 153; Brazilian dictatorship 123–155, 159; Cervantes's *Don Quixote* 140–141, 147; class 137, 139, 153; depersonalization 133, 152, 136–137, 139–143, 147, 151, 153–155; failure 124, 130, 137, 140, 148, 155; Foucault 137, 139–140, 148, 201, 204; freedom 132–133, 140–141, 152; historiography. See historiography; individualism 123–125, 129–134; Levinas' face-to-face ethics 142, 174; madness. See madness and Fonseca; martyrdom 142–143, 146; mass incarceration. See over-incarceration in Brazil; memory 125, 138, 153; mourning 135, 141; the multitude 129, 142–147, 149, 152–153, 155; the people 130, 135–136, 143–147, 150–154; personalism 7, 125–126, 129, 133, 138–139, 149, 155; the political 126–128, 135; politics 126, 129, 131–133, 135–137, 150; reading 139; sickness 129–135, 142; symbolic blindness 7, 132, 135, 142, 155; symbolic illiteracy 7, 139–140, 149, 155; symbolic muteness 7, 128, 131–135, 146, 154–155; symbolic paralysis 7, 124, 129, 131, 133–134, 139; symbolic unintelligibility 134–140, 142, 155; suicide 127–128, 133, 135, 141–145, 147, 151–153; Vargas. See Vargas, Getúlio
force: agency 88, 134–138, 141, 167; counter-force 57, 103, 119, 132, 185, 187, 190; hard-boiled toughness 39, 74; failure. *See* failure and force; immunity 57, 135–136, 185, 187, 190; knowledge 14, 39, 41–42, 55,

57, 69, 72, 113, 140–141, 167, 170; language 39, 41, 57, 111, 115–116, 170; legibility 55, 115; paralysis 117–120; as a symbolic disability 42
Fortunato, Gregório 127, 129, 150–153
Foucault, Michel 8; Cervantes 140; criminality 87; history 80; madness 139–140, 148, 201, 204; neoliberalism 76; police 87–88, 137; resistance 80; the state 75–78, 86–88; state-phobia 75–78
fragmentation: depersonalization 6, 103
France and the detective story 15, 38, 49, 87, 123–124
Franco, Jean 96, 120
Francoism 112
Francophone theory and the state 15, 42, 75, 88, 95, 137, 150, 192, 197
Franken Kurzen, Clemens 91–92, 104, 203
Franklin, Benjamin 178
French Revolution 15, 23–24

Galeano, Eduardo 138
Galtieri, Leopoldo Fortunato 125, 128
Gamerro, Carlos 64–68, 77, 88
García Márquez, Gabriel 93, 176, 179, 184
García-Roza, Luis Alfredo 1, 124
Garcilaso de la Vega 113
Gaulle, Charles de 192
Gelman, Juan 96
gender: class 48, 182, 187, 191, 198, 200; Dandyism 31–32, 48, 67; the detective 8, 14, 68, 177, 183, 200; feminism 8, 191; the *femme fatale* 14, 20; heteronormativity 32; masculinity 8, 14, 36, 78. See also Bolaño and Bourdieu's masculine domination and the people 191, 198, 200; queerness 31, 74, 78; race 191; the state 14, 182, 191, 198, 200; violence 14, 182, 191. See also *Ni Una Menos*

genres: Bourdieu's literary fields 4, 50, 52, 68–69, 111, 114; Zohar and Lambert's poly-systems 49, 64–65; imported 49; smuggling 50
Giardinelli, Mempo 1, 68, 76, 93; individualism 11, 13, 38; Latin American dictatorships 66; Anglo-American detective stories 2, 3, 13, 38, 64, 66, 76, 201; Latin American detective stories 63–65, 104; the state 66, 88–89, 104, 201–202
Ginzburg, Carlo 149, 151
global South 76, 195
globalization. See detective fiction and neoliberalism or globalization
Goldmann, Lucien 18, 23, 44–45, 203
Góngora, Luis de 183
González, Horacio 9, 58
González Rodríguez, Sergio 169–170, 175, 177
Goulart, João 126–127, 132, 150
Gramsci, Antonio 15–16, 145, 203
Grandis, Rita de 58–59
Great Depression (1930s) 11, 13, 24, 64
Great Recession (2008) 197
Groussac, Paul 49
guerrillas 83

Halperín Donghi, Tulio 9
Hammett, Dashiell 3, 31, 35, 39–40, 51, 82; individualism 13–14, 17, 21–22, 24–28, 30, 32, 44, 166–167; masculinity 8; the state 13, 17, 21–22, 30, 37, 41, 46, 62
happening. See Bolaño and performance art
hard-boiled fiction 1, 8, 11, 13–14, 22, 24–26, 29, 31, 39–45, 48, 50, 53, 64–66, 71, 74, 82, 88, 131, 153, 157, 161, 166–167, 204; cynicism 25, 44; influence of 1, 45, 50
Harvey, David 73, 76, 79, 94
Hayek, Friedrich von 76
Heidegger, Martin 198
Himes, Chester 4, 64

historiography 9, 82; mythology 7, 141, 147–149, 154
history: falsification 82; the historical novel 138, 147, 201; the linguistic turn 148; literary representation 82, 129, 146; martyrdom 142, 146; memory 65, 80, 82, 93, 125, 153; as a mirror 129, 145, 148–149; mythology. *See* historiography and mythology; positivist 147, 149, 153; rectification of 107; the state's narrative 61–62, 73, 82, 84, 92, 125, 147–148, 159, 197; social justice 62, 84; truth 147–148
Hobbes, Thomas: Contractualism 87; depersonalization 144; the people as a mirror of the state 7, 144–145, 147; the Jewish tradition 36; Rousseau 36; the state 7, 87, 144, 147; the state of nature 150
*Homme jetable* 180–181
*Homo Sacer* 181–182
horizon of expectations 6, 34; betrayal of 105
Horkheimer, Max 200
Hoyos, Héctor 67, 104, 196
Huidobro, Vicente 91, 116, 204
Hutcheon, Linda 50–52
hyperinflation (Argentina) 81

immunity: accumulation 178, 186–187; asymmetric 188, 190, 192; community 27, 57, 77, 153, 187; contagion 26, 185; constitutional 137; to corruption 26–27, 41, 131, 133, 135–136, 152–153, 163; to death 27, 35, 58; distribution of 188, 192; to failure 27, 56–58; Esposito's *immunitas* 5, 26, 57, 186–187; image 190; impunity 27, 62; as a lack 26, 186; loss of 53–58; money 26–27, 77, 178, 187; Esposito's *munus* 26, 186–187; oligopoly of 187; to politics 131, 133–137; of the private detective. *See* detective and immunity selective 111, 188, 190; to social disapproval 190; of the state 189; taxation 186–187
*impune occidi* 182
incompetence 13, 37, 69, arbitrariness 84; corruption 52; of the state 13, 40–41, 74, 84, 86, 123, 188, 202
individuals: community 18, 23, 198–200; the epic hero 18; the modern novel's hero 18, 29
individualism: accumulation 16, 56, 120, 178, 184, 186; anathematization of 46; attenuation of 44, 101, 201; autonomy 22, 27, 131, 136, 138; collapse of 7, 117, 159, 186; community 8, 18, 23–25, 27, 29, 139, 141, 153, 155, 196–202; the Counter-Reformation 20, 27, 46; counter-revolution 24, 119; as a derogatory term 24; endorsement of 5, 9, 19, 24, 28, 44–45, 52, 68, 70–71, 84, 88, 102, 129, 132–133, 186, 200–201; etymology of 98; fragmentation of 6–7, 98–100, 103, 109, 160, 164, 201; the Great Depression 11, 13, 24; history of 2, 14–20; individuals 204–205; the law 20, 34, 103–106, 191; myths of modern 4, 16, 20, 26–27, 31, 33, 44, 46, 50, 52 63, 151; the Manchester School 24; neoliberalism 3, 27, 46, 76, 82, 82, 91, 94, 99, 114, 159, 184, 186, 197, 200; omnipotence 8, 137; personification 5–7, 18, 20, 36, 97–103, 117, 164, 166–167, 184, 191–192, 199; personalism 7; persistence of 44–46; privilege 5, 27, 33; in Renaissance Italy 14; selfishness 23; the self-made man 76; transformations of 24; trickle-down economics 186; utopian socialism 24; within the state 91–121
individualism against the state: as an anarchist libertarian dilemma 159; as an asymmetric rivalry 20–22;

dissolution of 199; as *ego contra mundum*. See Watt, Ian and *ego contra mundum*; as a literary antagonism or rivalry 11–22; as an obsolete rivalry 158–159; as a stable rivalry 3, 11, 13, 20, 98, 159; subversion of 5, 6, 46, 52, 56, 84, 159, 202
industrialization of European cities 23
innocence: loss of 40, 60
Italy: Argentina 47–48, 52; avant-garde and fascist poets in 111; Borges 47–48; counter-revolution 96; language 39, 130; parody 47–48; Renaissance in 14

Jakobson, Roman 43, 100
Jango. See João Goulart
Jelly-Schapiro, Eli 167, 175
justice: absence of 103; restoration of. See restoration of social order; the multitude 191–192; the state 13, 34, 57, 59–60, 62, 66, 71–72, 84, 137, 188, 191–192; vigilantism 103

Kafka, Franz 192; individualism 200; the state 201
Katari, Túpac 146
*The Killing* (2011–2014) 45
Kirchner, Cristina Fernández de 126, 154, 191
Kirchner, Néstor 126, 144
Kissinger, Henry 94
knowledge: asymmetry of 37, 55; crime 32, 34, 37, 40, 48, 55–56, 61, 69–72, 86, 103, 162–163, 167; disembodiment 34; eloquence 33, 38, 40; erudition 33, 38, 70, 74, 162; failure 33, 38, 103; force. See force and knowledge history 127; illiteracy 5, 38–40, 55–57, 115, 140; imagination 33, 38, 103; individualism 17, 31–35, 50, 56, 61, 68, 70, 74, 100, 103, 119, 140, 162–167; language 33, 39, 41, 56–57, 68–70, 100, 115, 147, 169–170; legibility 39, 55, 70, 115, 167; loneliness 33; madness. See madness and knowledge; misreading 43, 54, 56; Positivism 147, 149–150; rationality 32, 34–35, 40, 138, 147, 162; success 32–35, 41, 48, 56–57, 68, 162; slyness 34, 52
Kracauer, Siegfried 34–35
Kraniauskas, John 180, 183, 187
Kubitschek, Juscelino 126
Kucinski, Bernardo 124
Kurnick, David 163–168, 176, 179, 184, 188

labour: amateurism 15, 28, 31–32, 51, 67; Calvinism 27; capitalism 27–28; class 28–29, 32; the detective's domestic *vacuum*; 24, 27–28, 151; the figure of the detective 44; individualism 27–29, 32; Judaism 29; loneliness 27–29; the market 28–29; money 27–32; myths 27–28; neoliberal workaholism 27; the people 29; power structure 28; professionalism 28, 32; Protestant work ethics 27, 29; the private sector 28; religion 27; the state 28–29, 32; success 28, 32
Lacan, Jacques 8, 19, 26, 36–39, 42, 69, 147
Lacerda, Carlos 126–127, 131–132, 136, 146
Lafforgue, Jorge 51
Lambert, José 49, 64–65
LAPD 17, 28, 37, 45
the Latin American Boom 93, 176, 179, 184
the Latin American left 96, 105; human rights movement 114; *indigenismo* 114; literature 96; politics 96, 177; representation 175–177; the Latin American right 114; Sartre's *littérature engage* 114; *testimonio* 114

Laurini, Myriam 8
Lévi-Strauss, Claude 9; illiteracy 115; history 148; myth 78, 148: writing 114–117
Levinas, Emmanuel 142, 174
Levinson, Brett 158, 178
linguistics 39, 67, 69, 71, 164–165, 170, 172, 173, 192
linguistic turn 148
Link, Daniel 34
literacy 5, 33, 35, 38–39, 42, 55–57, 70, 72, 79, 100, 106–111, 114, 115, 117, 121, 140
literature 4, 14–15, 18–19, 34, 48, 50, 53, 58, 63–65, 68, 71, 81, 84, 87, 92–94, 101, 113–114, 127–129, 147, 149, 162, 166, 175–176, 183, 201
locked-room mystery case 11, 99
London 16, 19, 28–29, 48, 51, 123
loneliness 25–33
Ludmer, Josefina 12, 87, 180
Lugones, Leopoldo 112, 114
Lula da Silva, Luiz Inácio 126, 154
Lukács, György 9, 18–19, 23, 28–29, 33

Macri, Mauricio 191
madness: Bolaño 160; Cervantes's *Don Quixote* 63; class 139; community 139, 141, 201; exclusion 70, 139–141; failure 140, 162; Fonseca 130–131, 135–141, 147, 162; Foucault 139–140, 148, 201; knowledge 70, 138–141, 162; meaning 70, 139–140; mirrors 148; Piglia 67, 70; reading 70, 139; as a symptom 130, 135–136, 147; truth 140, 147–148; unintelligibility 70, 140, 162
malfunction 6, 68–69, 89
Mandel, Ernst 9, 15–16, 18, 28, 34–35, 38, 81, 104–105
Mankel, Hanning 50–51
Mann, Thomas 200
*Mare of Easttown* (2021) 45
Marlowe, Phillip 13, 17, 26–34, 37, 44–45, 58–59, 63–64, 157

market 15–16, 28–29, 45, 79, 81, 93–94, 99, 114, 167, 177, 180–188, 190–192, 196
Marsh, Ngaio 14, 123
Martínez, Guillermo 65, 68
martyrdom: Catholicism 142; Latin American political history 142–143, 146
Marx, Karl 9; accumulation 176; Bonapartism 151; crime 87, 181; history 151; Italian Post- Marxism 8. *See also* Negri. *See also* Virno; the Latin American left 175; Marxism 9, 44; Marxist jargon 107; money 79; personalism 145; proper nouns 145; socially necessary labor 177
masculinity: fantasy 8; individualism 8, 14; force 14; detectives 8, 14, 32, 36, 78, 200; the state 8, 14, 32, 36, 78, 137, 145, 152, 182, 200; Bourdieu. *See* Bourdieu and masculine domination; Segato. *See* Segato and masculinity; Nyman. *See* Nyman
Mattalia, Sonia 48–49, 69–74
meaning: signifiers 56, 116, 121, 139, 145, 167–168, 170–172; myths 78–79, 148–149
Ménem, Carlos Saúl 73–74, 81–83
memory: forgetfulness 116; the market 93–94; official 82; parody 62–66, 93, 124; post-dictatorship 62–66, 80, 138
Mexican-American border: accumulation 161, 176–187; as an anomic threshold 182; as an aquatic desert 157–158; bilingual interference 168–171; crisis of representation 158; the drug trade. *See* Bolaño and drug-dealing; infertility 177–185; as a literary hell 184; as a *locus eremus* 184; migration 163, 186, 191; money 158, 177–180, 183, 185, 187; as a narco-territory 187; as a porous border 158, 161, 185; Southern

Cone dictatorships 172, 173, 175, 178–179, 183, 188
Mexico 3, 63, 92–93, 157–193; as a *narcoestado* 192
Mises, Ludwig von 76
misogyny 8, 169, 179
monetarism 81–82
money: burnt. *See* Piglia and money; class 31, 76, 82, 139, 187; corruption 32, 40; counterfeit 79; the early detective story 26–32; hard-boiled fiction 26, 31, 40, 82, 131; history 79–84; immunity 26, 77, 131, 187–188; impunity 77, 79, 81, 82, 187–188; laundered 79, 187; meaning 79, 83–84, 178; metaphorical uses of 79, 81, 157–159, 204; productivity 79–80; rationality. *See* Weber and money; social distinction 76, 101, 139; sublimation of 31; sweet 81; unintelligibility. *See* Piglia and money
Montevideo (Uruguay) 63, 65, 74–76, 157, 159, 191, 195
Moreiras, Alberto 175–176
Mulroney, Brian 76
multitude: definition of 144–145, 204; Beasley-Murray 86. 192 Bolaño. *See* Bolaño, Roberto
the multitude: the Chilean diaspora 6, 199; the common 192, 200; community 8, 57, 155, 199–200; as constituent power 8, 190–191; Contractualism 192; contracts 143–147, 155; depersonalization 6, 8, 117, 119, 152, 155, 160, 163, 178, 190–193, 199; feminism. *See* Ni Una Menos and Fonseca. *See* Fonseca, Rubem and the multitude; individuals 204–205; individualism 6, 8, 16, 117, 143, 191–192, 199–200, 204–205; literacy 7, 115–117, 155; *Ni Una Menos* 191; orphanhood 142, 145–146, 165; paternalism 145; the people. *See* Virno and the multitude and the people; Negri. *See* Negri and the multitude and the people; the state 6–8, 16, 86, 115–117; subalternity 134, 145, 176; unintelligibility 115, 117, 142, 155, 176, 190–191; Virno *See* Virno and the multitude and the people
murder mystery narratives 13
myths: Barthes *See* Barthes, Roland and community 18, 23, 25, 141, 199; historiography 7, 82, 141, 147–149, 201; Lévi-Strauss *See* Lévi-Strauss and myths; literature; *See* Watt, Ian and myths; time 148–149; Watt. *See* Watt, Ian and myths

NAFTA 159, 161, 185, 187, 196
nation 178: the people 191; the state 143
Nazism 75, 110, 116; in Argentina 101; in Chile 92, 101, 113, 116, 158
Negri, Antonio 9, 89
neoliberalism: anomie 182; Argentine dictatorship 73, 83; communism 112; depersonalization 185–189; globalization. *See* detective fiction and globalization; the fall of the Soviet Union 76; Foucault 75–76, 86; Harvey 73, 76, 94; history of. *See* neoliberalism and Harvey and neoliberalism and Foucault; modernization 116; Pinochet. *See* Pinochet as a redefinition of the state's contours 73, 86, 96; selective privatization 73; state terrorism. *See* state terrorism.
Neruda, Pablo: personification 176; literature 96, 176; the Latin American left 96, 176
*Ni Una Menos* 191
Noguerol, Francisca 57
Nyman, Jopi 8

Ogilvie, Bertrand 180–183
Operation Condor 3, 65, 94–96, 124

Padura, Leonardo 1, 3–4, 45
paranoia 75, 84
Paris 2, 12, 15, 17, 20, 28–29, 36–38, 40, 42, 48, 51, 65, 123
Parodi, don Isidro 47–54, 68, 125
parody: Argentina 47–53, 62–65, 91; Brazil 124–125, 203; Chile 91–92, 111, 203; tribute 50
Paz, Octavio 116
Pellicer, Rosa 76
the people: Brazil. *See* Fonseca and the people; contracts 144; constituted power 87, 105, 115, 153–154, 191; the multitude. *See* Virno and the multitude; the people and Hobbes 7, 144–145, 147; personalism 7; personification 7; Virno. *See* Virno and the multitude and the people and the state. *See* the people and Hobbes
perfectibility 59–60, 63, 82, 88–89, 201–202
Perón, Eva 146
Perón, Juan Domingo 70, 126
Perón, Isabel Martínez de 70
Peronist resistance (1950s) 83
personalism: in Argentina 125–126; in Brazil 7, 125–127, 129, 133, 138, 149, 155; in Chile 125, 126, 155; personality 7, 126; personification. *See* personification and personalism against liberal democracy 138
personhood 7–8, 128, 143, 164, 166, 174, 192, 199
personification: as a prosopopoeia of the dead 176; of crime 6, 66, 88, 97, 166–167, 192 of evil 66, 102, 166–167, 179; of individualism. *See* individualism and personification; malfunction 6; personalism 7, 125–127, 129, 149, 155; resistance to 95, 97–98, 102, 110, 128; of the state 5–7, 18, 35–36, 73, 78, 88, 97–99, 111, 117, 125–126, 129, 134, 160, 167, 184, 190–192, 199
Pessoa, Fernando 101

Piglia, Ricardo: Borges 2, 5, 64, 66–67, 71–72, 80, 86, 88–89, 92, 97, 121, 130, 200; Brecht 2; defeat 69, 72, 74, 84, 196; (post)dictatorship 2–3, 5, 9, 64, 67, 69–73, 76, 80–84, 86, 92–93, 97, 121, 196–197, 201; Renzi. *See* Renzi, Emilio; failure 9, 27, 68–79, 81–84, 104, 121, 130, 175, 189, 196–197, 200–202; gender 74, 78; his generation 64, 93, 196; immunity to corruption 41, 131; individualism 2, 4–5, 21, 26, 68, 70–84, 121, 201–202; language 67–72, 100; *Los diarios de Emilio Renzi* 66; knowledge 5, 68–70, 72, 74, 86; Marlowe 26–27, 31, 64; madness 66–74, 201; meaning 70–71, 79, 83–84, 117; memory 64, 66, 80, 82, 93; money 26–27, 31, 40, 72, 74, 76–77, 79–84, 131, 180; *Plata quemada* 5, 68–69, 74, 77–84, 128, 154, 158, 180, 196, 200; *Respiración artificial* 47, 69, 196; the state 2–3, 5, 9, 21, 27, 71–84, 86, 88–89, 92, 97, 154, 189, 196–197, 200–202; Walsh 5, 64, 67–72, 77, 80, 83–84, 86, 88–89, 92, 97, 121, 200
Pinochet, Augusto 6, 92, 94, 96–97, 99, 103, 109, 113, 116, 118, 125, 128, 159, 199; death flights 95; personalism 125–126, 129
Piñeiro, Claudia 1, 8, 68
Plan Cóndor. *See* Operation Condor
*población chatarra* 180–183
Poe, Edgar Allan 2–3, 5, 11–20, 23–24, 29–31, 33–34, 36–38, 40, 42, 45–46, 52, 57, 61, 88–89, 103, 130, 166–167, 172, 192, 202; individualism 2–3, 5, 11, 13–20, 23–24, 31, 36, 45–46, 89, 166–167, 201; failure 18, 30, 34, 42, 52, 57; personification 5, 18, 20, 36, 88, 166–167, 192; success 5, 11–12, 18, 20, 23, 34, 52–53, 103, 202; the state 2–3, 5, 11–18, 20, 24, 31–46, 52, 57, 61, 88–89, 202

Poirot, Hercule 16–18, 22–23, 26–28, 31, 34, 36–37, 40, 43, 48, 56, 99
police: history of the 15–16; hostility towards the 15, 17, 21–22, 55, 74–75, 129; as a metonymy of the state 5, 35, 56, 73, 94, 97, 117–118, 129; post-dictatorial democracy 66, 124, 138; the political 2, 8–9, 16, 20, 24, 46, 59, 64, 93, 104–105, 108, 126–128, 135, 159, 166, 179, 185
post-dictatorship 3, 9, 45–46, 57, 60, 62, 64–69, 80–81, 83–84, 92–93, 99, 101, 106, 119–121, 123–125, 127, 129, 131, 134, 137–138, 150, 152, 155, 159, 177, 195, 197, 199, 201
power. *See* individualism, sovereignty; the state; Foucauldian normatization of 74; physicality of 37–38, 149, 152
Premat, Julio 74, 76, 78, 80–81, 83
private eye. *See* detectives
private sector 28, 73, 161
public sector 82, 99, 123, 163
Prohibition 64
proper nouns 59, 127–129; personalism 143, 145–147
pronouns: language 164–170; politics 164–70; the third person 9, 164–166, 179, 182, 190, 198–199; the first person singular 58–59; the first-person plural 164
prosaism 2
prostitution 70–71
punishment. *See* crime and punishment

queerness 3; detective fiction 31; Piglia 78; the state 32

Rama, Ángel 58–59
Reagan, Ronald 76
religion 20, 27, 29, 46, 142, 184, 198, 203
Renzi, Emilio 66–74, 76–77, 81, 84, 100, 130, 139, 162, 164, 167, 200–201

representation: crisis of 72, 95, 107, 118, 146, 158; literary 16, 82, 129, 155; political 6, 16, 126, 129
resistance and history 79–80, 113, 132
restoration of social justice/order/fabric. *See* detective fiction and restoration of justice/social order
revolution: counter-revolution. *See* counter-revolution; Chile 72, 96, 105, 110, 112–113, 116, 119; neoliberalism 96, 105, 112–113, 116; poetry 96, 110, 113, 116, 119
Richard, Nelly 112, 116
Rio de Janeiro 63, 65, 123, 124, 131, 133, 135, 137, 145, 149–150, 154, 157, 159, 174, 195, 199
Robinson Crusoe 4, 19, 26–27, 29
Rodríguez Pérsico, Adriana 2, 78, 81
Romanticism 9, 14, 17, 29; detective fiction 24; individualism 23; hard-boiled fiction 24
Rousseau, Jean-Jacques 36, 143–144
Roussef, Dilma 154, 191
Rosende, Mercedes 8
ruins 182–183, 196–197, 199
Ruiz-Tagle family (Chile) 92, 101–102
Rulfo, Juan 184

Sacheri, Eduardo 68
Saer, Juan José 64–65, 69, 93
Santillana, Marquis of 113
Sarlo, Beatriz 2
Sarmiento, Domingo Faustino 48
Sasturain, Juan 63–64
Saussure, Ferdinand de 9, 121
Scandinavia 50, 54, 65
Scapegoating 188–189
Schmitz, Sabine 82, 183
Schnaiderman, Boris 131, 139–140
Segato, Rita 8; feminicides 158, 171, 185, 192; masculinity 8, 32, 36, 78, 192; the state 8, 32, 36, 78, 192; unintelligibility 171, 185; Setton, Roman 48–49
the Seventh Circle 49

*Sherlock* (2010–2017) 45
Sherlock Holmes 1, 5, 12–13, 15, 17–23, 25–45, 48, 50, 54–59, 63–64, 100, 123–124, 136, 139, 162
Shklovsky, Viktor 109
sickness 129–135
sidekicks 12, 18, 21, 23, 25, 30, 37, 42, 56, 100, 129
signifiers 5, 43, 55–56, 100, 107, 109, 116, 121, 132, 139, 145, 167–172
silence. *See* symbolic disabilities and muteness; brevity. *See* writing and brevity; communism 108; crimes against humanity 6, 11; crisis of representation 107, 118, 146 in Bolaño's *Estrella distante* 6, 106–107, 111, 117, 121; Imposed 62, 85, 110; in Fonseca's *Agosto* 130, 132, 134, 146; literature 175; of the state 6, 21, 37, 62, 69, 85–86, 106–111, 117, 118, 121, 130, 132, 134, 146, 175; writing. *See* writing and silence
Simenon, Georges 123
Skepticism 48, 72, 192, 200–201
social contract. *See* Contractualism
Sonora Desert 93, 157–158, 188
Soriano, Osvaldo 62, 67
south. *See* Global South.
sovereignty 8, 32, 36, 38, 42, 68, 75, 78, 87–89, 97, 114, 116, 126, 137, 144–145, 161, 171, 182, 187, 195, 199–200, 202; the detective as the sovereign 20
Soviet Union 76, 196
Spain 60, 93–94, 101, 126; post-dictatorship 3; Golden Age Poetry 113, 173, 183
Spinoza, Baruch 144, 205
Spitzer, Leo 102
Spivak, Gayatri 145
state: abuse of authority 124; Althusser 150; apparatus 15–16, 57, 65, 72, 86, 88, 123, 136–137, 191; apology of 9, 89, 159, 189, 202 and anti-statism. *See* Foucault state-phobia.

Bourdieu's symbolic domination 85; collapse of the sovereign 195; crime. *See* connivance between the state and crime; critique of the 3, 5, 36, 46, 88–89, 149–150, 202; corruption. *See* corruption; definitions of the 42, 77; depersonalization 6, 103, 159–160, 162–167, 173, 177–180, 182, 184, 188, 190–191, 199; of exception. *See* Agamben and state of exception; fear of. *See* Foucault and state-phobia. Taussig's state fetishism 86–87; fictional silhouette of the 9, 78, 135, 197; fictions of benevolence 59–60, 76, 87, 133, 162; hindrances of the 19, 21, 31, 136; hostility (or contempt) towards the 15, 17, 21–22, 55, 74–75, 129; hollowness of 36, 77–78, 87, 135; incompetence. *See* incompetence and knowledge 5, 14, 17, 35, 37–42, 55, 61, 72, 86, 96, 109, 115, 140–141, 162–163, 170; lacks 5, 25, 35–36, 38, 41–42, 61, 69, 78, 89, 186, 198–199; metonymies of the 35, 73, 94, 184; monopoly of force (or violence). *See* state's monopoly of or violence; monopoly of literacy 100, 108; mutilation 5, 36, 131; outsourcing of the. *See* state and privatization omniscience of the 86; personalism 7, 125–126, 129, 133, 138, 149, 155; phobia. *See* Foucault and state-phobia and privacy 135, 141, 149–152, 154, 159, 160; privatization 73–74, 99 and the public eye. *See* detectives as public eyes and queerness. *See* queerness. resistance to embody the 97, 109–110, 128; second 192; selective absence of the 85–87, 151; space 38, 56, 87, 94, 109, 123, 139, 149–152, 157–158, 184–185; against the state 7, 123–155; state terrorism 70, 86, 110, 120–121, 159; state-sponsored

violence 58, 60, 77, 92, 106; Strange's Westfailure system. *See* Westphalian Sovereignty: suicidal 143, 155; technology 42, 77, 113, 115; voice. 77–78, 171. *See also* symbolical disabilities and muteness and silence.
Stavans, Ilan 1, 3
Stevenson, Robert Louis 101
Strange, Susan 195–197
subalternity 101, 134, 145, 176
suicide: history 126–127, 143, 147, 153; individualism 43, 56, 128, 133, 135; intimacy 151; mythology 142, 147; political 142, 147, 152; the state 126, 141, 144–145, 147, 153
*Sur* 15, 49
symbolic disabilities: blindness 5, 7, 35–40, 44, 56–57, 103, 118, 133, 135, 142, 155, 172–177, 185, 190–191, 199; deafness 36, 62, 72–73, 85, 87, 107, 125, 174, 199; illiteracy 5–7, 35, 38–40, 48, 54–57, 95, 106, 10–109, 111, 115–118, 120, 139–140, 149, 155, 199; impotence. Bolaño and symbolic impotence; infertility 177, 180, 184–185, 199; immaturity 37; muteness 5–7, 35, 37, 61–62, 71–74, 85, 87, 103, 106–111, 117–121, 128, 131–135, 146, 154–155, 168, 174–177, 189, 191, 199; negative affect 37, 142; paralysis 6–7, 37, 41, 69, 106, 115, 117–120, 131, 133–134, 139, 168, 187–188, 199; unintelligibility 7, 106–108, 111, 115–118, 134, 140, 142, 155, 162, 167–176, 185, 190–191, 198–199
symptoms 6, 36, 49, 104, 130–131, 134–136, 147

Taibo II, Paco 1, 3–4, 63, 159
Taussig Michael 33, 85–86
Thatcher, Margaret 76
Tocqueville, Alexis de 16
Todorov, Tzvetan 8; detective fiction 26–27, 58; the *fantastique*'s pan-signification 172
Tönnies, Ferdinand 153
torture 73–74, 86, 110, 121
Tournier, Michel 200
translation: of Anglo-American detective fiction; of Bolaño's *2666*
Trelles Paz, Diego 104–105, 111, 113, 177
*True Detective* (2014–2019) 45
*Twin Peaks* (1990–1991) 45

unemployment 81, 180–181, 197
unintelligibility 7, 106–108, 111, 115–118, 134, 140, 142, 155, 162, 167–176, 185, 190–191, 198–199
United Kingdom 3, 13, 45, 49, 65, 94
United States 1, 3, 13, 15, 23–24, 45, 49, 65, 94–95, 157–158, 161, 173, 186–187, 201
*Unsolved. The Murders of Tupac and Notorious B. I. G.* (2018) 45
Uruguay 74; detective fiction in 8

Valenzuela, Luisa 8, 64–65
Valle, Amir 1
Vargas, Getúlio: benevolence 133, 135, 137–138; the multitude 7, 129, 142–148, 152–153, 155, 160, 199; the people 7, 135, 143–147, 150–154, 160; personalism 7, 126, 129, 133, 138, 149, 155; personification 7, 126, 129, 149, 155, 160, 199; suicide 126–128, 133, 135, 141–147, 151–153
Vargas Llosa, Mario 1, 93, 126
Vázquez Montalbán, Manuel 3
Veríssimo, Fernando 124–125
Videla, Jorge Rafael 81, 125, 128
Vidocq, Eugène-François 38, 88
Vienna 76
Vila-Matas, Enrique 105
Villalobos Rouminot, Sergio 184
Viñas, David 47–48

Virno, Paolo 9; counter-revolution. 96, 112–113. *See also* counter-revolution; Hobbes 144–145, 147; the multitude and the people 144–147
vigilantism 103, 106, 118–120; Esposito's *compensatio* 103, 119; individualism 103, 119–120; state terrorism 120; justice 103
violence: domestic 130; language 41, 171, 183; Benjamin's critique of 41, 61; gender. *See* gender and violence. Bourdieu's symbolic 42; the state's monopoly of 42, 77, 137

Waldemer, Thomas 131, 147–149
Walsh, Rodolfo 5; chess 58, 130; detective/hard-boiled fiction 5, 53, 58–61, 64, 67–68, 71–72, 80, 84, 86–89, 92;dictatorship 5, 53, 58–62, 64, 70, 72, 83–86, 92, 97; individualism 5, 58–62, 68, 71, 121, 200; knowledge 5, 61, 68, 72, 86; loss of innocence 60; non-fiction 53, 58–59, 64, 67, 200; *Operación massacre* 53, 58, 60, 62, 72, 77; restoration of the social order 60, 62, 64, 68, 71–72; silence 62, 85–86; the state 5, 58–62, 70–72, 77, 80, 83–89, 92, 97, 200; the state of exception 61; state's perfectibility 59–60, 88–89
war: Colombia's dirty 86; First World 44; the interwar period 44; post-75, 158; Second World 53, 75

Warhol, Andy 95
Washington Consensus 82, 161, 187
waste 180–185
Watt, Ian: *ego contra mundum* 4–5, 7, 19–20, 42, 94, 117, 132, 141, 143, 150, 159, 200, 202; failure 44; individualism 4, 15–29, 44–46, 63, 81, 117, 159, 200, 202; myths 4, 17, 19–20, 23–28, 44, 63, 81, 143, 148, 200; the state 15, 20, 28–29, 81, 117, 202
Weber, Max 27: money 178, 182; the state 42, 77, 86, 109
Westphalian sovereignty 195–197; failure. *See* state and Strange's Westfailure system
whodunit 58, 97, 120
Williams, Gareth: *Estrella distante* 111; *2666* 135, 158
Wilson, Jason 83
Wimmer, Natasha 164, 179
*The Wire* (2002–2008) 45
writing: brevity 108–109; hermeticism 108, 111, 115; oppression 9, 109, 115–117; silence 108, 111, 117, 121

Yates, Donald A. 1, 48, 53, 203
Yrigoyen, Hipólito 53, 56, 60

Zizek, Slavoj: detective fiction 50–51, 93; the invisibility of the Schmittian enemy 179; Lacan's understanding of symptoms 147
Zurita, Raúl 111, 113–114

# About the Author

**Dr. Fabricio Tocco** (Buenos Aires, 1985) is assistant professor of Spanish and the Portuguese Convenor at the Australian National University. He was raised between Argentina and Brazil, and he has lived in Spain, France, and Canada, where he obtained a PhD in Hispanic Studies at the University of British Columbia. He has published several articles in Spanish and English, in Europe, and in North and South America. His writing deals with the intersections of literature and history, especially with the way popular genres inform and are informed by literary and political theory in Latin American cultural studies. *Latin American Detectives against Power* is his first book.

www.ingramcontent.com/pod-product-compliance
Lightning Source LLC
Chambersburg PA
CBHW020742020526
44115CB00030B/842